SUNRISE IN THE VALLEY OF DEATH

God`s love and transformation in Yemen

AMIIRA ANN

YWAM Publishing
Seattle, Washin

D1279487

YWAM Publishing is the publishing ministry of Youth With A Mission (YWAM), an international missionary organization of Christians from many denominations dedicated to presenting Jesus Christ to this generation. To this end, YWAM has focused its efforts in three main areas: (1) training and equipping believers for their part in fulfilling the Great Commission (Matthew 28:19), (2) personal evangelism, and (3) mercy ministry (medical and relief work).

For a free catalog of books and materials, call (425) 771-1153 or (800) 922-2143. Visit us online at www.ywampublishing.com.

Sunrise in the Valley of Death

Published by YWAM Publishing
a ministry of Youth With A Mission
P.O. Box 55787, Seattle, WA 98155-0787

Library of Congress Cataloging-in-Publication Data — Pending

ISBN 978-1-57658-669-3 (paperback)
ISBN 978-1-57658-683-9 (e-book)

First printing 2019

Printed in the United States of America

International Adventures

To Jesus

To my beloved and precious husband and sons

To my brothers and sisters in Yemen

You are heroes indeed and I am privileged to tell your story

Contents

Fire!

September 17, 2005

A DEAFENING EXPLOSION jolted us from our sleep. My husband, Chris, jumped out of bed and tore open the door to the balcony of the bedroom. It was 2 a.m., and we were both wide awake. He looked down below and saw that our car was on fire. He knew right away that the house was also in danger of going up in flames.

"Amiira, call the neighbors to alarm the fire department!" he yelled with a hoarse voice and slipped on some shorts and a T-shirt.

We had just returned to Yemen from Germany two days before, and were still feeling the jet lag. But the rush of adrenalin put us on high alert.

I had so many questions as I rushed over to the phone. "Was that an explosion? What's happening? What's the Arabic word for 'fire department'?"

But the questions would have to wait. Chris, usually calm and level-headed, stormed down the stairwell, taking three steps at a time. This was a precarious situation. The car could explode any minute. Soaring flames were about to reach the parched 25-foot neem trees in our front yard. If that happened, the fire could expand and endanger the whole neighborhood.

Chatija—one of my best friends in Yemen—lived right next door. Our houses were separated by only two narrow alleys and a six-foot fence. The flames could easily leap from house to house.

Chatija had always been the nervous sort. Whenever her husband went to work in his restaurant in the city 12 miles away, she felt abandoned and frightened. Now she ran out onto the street, dressed in her *nuqba,*[1] *lithma,*[2] and *balto*[3] and screaming hysterically. Grabbing her four boys, still half asleep, and the frightened goat that lived with them, she sat down at the side of the road and sobbed over her bad luck: *"Ya Allaaaah!!!!"*[4]

She completely forgot that she was supposed to call for help. But it didn't matter anyway, because as we found out later, there was no fire department in South Yemen.

Meanwhile, Chris tried to contain the blazing fire with water from the garden hose. But it was too short and the water pressure too weak to do any good. He stood behind the front door of our house, even though he knew it wouldn't protect him if the car's gas tank exploded.

Our three boys, David, Martin, and Tim, were asleep in their room in the back of the house. Since I figured they would be safe, I ran down the stairs to wake up Enrico. He was our kids' 19-year-old teacher, who had just graduated from high school and had joined us here in Yemen. He jumped out of bed and rushed up to the roof of the house where the water tanks were. I grabbed a few buckets and bowls to fill with water. From above, Enrico emptied the buckets onto the engulfed car, trying to douse the blaze. But the towering flames and biting smoke made it difficult for us amateur firemen. Even the damp rags we had used to cover our mouth and nose didn't help much.

---

1   headscarf that covers the entire head down to the chest
2   face veil that covers the entire face, but can be folded over to allow for eye slits
3   black, floor-length cloak
4   Oh, God!

I was amazed that the water tanks were still full of water since we had had a water shortage for quite some time. About three months before we arrived in Yemen, the city had done a lot of construction work, because the president, his son-in-law, who was the governor of Hadhramaut and all his ministers were coming to celebrate the fifteenth anniversary of the reunification of North and South Yemen. The construction work had damaged many of the water pipes in Mukalla, allowing much of the city's water supply to leak out. Whatever water remained was used for mixing cement and building new streets. They also planted trees and bushes along the entire road leading to the airport. Keeping things green here was however a huge waste of precious water. Since the work had begun, water had had to be transported in tank trucks from far away to fill the water tanks in the city.

The fire was still crackling loudly when we heard somebody impatiently pounding on our gate:

"*Salaam aleykum.*[5] Open up! We want to help!" It was Fuad, our young neighbor from across the street.

"I can't! It's too hot! The car could explode any minute! I can't get past the fire!" Chris was thankful for the offer, but he was also very frustrated.

All of a sudden, the car horn began to blow. It was as if it were sending out a continuous distress signal.

A cold shiver ran down my spine, and I screamed, "Chris! Chris! Chris!"

Suddenly, the car engine started up. I screamed even louder. The car rolled a few feet forward toward the gate. It was strange.

I was still on the roof looking down at this strange happening. I couldn't see very well due to the thick smoke, but I thought maybe Chris had jumped into the burning car to try to get it away from the house and protect his family. Perhaps he was unconscious with his head on the wheel. That would explain the incessant honking of the horn. My face grew pale, and I feared I was losing my balance. I panicked.

"Chris! Where are you?!" My desperate cry echoed across the roofs of the sleeping city.

---

5   peace be with you (good day)

Map of Yemen

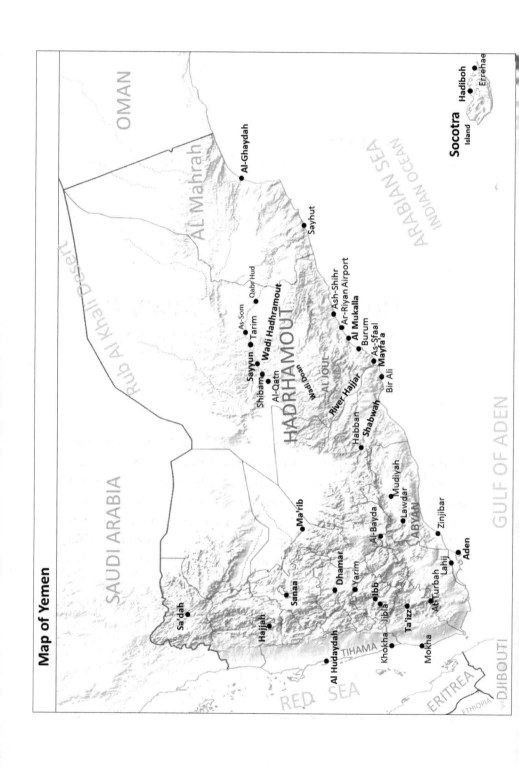

First Visit to the Valley of Death in October 1999

OUR TWO SONS, David (5) and Martin (3), pressed their faces to the window of the Yemenia Airways Boeing 737. They certainly didn't want to miss the fascinating sight of the oriental airfield, brightly illuminated in the blackness of the night. We were about to land in a mysterious Arab city. Our boys were not the least tired, in spite of the hours-long flight, and I envied them for their endless energy! The flight attendant smiled and didn't even attempt to get our playful boys to buckle up for the landing. I guess she sensed that they would undo their belts again anyway as soon as she turned her back!

My mind was buzzing with thoughts about this amazing country in which we were just about to land. It was called the "Home of the Queen of Sheba."

But I felt a joyful anticipation rising within me. I could hardly wait to get to know this country of Bedouin tribes, ingenious architectural structures, and amiable, hospitable people. Of course, we had heard that there were radical and extremist Islamist groups here in this country, which is probably the most impoverished on the Arabian Peninsula. The world press had often run headlines about Al Qaeda attacks or tragic ransom situations here. But we were not afraid. After all, we were young, enthusiastic, and full of idealism! And we were coming as ambassadors of the Most High God!

A couple of young German-speaking pioneers had invited us to visit the Yemeni province of Hadhramaut, what means the "Valley of Death." They asked us to consider moving there soon since they were beginning a project for which our talents and skills could prove helpful. We couldn't have imagined what was waiting for us in this undeveloped region!

Six years earlier before Yemen was in our thoughts, I had had a dream.

In this dream I had to stay home while my husband was in a disaster area that was constantly in the news. Every day there were reports of casualties, and I wasn't even sure if he was still alive. All the telephone lines were cut off, and there was absolutely no way to reach him. I waited anxiously for a word from him but to no avail. My heart was heavy. I was weighed down by worry and the pain of being separated from him, and I became increasingly restless.

Then early one morning, Chris stood over my bed and woke me with a kiss. I was relieved. I listened intently as he told me about his assignments: "I was standing on a wall next to Jesus. I could hear people screaming, and I was horrified to have to watch as defenseless people were sinking, being drawn down by an irresistible undertow. The clamor was deafening and flames were blazing. I could hardly breathe. The situation was extremely agonizing. But Jesus was with me, and placed his hand on my shoulder. 'Pull out that man over there!' I did as I was told. I was able to help several people out of this lake of flames, and their lives were saved. During that whole time, I was thinking about you, Amiira. I knew you would be worried about me. Since I wasn't able to get in touch with you, I asked my Boss to allow me to go home so I could set your mind at ease."

Upon hearing this report, I was moved by how Jesus had used Chris. My husband had played a very important role in this rescue mission!

At the same time, though, I was aware that my husband's assignment also had a sobering side to it. It meant he would not be staying at home with me! It wouldn't be long before he would be off again on a mission to save more lives from this lake of fire. And sure enough, just a short time later, he told me he would be leaving soon. My heart bled, and I pleaded with him: "Please don't leave me behind this time. I want to go with you."

Chris hesitated. He warned me: "It's very hard for women there. It's definitely not a family-friendly place And there probably wouldn't be very much for you to do. Your only assignment would be to pray. Are you ready for that?"

When Chris asked me that question, I was taken aback for a moment. I am a very energetic person and like to stay busy! But then I replied, as determined as Ruth from the Bible story when she answered her mother-in-law: "Yes, I want to come with you! Wherever you go, I will go, and wherever you live, I will live!"

Shortly after that, I tried to persuade my friends to join us. I was relentless: "You guys have heard the reports about the crisis zone where masses of people are dying every day. Please come and join us! There are so many people in distress who need our help!"

But our friends did everything they could think of to dissuade us from following what they thought were just the fanciful delusions of a whimsical young couple. In our circle of acquaintances, nobody was thrilled about my proposition! I looked into my friends' faces and was disappointed. One of them frowned at me. She was fearful and tried to persuade me to stay: "Be reasonable. The risk is too great for us and for you!"

Someone else chimed in: "It's way too hot there and dangerous as well! Besides, you're needed here."

Another asked: "Why do you even want to leave? You have such a good life here. Chris has a well-paid job he truly enjoys where he can advance his career. You guys have such a great job."

Bravely I tried to disarm my friends' misgivings. Was it actually some craving for adventure or naiveté that led us to make this decision? Was it worth the risk we were taking? Had Chris only imagined God's call? Doubts began to settle into my mind and tug at my heart, as the wind tugs at a boat's sail. But then I remembered that Jesus had called us, and that it was a matter of saving lives. Our comfort and security were no longer important. Even if it meant leaving our family and home behind, my mind was made up: "We'll do our best! We know we have to go. We *are going to obey!" And then in a whisper: "Even if that means going on our own."*

In my dream, Chris and I followed along some railroad tracks. It seemed like we were floating above them. Hours went by until we finally arrived at an ocean shoreline. The railroad tracks disappeared, and the path continued seamlessly on into the ocean. Across the waves on the horizon, we could see a desert region covered by volcano-like mountains.

When I woke up from that dream, I immediately knew that it hadn't been a normal dream. And I could see that God was trying to tell me something.

* * *

We got off the plane and stepped onto the runway of the Riyan Airport. We were full of anticipation. Within seconds, we were soaking wet with sweat. A few days later, it dawned on me that we had literally landed in the country from my dream! It was strange: This foreign oriental world was entirely different from where we came from, but somehow everything felt unusually familiar like we belonged here. A sort of *déjà vu.* I felt as if I had finally arrived home! Neither the unbearable heat nor the constant noise bothered me, nor did the filth and the oppressive poverty of the people around me. It was like I had fallen in love. I looked at everything through rose-colored glasses. I felt like I was floating on clouds. My dream from six years earlier came alive again, and I knew that the place I had seen then had a name: "Hadhramaut—the Valley of Death."

The wonderful people I had seen in my dream actually existed, and they certainly needed our help! They had captured my heart, and right away I instinctively knew that this was the place we were supposed to be! That assurance would give my husband and I strength in the days to come. Even now we were already sensing that things wouldn't always be easy for us here in this part of the Orient.

The following day, en route to Mukalla itself, we sat in silence as we admired the unique and fascinating countryside from our car. The noon sun reflected in an ocean of turquoise that stretched to the far horizon. The innumerable grains of sand, sparkled on the vast shore.

Camels swayed through the dunes of the wide swathes of sand like ships in the desert.

After we arrived in the city, we strolled side by side along the busy alleyways and observed the scores of dark-skinned people with keen interest. We heard loud voices coming from everywhere: persuasive merchants selling their products, fully veiled market-women attempting to attract customers, streets overfilled with honking automobiles and interspersed with simple donkey carriages. And all around us, a colorful swarm of Yemenis —many of whom looked African—shoving their way through the crowd.

It was absolutely fascinating. This fair city was tucked between the dark mountains and the blue Indian Ocean, and the golden light from the sun made the provincial capital shine like porcelain. No wonder they call this beautiful city in southeast Yemen "The Pearl of Arabia." The port of Mukalla was full of picture-book fishing boats and rustic wooden sambucas with their distinctive keel design.

From the shore, we watched the dolphins play. We were told that farther out, we would find magnificent coral reefs. This fascinating city was covered by a blanket of heat, and yet a light breeze came in from the ocean. We were experiencing the Orient in its purest form. I felt like we had stepped into a time machine and gone back a thousand years. I almost thought I was living out the story of the Arabian Nights.

The city was full of life. The marketplace teemed with colorful shops that stocked dresses, scarves, baskets, and lots of other merchandise. Brightly painted booths with stacks of fresh fruit and vegetables. Odors, which were difficult to recognize. Fresh meat hung from the hooks at the butcher's shop, dripping with blood and surrounded by a swarm of flies. The fish market was right next door. A tourist with a queasy stomach might have felt ill at the unmistakable fish stench, but it didn't seem to bother anybody else.

In the afternoon, when the heat died down, the women came out to the marketplace. They strolled past the sales booths, their bodies completely covered in black fabric. In spite of the heat, they wore black cloaks that touched the ground, carried heavily laden baskets on their heads, and often had their youngest babies strapped to their backs. I could only distinguish their fronts from their backs by the direction they were heading since veils covered their faces entirely. I couldn't even see their eyes. The mothers went about their shopping, completely ignoring their dark-skinned children running around about them. I thought they might want to hurry up with their errands so that they could get out of the scorching heat, but they seemed to have all the time in the world. Perhaps they were just happy to get out of the house and for a few fleeting moments leave all the chores behind.

The children ran around barefoot on the sand or splashed about in the water to cool off. The girls wore dresses worthy of a princess, except that they were torn in various places and had been faded by the sun and by inexpensive washing detergent.

Many men sat cross-legged on the floor at the teahouses or in the marketplace. They smoked their *shishas*,[6] drank tea and chewed *khat*[7] with their overstuffed jaws. They would always choose the cleanest stalks and leaves, pluck them off with their fingers and stuff them into their cheeks.

Chris whispered into my ear: "That's a drug. It tastes like grass and is very expensive." Many people are obsessed with the chewing of khat, spending irrational amounts of money and time on the habit. The cultivation and marketing of khat also puts an enormous strain on the nation's water resources through the irrigation of the plantations and the demand for the leaves to get to market fresh, firm and green. A lot of time is spent by buyers in the market fingering the leaves and stems before making a purchase. Chewers praise the energizing effect of the drug and claim that it increases the powers of reason, imagination and sexual potency. As a side effect, it also takes away the feeling of being hungry. But they forget the reality of their lives.

Here in the Southeast, the Yemeni men, most of whom were rather short in stature, wore *futas*,[8] along with a shirt. Their colorful scarves, which most of them wore casually on their shoulders, gleamed brightly in the sun, each one boasting its dazzling hues, often with metallic thread woven through them.

---

6   water pipe
7   native tree leaves chewed for their effect (drug)
8   finespun wraparound skirt with lovely patterns

The loud hustle and bustle somehow seemed very laid-back and relaxed. "Hurry up" apparently wasn't in their dictionary. Their motto was more like the old saying, "If I don't show up today, I might show up tomorrow." *Inshallah!*[9]

When the muezzin called the *marib*,[10] all the men dropped everything and hurried to the mosque where they dutifully said their prayers, always bowing toward Mecca. Countless pairs of shoes could be seen at the front door of the mosque. Just as quickly, all the women fled to their homes to pray.

Only the local boys remained behind, playing unsupervised. They weren't about to let the preacher of the mosque interrupt their games. They were kids and were going to enjoy their carefree childhood.

The girls went home with their mothers as tradition required. Most of the girls here were illiterate since it would have been unseemly for them to leave the house, much less go to school. Besides, school materials were too expensive for most of them.

Most of the women in this village dressed entirely in black, with only their high-heeled shoes peeking out from under their black *abayas*.[11] Black scarves were draped tightly, but elegantly, around their heads, completely hiding their hair. On top of that, black veils enshrouded their faces. Some were more transparent than others. Some had eye slits; others didn't. The women usually had elegant handbags as accessories to their black apparel.

"I am going to have to get used to this all pervsive black," I sighed.

From our time in Jordan, we were fairly familiar with the Arab culture but discovered that in Yemen views on women's clothing were much more fundamentalist.

"It's strange not to be able to see the women's faces," I muttered self-consciously. "You can't tell whether or not they're smiling. I wonder how it feels to be so shielded and concealed. And how much can they even see through those tiny slits in their veils, anyway?"

---

9   "If God wills", also used to mean "perhaps" or "I don't know".
10 evening prayer
11 traditional black floor-length coat women wear to completely cover themselves in public

At least the innumerable brightly dressed children all around were a glaring but welcome contrast to the "women in black."

* * *

I glanced over at Chris, my good-looking husband, and smiled. With his broad shoulders, dark complexion and mustache, he fit in perfectly in this Arab world! By nature he is usually very cheerful, friendly, and laid back. He was taller than most of the relatively short locals, but when he placed his scarf casually around his shoulders and wore the traditional *futa* and a shirt, as they did, he looked just like one of them. Even though it was obvious to them that he wasn't a native Yemeni, the locals assumed he was from a different Arab country. Perhaps from Syria? Although he spoke flawless Arabic, he did have a slight accent and also expressed himself a bit awkwardly sometimes, but they would never have suspected he was from Europe. Because they see reports on television about this exquisite "Continent of Plenty"; many Arabs want to go to Europe. Why a European would leave a life of luxury and come to a country known for its unbearable heat, poverty, and barren deserts would be a mystery to them.

I was very aware that I didn't have Chris' advantage. I stuck out like a sore thumb among the other women. My skin had a nice tan from the sun and the wind, but I still looked pale in comparison to the southern Yemeni locals, with their hint of African descent. At least my height didn't stand out since I am not much taller than most of the native women. I wore metal-rimmed glasses, which kept anyone from seeing my brown eyes unless they looked closely, which was of course strictly forbidden (for the local men, at least).

My husband described me like this to the team we were to be joining:

"My cute little blonde wife is outgoing, friendly, warm-hearted, and affectionate in her very special way. She has no problem opening up to people, but she doesn't enjoy shallow conversations. She gets to know people surprisingly fast and forms really strong friendships."

During this initial visit, we had the opportunity to get to know the two couples and the two single women on our team who had arrived a few months earlier. Our team's purpose was to do developmental work in a certain project area outside the city limits. We wanted to help the needy any way we could. Our young team leader had learned Arabic after completing his dental studies and marrying his wife, a physical therapist. He had a strong passion for the vision, but very little practical experience.

The task force also included the Webers and their five children, Samuel, Benedikt, Tabea, Tobi and Gideon. Eva, their mother, was a very kind woman who took care of their children and the household very well in this foreign land. Her husband, Udo, was a friendly and outgoing man, who emanated a natural, charismatic authority.

And then there was Heidi, a Swiss midwife whom we had gotten to know during our time in Jordan. She had helped deliver our son David and was happy to see us again. We looked forward to the possibility of working together, after we would finally move here. There was also a nurse from Germany and a high school graduate who taught the schoolchildren during the first year.

On our first walk through town, I wore a blue, long-sleeve, floor-length robe and a large headscarf that modestly covered my blonde hair. I still felt like I was on display. Even though I had everything tucked away neatly, I felt all the people around me staring, and that made me uncomfortable! In Jordan, I would have felt comfortable around the locals in a knee-length skirt, elbow-length sleeves, and no headscarf at all. But here, without being in full black array, I felt like I was walking around the shopping area in my bathing suit.

"Chris", I exclaimed, "I stick out here like a sore thumb! I don't like people staring at me like that. Look at all those women. They're all wearing black, black, and more black. Most of them have their faces covered. You can't even see their eyes. Still, I feel like they're all staring at me. Look, some of them are even wearing gloves and stockings in spite of this heat. There's not an inch of skin in sight. It's incredible!

"Now I understand why the women on our team are required to wear black, full-length robes and headscarves. By covering everything up, we're trying to show respect for the locals. We want to meet them at their level. Having said that, I'm relieved the scarves don't have to be black and we can wear whatever we want under the robe. Maybe I should get one of those black robes, and the sooner the better!"

Chris tried to encourage me. "One street over are some shops that sell dresses and *abayas*. Why don't we see if we can find something you like?" He turned onto an intersecting road, and after a few minutes we found ourselves in "Dress-Alley."

At first, I was overwhelmed by this extremely narrow shopping area. It seemed like there were endless shops that offered black garments for sale. Because the high buildings were so close together, the sun was blocked out making it very gloomy. Chris led me directly to a shop where there were a lot of *baltos* hanging outside on clothes racks and fluttering in the wind. A dark-haired man with a black beard and a frowning face stood in the doorway. He immediately escorted us into the shop, which had no windows and thus was extremely dark. He pulled a few black cloaks off the rack and presented them to me. Feeling a panic attack coming, I tried to take a deep breath. Even though the door was open, I felt uneasy and cramped, as if I were in a cave. It was stale and damp in that little room, which was stuffed wall-to-wall with black cloaks and matching headscarves. The air was muggy and stagnant. Not even a slight breeze. Apparently, there was a power cut. The merchant placed himself cunningly in the doorway so that nobody could get past him, at least not without brushing up against him. The whole situation overwhelmed me. Everything around us was black, pitch-black. And what was that smell? Was it incense? Perhaps mothballs?

Suddenly, I realized I hated the color black. Why hadn't I noticed that before?

And anyway, all the cloaks the merchant showed me were way too long for me. I shook my head each time he showed me one. But he went on promoting his merchandise, singing its praise in a strange Arabic chant, and pointing out the quality and beauty of each *balto* and its matching headscarf. Surprisingly enough, despite his exaggerated enthusiasm, I could sense a certain caution in his behavior, even a hint of standoffishness.

Finally, I couldn't stand the dark, narrow confines any longer and begged my husband to get me out of there instantly!

I ran out of the tiny shop, passing right by the merchant, who continued to advertise his products. Once outside, I took a few deep breaths to try to alleviate my lightheadedness.

Chris forced his way past the confused and unsuccessful merchant and muttered that we might be back later, *"Inshallah."*

Outside, he looked anxiously at me and asked: "What's going on? You're so pale. You looked like you were going to pass out."

"There wasn't enough room in that place to pass out, certainly not with all those foul-smelling black cloaks everywhere you looked!" I tried to smile again. "It was terrible. My heart began to race, and I felt like I was in a cave with a host of dark monsters just waiting to attack us. I don't ever want to go back into one of those gloomy *abaya* shops again."

But as soon as we got to the next shop where black *abayas* were out front, my curiosity got the best of me, and I paused to inspect the quality of the material. The owner of the shop tried to lure me inside, saying he had better and more beautiful merchandise in his shop. But I was adamant that I would not go in.

"Wild horses couldn't drag me in there. You couldn't get me to come in, even if you did a handstand and wiggled your ears at the same time!" I said in German, all the while smiling at him in a friendly way and hoping he couldn't understand what I was saying.

I looked to Chris for help: "Maybe I'll just have to get you to buy me one of those black things," I said with my "begging" eyes, which I knew he couldn't resist.

He didn't hesitate, not even for a second. He just passed me the first cloak he could get his hands on. I held it up against my short frame and examined it.

"I suppose this one could sort of halfway fit me without having to alter the hem," I said rather skeptically.

The robe had simple black stitches on the neckline, the wide sleeves, and the hem.

The merchant tried intensely to convince me that he had even better designs. When he realized it was no use, he tried to persuade me with a deluge of words and gestures to purchase the matching headscarf, which he said was "unique and of the highest quality."

"I'll make a special price, just for you," he promised, like I guessed he did with every customer.

But I vigorously declined his offer. I didn't like the color of the scarf. It was black, and I didn't want to add any more to my "black collection," especially since I knew I wouldn't wear it anyway.

Chris bargained with the merchant until they agreed on a price and without further ado handed him the money, closing the deal. He gave me the cloak, and right then and there in the middle of the alley, I slipped it over my dress and adjusted my colorful headscarf. I ignored the countless onlookers curiously staring at me. Apparently, they didn't get to see something as interesting as this very often.

"So, we made it! Thanks for helping me out there. Wow, it's even hard to buy a black *balto* around here." I was relieved and able to smile again.

As soon as we left the shopping alley, I relaxed. That presence of a dark, powerful entity I had felt so strongly only a few moments earlier had now completely disappeared.

* * *

After a few days in Mukalla, we drove with our team to Sayun, where we planned to spend a few days at a team retreat.

We spent time there getting to know each other. The children splashed around in a tiny swimming pool surrounded by high walls. Each evening, the families took turns telling their story. That made us feel like we were a part of the team. Unfortunately, we had to say good-bye all too soon. It had been such a nice time together!

Our team's driver, a gray-haired Yemeni named Abu Rashid, drove us to the airport. We flew out from the capital of Sanaa and back to Germany. It was time for us to prepare for our move to Yemen. Chris would have to quit his well-paid job.

CHAPTER 2

Tales from the Arabian Nights

February 26, 2000

When we finally moved there five months later, we could hear loud voices coming from the airport speaker system. The hard white light of glaring neon lamps lit up the strange-looking airport and all the passengers waiting for their luggage. We stood at the customs counter at Sanaa Airport, which appeared somewhat worse for wear. Despite being exhausted, we could hardly wait to reach our destination. But before we could move on, we had to pay the entry fees and buy our pre-ordered visas at a separate counter. A man in a dark suit stood next to the door in the lobby. His elegant clothing made him stand out from the rest of the men there, who were all clothed in traditional Yemeni fashion: floor-length white robes and suit jackets, the *ya*[12] around their waists, and Arab scarves looped around their heads. This courtly dressed man held a sign in his hand, which read in large letters: "Transit to Mukalla."

---

12 Yemeni dagger

He smiled at us and asked, "Are you continuing to Mukalla?"

We probably looked like we were, for he was already motioning his hand at us to go left:

"You have to go to Gate 2. That's where your connecting flight will be leaving soon. It will take you to your final destination, the Riyan Airport in Mukalla!"

David suddenly yelled out enthusiastically, "Our bags and one of our chests are over there on the baggage carousel!"

"Good job, David! Our luggage was supposed to be checked through. You just saved us from a huge headache! Hurry, go grab a couple of baggage carts. We've got to get everything through customs."

Many passengers were already waiting in a long line to get their bags from the carousel. We loaded up our baggage and took it to the customs counter, where soldiers scanned one person at a time and inspected the luggage. Chris was the first in line. Quickly adapting to the local manners, he had already jumped the line. Our friends who were accompanying us came next, followed by Grandma and Grandpa B., then the children. To make sure neither of our two boys got lost, I brought up the rear with the bulk of our luggage.

The transit assistant hurried us along: "The plane is ready for take-off. You need to get to Gate 2 quickly!"

But the local customs officials couldn't read what was on the departure screen. They also seemed to turn a deaf ear to our demands and requests. It probably wasn't very important to them whether or not we as foreigners arrived on time.

"I'll go get the visa. You guys wait here," Chris called to us and rushed off without waiting for a response.

Meanwhile, our 3-year-old son, Martin, was sitting on the floor—his stroller hadn't arrived yet. He was playing happily with discarded drinking cups and checking out the cigarette butts lying all around. Grandma B. and David were just going through customs with two fully-loaded baggage carts.

"Do we have everything?" I counted out loud: "Let's see: eight boxes, three large suitcases, two smaller bags, three trolleys, and the carry-ons."

"Don't forget the two bags from Grandma and Grandpa B. And where is the cart with the rest of the luggage?"

I suddenly realized that Chris was far up ahead of me. I couldn't even see him anymore. Grandpa B. had just finished getting through customs and was putting everything back on the carts. He took Martin and went through the customs barrier.

I was the last of our group to go through. The others in my travelling party were now nowhere to be seen. I was in a hurry to catch up with them. At the very bottom of my pile was a box marked "Microwave—Caution! Fragile!" On top of it were two suitcases, a traveling bag, and the carry-on luggage

"Please open that box at the bottom," the customs officer said harshly.

I began to sweat. I prayed under my breath, "Lord, please help me! I don't want to be left here all alone."

It took a lot of effort to get the heavy luggage off the cart. When I reached the box, I opened it, carefully removing the tape and twine we had used to seal it. I attempted to explain to the officer in English that it contained a kitchen appliance. But he just shook his head unapologetically, determined to inspect this apparatus more closely.

His snooping manner was beginning to get the best of me, so I made a quick decision. The only thing important to me now was to catch up with my family. I looked the customs officer straight in the eye and said:

"Just keep it. I've got to get going! My plane, my children…"

I had totally forgotten that I was told not to speak Arabic at the airport!

But the man in uniform just smiled at me. He had understood what I had said, and I could see a touch of goodwill flashing in his eyes.

"I have children, too. They need their mother," he muttered in Arabic under his breath.

I was quite surprised to see this officer, who had been rather aloof up until then, help me reload the cart with all our things. We crudely sealed the frayed box with some twine. I nodded a quick and friendly good-bye and went looking for the proper exit. I looked around but couldn't see anybody, not even the transit assistant.

I rushed for an exit, pushing the baggage cart with the rest of our luggage. Completely out of breath, I ran out onto the runway, but there was only one airplane there, and it was a very small one.

I wondered, "That couldn't be our plane, could it?"

Despite the panic stirring in me, my legs carried me almost instinctively to the airplane stairs.

Meanwhile, all the other passengers were in their seats, the propeller was already rotating, and the engines were getting up to speed. My heart was in my throat by the time I finally reached the stairs, using my last ounce of strength.

Somebody offered to help heave the massive suitcases into the plane. I breathed a sigh of relief. Apparently, this tiny plane was the right one, after all! Then, all of a sudden, I saw that handsome, familiar face.

"What took you so long?" Chris asked, his scalawag face grinning mischievously.

But he saw me gasping for air and knew I wouldn't be responding anytime soon. Panting heavily,I dropped into the last row onto an empty seat.

"Whew!"

There was only one flight attendant on board this mini-plane. She opened the door to the rear lavatory and placed all my bags on the toilet seat. Then she quickly shut the door and sealed it from the outside by jamming another bag flush under the doorknob. Almost immediately the tiny plane was in the air. The attendant quickly went to her seat and buckled up. She didn't even take the time to rattle off the security procedures. There were only a few passengers on the plane, and they all seemed to be regular fliers anyway.

It was only a one-hour flight, but we experienced heavy turbulence several times. Yemenia Airways decided, without even batting an eye, to skimp on the little snacks they usually serve on this flight.

The plane landed at Riyan Airport on time, at one o'clock in the morning. All the passengers got off the plane, excited and thirsty. Even before our feet touched the ground, we were drenched with sweat.

When we had left Germany, the temperature had been freezing cold. Arriving now in Yemen, the heat and humidity slapped us in the face like a hot washrag. Our friends, "Grandpa and Grandma B" were having an especially hard time dealing with the humidity. We were grateful they had agreed to join us for a week to help watch the kids while we focused on finding an apartment.

All of our boxes, bags, and suitcases had made it to the conveyor belt, although some of them were a bit worse for wear. At least nothing was missing—except for the buggy. Martin had taken his place again on the dirty floor, and I had to hold back a gag reflex.

I tried to rationalize my letting him sit there: "Well, he's going to have to toughen up sooner or later. From now on, his immune system will have to deal with a lot stronger stuff."

I tried to ignore my instinctive standards of hygiene. But alarms were going off left and right! I just had to grit my teeth and ignore it!

For a little *baksheesh*,[13] we hired a few guys to help us with the luggage. Chris was already fervently negotiating with cab drivers in Arabic. Gesticulating wildly, they were all trying to get him to pick them. During our flight, Chris had found out that one of our fellow passengers, a young, dark-haired German named Tom, was working as a diving instructor at the Hadhramaut Diving Center. Like us, Tom was heading for the parking area. He glanced over in our direction with an inquiring look on his face. Chris went over and introduced himself.

"Hi, I'm Chris. We've got quite a lot of luggage. Do you think you'd have room for it in your van? And maybe you could let these two ladies here and the kids ride with you to the Hadhramaut Hotel?"

Tom gave him a friendly nod and motioned to the van. His driver came over right away, carried our luggage to the van, and put it in the back. Wearily, I squeezed into the backseat with Grandma B. Each of us took a child and a carry-on bag on our laps. Now Chris could retrieve our entry clearance documents without having to worry about us. Grandpa B. helped him gather up the rest of the luggage, and they joined us shortly after that.

The night was clear and beautiful. The constellation named the Southern Cross shone brightly in the night sky, and we saw it as a sign of God's comforting presence. It was still very humid, but the breeze gently caressed our skin and cooled us off quite nicely. Despite the bright stars, it was still so dark outside that we couldn't see the countryside. But we were too tired to care. The kids had not slept a wink because of all the excitement. They bombarded us with questions:

"How do you say 'thank you' in Arabic?"

---

13 tip

"Will I die if a mosquito bites me?" (They had heard that we were moving to an area, where people could get malaria.

"Are we going to sleep in the same room as Grandma and Grandpa B.?"

"How come we only get to stay two nights in the hotel? Why do we have to move into the office? Can't we stay with our friends?"

"When are we going to eat?"

"I'm thirsty. Why don't we have anything to drink?"

Shortly after 2 a.m., we finally arrived at our hotel. While we were getting the van unloaded, Chris and Grandpa B. rode up in a taxi. They got out and stretched. A friendly hotel page came over, smiled, and dutifully helped us take our luggage to the garden bungalows, which Chris had reserved. The men had to go back and forth a few times, but everything was soon piled up neatly in the corner of our holiday residence. We were surrounded by swarms of relentless mosquitoes. Then out of the blue, a fat rat appeared and hid behind our gray suitcase. That was the straw that broke the camel's back, the camel being me. I wept.

"I can't sleep here! I can't share a room with a rat!"

Chris rolled his eyes and heaved a sigh of exasperation. He just wanted to go to bed.

"It's just a rat!" he said in a weary, irritable tone.

He was just stressed out. But I was suddenly wide awake again and was fiercely determined to let him know how I felt.

"Please, get us out of here! I can't stand it here!"

I did my best to discuss the situation calmly and objectively, but I was upset. I had experienced enough adventure for one day!

After a few minutes of arguing in vain, Chris reluctantly gave in and went to the reception area to ask if there was another room available. How embarrassing that must have been for him!

I stayed behind with the kids, who were tired and grumpy by now, hardly daring to breathe. I remained completely still and kept staring intently at the corner of the room where that detestable little creature had disappeared. A few minutes later, Chris returned with Mohammed, the friendly hotel page who had been so helpful. Once again, he took our luggage to the new room, all the while smiling respectfully. I was very grateful and rewarded him by returning his smile. If he had not been an Arab, I would have given him a big hug and a kiss on the cheek. Fortunately, I remembered the rules of etiquette just in time. I quickly pulled myself together and at least was able to avoid one embarrassing situation.

Our new hotel room, which was in the main building, was about a five-minute walk from the bungalows through a rather dreary garden. While Chris and Mohammed were getting the luggage, I made the kids' beds in the new room. After all the bags had finally been stowed away, we fell into our beds. Despite being so exhausted, I had a hard time falling asleep. There were just too many impressions my mind had to process.

"This is an entirely different world!" Those were my first thoughts the next morning when Chris woke me up with a kiss on my cheek. I was amazed and fascinated by it all.

The tension between us was gone, and I could see everything in a different light.

"The people here are really friendly. And they're willing to lend a helping hand. It's just wonderful here!"

"But the language here is so different from what I am used to, and I don't think it's just the Yemeni dialect!" Chris remarked. "I find myself in awkward situations again and again and begin to ask myself: What have we gotten ourselves into?"

* * *

The odors here were so unlike those I was familiar with, and wherever we looked, we saw filth and trash. It was almost as if plastic bags grew on trees. We also found it difficult to adjust to the intense humidity. David and I were constantly exhausted. The sun was always very hot and the sky usually clear. The only time we saw any clouds was when a sandstorm was approaching, which was very rare.

During the first few days, Chris and I were able to concentrate on finding an apartment. The kids were in good hands with Grandma and Grandpa B. taking care of them. They would get into the pool with the boys or help them with various craft or painting projects. Sometimes they just would sit in the hotel room and read them stories. That put my mind at ease about leaving the kids behind in an unfamiliar environment. I knew that they loved their "grandparents-on-loan" and were happy to let them take care of them and, of course, spoil them.

"Maybe we'll find a place by the end of the week while our babysitters are still available," I said hopefully, although we had been told it wouldn't be easy.

Sebastian, our team leader, had told us it could be a rather complicated and time-consuming task. But we were convinced things would go smoothly. We had experienced so many difficulties up to then that we felt like we deserved a break! Fortunately, we had no idea what was awaiting us!

Udo had set up an appointment with a *wakil*[14] to look at a house. We took a taxi to the broker's office and were quite optimistic. The real estate agency was located on a back road of the city. The air was hot and humid, the temperature over 110° F. The sun burned down on us with its cruel heat. It was scorching outside, and the sweat trickled down our foreheads and necks. The minutes passed by very slowly. It seemed like time had come to a standstill.

"Thank God the kids didn't come along. Can you imagine them in this heat? And right in the middle of the city with all this crazy traffic? We could never let them play or run around out here."

We checked our watches, then checked them again, but that didn't speed things up.

"Are you sure the appointment was for today and not yesterday? Was it in the morning or later in the day after the *asr*[15] prayers?" We weren't so sure anymore.

Unfortunately, we hadn't brought anything to drink and were beginning to feel dehydrated.

"How I'd love a cool glass of water or even some coffee! Next time, we need to remember to bring something to drink!" I was hoarse, and my voice cracked.

An hour later the real estate agent finally showed up. By then, both of us were not only thirsty but also very tired and frustrated. After we had introduced ourselves, we accompanied the broker to his

---

14　real estate agent, landlord, house broker
15　afternoon prayer

pickup which he had parked a few blocks away. When we got there, he motioned for us to get in.

Chris politely held the door open for me and whispered, "Keep your feelings to yourself! People here are really good at reading gestures and facial expressions. We don't want to spoil our chances with this guy!"

His facial expression let me know he was serious. He probably wished he could have hypnotized me to keep me from telling the man off, as my German straightforwardness would have inclined me to do. But I just smiled and batted my eyes at him to let him know I wouldn't let him down. He had already told me many times before that I would have to learn to tame my temper in this environment. Chris was relieved. He took his place in the front seat next to the *wakil* and started up a conversation with him in Arabic. We headed east on a wide road. Fifteen minutes later, we arrived in Fuwah, a remote district of Mukalla. The driver took a right then stopped. We got out of the car, drew in a deep breath of humid air, and walked another short distance until we reached an unplastered, half-built house.

Trying to keep from stumbling, I followed the dusty path in silence. I stepped over a pile of rubbish lying directly in front of a rectangular opening in the building where the front door would eventually be.

Upon entering the hallway, I saw more piles of garbage and construction litter. A rat scurried into its hole. The stairway to the first floor hadn't been built yet so the *wakil* did a balancing act on two narrow boards and climbed to the upper story. Boldly Chris and I followed. When we arrived outside the apartment door, it was locked.

The well-dressed Yemeni pulled out an impressive key ring from his pocket as if to show off. He went through all the keys, but none of them fit the lock. I breathed a sigh of relief. But the man was not about to give up. He tried them all once again.

The broker said: "*Bukra inshallah*[16] I will have found the key. But I have another place I'll be happy to show you. The key is at the home of my friend's uncle. His house is only a couple of miles from here."

We headed out full of anticipation. When we arrived, Arab hospitality took over: We all took a seat in the living room and drank some coffee together. The women of the house remained in hiding, which

---

16 hopefully tomorrow

made it awkward for me. I felt out of place as the only woman among men, even though I knew they would ignore me anyway. Besides, I was exhausted and couldn't understand most of the political conversation the men were having. It was shortly before nighttime prayer. The man with the key finally arrived. Even though the sun was setting rapidly and the day was being swallowed up by the night, we made our way by foot to the other house. We were eager to see if this house might be the right one for us. This building was only half-built, just like the first one. It was surrounded by piles of rubble and paint cans. There were no apartments on the ground floor because it was reserved for businesses. That meant that there would be no backyard, and the front door would lead directly onto the street.

Lo and behold! The key actually fit! It was almost completely dark inside, and although there was no electricity, I could still see the debris and filth all around.

"I guess I'll just have to get used to that," I mumbled to myself.

We went up a staircase with no handrail. The kitchen was a very tall, rectangular, windowless room. The walls were dark gray. I didn't even look at the rest of the place. I had had enough! Out of nowhere, a swarm of mosquitoes attacked me, and just as unexpectedly, a surge of fatigue and discouragement got the better of me. I just wanted to return to the hotel and be with my kids, then hit my bed ASAP. All the struggles of the past few days, the farewells, the flight, the jet lag, and all the impressions of this foreign culture began to take their toll on me.

The next day, we waited for two long hours in the afternoon heat for the real estate agent to make his appearance. The time ticked by very slowly, but we didn't want to give up, so we just stuck it out! After a while, we decided to accept the fact that we had waited in vain. Unsuccessful and frustrated, we returned to our hotel.

Meanwhile, Wednesday arrived. Chris warned me not to get my hopes up:

"We shouldn't expect too much today. Tomorrow is Thursday, the first day of the Arab weekend, which continues through Friday. Businesses are closed, even the post office and the banks."

The first house we looked at was located on a noisy, busy market road. We were greeted by a conglomerate of people, goats, and the obligatory piles of garbage. The house was just as dingy as the others we had seen so far.

Chris took a look at the frown on my face and said to the agent, "No, I don't think this is the one." He didn't even give him time to ask.

"I have two other houses on the beach side," the agent said and led us outside again onto the dusty road.

We arrived at the beachside and were surprised to hear that electricity was already available for this region and only needed to be hooked up to the building in front of us. However, there were no telephone lines on this remote street, just like everywhere else in eastern Yemen. "Perhaps we will have a telephone connection by next week. *Inshallah?!*"

Chris and I chose to ignore the piles of garbage and rubble in and around the house. We checked out the two available apartments and were pleasantly surprised. You could actually breathe in here! They even had sliding glass windows imported from Saudi Arabia, which would keep the apartments cool. The living room, bedroom, kitchen, and children's bedroom all had individual balconies. That was a big bonus that would afford us extra space. The entire 650-foot area of the building's flat roof was covered by a roof-deck expansion. If we got up on our tiptoes, we could enjoy a picturesque view of the nearby ocean and the city.

"So there *are* better houses than the ones we've already seen!" I sighed relieved.

I had to be careful, though. If the agent detected my enthusiasm, the price for the apartment would skyrocket.

"The upper apartment would be ideal for us," I thought, and suddenly the disappointment and indifference from the previous days disappeared into thin air.

I was thrilled. But my level-headed husband Chris was still a bit skeptical. He enjoyed haggling over prices, and the rental fee the agent was asking seemed too high, especially when compared with the other less attractive apartments we had seen.

"I have another apartment I could show you in the building two doors down!" the passionate real estate agent said.

It was worth looking into. Perhaps the next one would be less expensive and more attractive than this one. The *wakil* led us down the now familiar road to a semi-detached house.

I tried to look at it with an open mind. But then I saw rubbish and rubble lying around everywhere. Quran verses handwritten on the walls showed us that the previous tenant had been a very religious person. The apartment was dark and only half as big as the last one. And there were no beautiful sliding windows to let in light and air from the outside. The windows here were made of brown, patterned glass, somewhat similar to what the Germans use in their bathrooms. They could only be opened a crack.

I knew right away I didn't want to live here. The thought of living in this dungeon made my skin crawl. Chris looked it over meticulously. But as soon as the unethical landlord named the bloated rental price, it was clear that this house was not for us. It was badly in need of renovation and would have cost only thirty dollars less than the previous apartment. But Chris was still not convinced that the clean new building we had seen was the right one. He wanted to see some other buildings first and then sleep on it. That meant our house hunting would go on a few days longer, continuing on Saturday.

Meanwhile, the time had come for our friends to leave. We remained behind, alone. The farewell was hard for me, especially because Grandma B. had always had a comforting and understanding ear for me. And Grandpa B. had been our trustworthy adviser. We were going to miss them both!

After spending the first few days in a hotel, we moved into a small room in the office part of the building where our other team members lived. We shared a bathroom and a tiny kitchen with the Arab coworkers. That was quite a restriction on my freedom since now I'd have remember to wear a headscarf and loose-fitting, floor-length garments that covered the arms and neck. These were very cramped quarters. I was already making plans about how I would furnish my dream apartment and praying that my husband would soon be just as excited about it as I was. I didn't want to waste any more time.

A couple of days later, we went to take a second look at the new building by the ocean. Shortly after that, Chris agreed it was the right place for us after all. Many days of negotiations with the *wakil* were to follow. He and Chris haggled and bickered until they finally agreed on a price.

"We need a gate in the yard to separate the two yards, just in case a Yemeni family decides to move into the ground-floor apartment. We need the entire roof for ourselves. In the largest room, we need a sliding door so that we can make a separate room for the children."

The landlord agreed and promised: "You'll get your yard gate, and I'll arrange for ceiling fans in the various rooms to be installed and the railing on the balconies to be attached. I'll have the electricity and water up and running and take care of the piles of debris in and around the house."

If we signed the contract and paid an entire year's rent in advance, the apartment could be ready for us in two weeks' time!

We didn't want any construction workers in the house when we moved in. So we had to figure out a way to get this money together as quickly as possible! That wouldn't be easy without a bank account. And setting up a bank account was a complicated matter.

But in the end, Chris was able to sign the contract and make the payment for one entire year's rent.

Meanwhile, we were refreshing our Arabic vocabulary, which had become a bit rusty. It was quite a challenge upon arriving here to learn an entirely new dialect. Many words were different from those used in Jordan. Our brains' hard drives had to be re-configured. We were mostly able to convey our thoughts to the locals, but understanding them was quite a different story! It took some time for our tongues and ears to adjust.

As soon as the paperwork for the apartment was signed, we contracted a carpenter to build wooden cabinets for the kitchen and a special bed according to our specifications. The furniture from the carpenter's shop was cheaper and certainly more attractive than the plastic furniture in the local furniture stores.

CHAPTER 3

Prayer Times Define
the Daily Routine

IN THIS PART of the world, nobody asks what time it is. Meetings are set up around the prayer times.

Yemenis often say: "In the West, you have clocks. Here we have time."

Around 4:30 a.m., at the crack of dawn, we heard a loud sputter and a voice blaring from the loudspeakers of the seven mosques in our densely-populated area. The muezzin had called everyone to *fajr*.[17] The entire city was rudely awakened by a thunderous echo: *"Allahu akbar!"*[18] All the men of the city, still drowsy and disheveled, hurried to complete the ritual washing of their hands, face, ears, nose, and mouth. Then they rushed off to the mosque, where only men were allowed to pray. Due to strong group dynamics and mutual accountability checks, all the men participated in this exercise, including the less devout ones. Even during a water shortage, there was always water near the mosque, so that

17 early prayer
18 Allah is greater

each man could indulge in a brief wash several times a day. If necessary, water would be delivered in tank trucks.

As soon as the sun was up and the *fajr* prayer was over, the regular daily clamor and hubbub took over. Our apartment was in a new housing area, so we were often surrounded by construction noise from power shovels, jackhammers, and the like. Stores didn't open until around 9 a.m. and closed for *dhuhr*[19] at around 12:30 p.m., or whenever the sun reached its peak. Islamic prayer times restricted the lives of everyone without exception—the rich and the poor, the educated and the laborers, the natives, and the foreigners.

The stores opened again directly after *asr*, which is around 3 p.m., depending on the position of the sun, and closed for the day at *maghrib*.[20] Between these two prayer times, women could get out and about. They would usually get all dressed and made-up before going to visit their friends and neighbors.

Whenever women left the house, they would dress in a black garment they viewed as a priceless robe, more valuable even than a diamond necklace. They felt very pretty in these special costumes! That's the fashion here. It's their culture and lifestyle.

The dress code made a statement: "I am a religious Muslim. I keep the hadith and the Quran. I submit to the laws. I desire to keep our family's reputation blameless."

Many religious people lived in our neighborhood. The women were very legalistic about wearing full face and body covering. They would instruct and monitor each other, making sure that no one accidentally or deliberately revealed anything that had to remain hidden. When I first arrived in Yemen, all these women covered in black looked the same to me. Sometimes I couldn't even tell the front from the back. After a while, though, I could discern certain details, which highlighted the differences. Not all *abayas* were identical. For instance, older and very religious women wore bulky ones to hide their figure. On top of the *abayas*, they wore long face veils, which extended down to their waists and completely concealed any curves.

---

19 noontime prayer
20 prayer at sunset

The younger generation had more fashionable garments. The oriental teenage beauties often wore black overcoats, which were tailored at the waist and accentuated their figures. They were made of black satin or silk and adorned with delicate embroidery. A matching headscarf rounded out the wardrobe. These flowing, floor-length robes were very attractive.

High-heeled sandals or modern platform shoes, as well as dainty handbags decorated with sequins, enhanced the *baltos* elegance. Flashing through narrow eye slits in the veils, brightly painted, almond-shaped eyes would make men's hearts beat faster. I was surprised to discover that outright flirting was still possible, even with a veil. Maybe the mysterious black disguises made the women more appealing. Men could let their imaginations run wild and envision a beautiful exotic being with perfect measurements under the veil.

After *maghrib,* which started at sunset, no more women or girls were allowed in the streets. They normally spent their evenings at home in front of the television. The men usually hung out in tea shops or the marketplace.

The last prayer of the day, *isha'a,*[21] began when the sun had set and its white afterglow had disappeared.

The Yemenis were easygoing people. We had to be careful not to make too many plans for any given day because things usually turned out differently than we planned. We needed to learn to take into account the major role the prayer times played in defining the daily routine. Otherwise, we might easily find ourselves in a state of constant disappointment. As soon as the *muezzin* called to prayer, everyone dropped everything they were doing. If you were shopping, the store owner would not finish waiting on you. He wouldn't even lock up the store. Once, we were left alone in a shop when a prayer time was suddenly pronounced. We could have cleaned out the store, and nobody would have noticed. Business deals were made through relationships and usually took a lot of bargaining. That required patience and time, and I was often frustrated.

It seemed the long-bearded fundamentalists had made a science out of ignoring women. That gave me the shivers. I learned very quickly,

---

21 prayer at night

though, that these religious Muslims were not only ignoring me. They avoided eye contact with all the women, including the Arab ones. This kind of behavior was commanded by the Quran and by the traditions passed down through the *hadiths*,[22] but I thought it was condescending and contemptuous. Every woman was considered to be a potential "seducer." So men ignored them altogether, at least in public.

Some of the laws in the Quran seemed full of contradictions to us Westerners, especially those which dealt with women. For instance, it was a sin for a woman to allow anyone to see her legs or hair. Of course, according to Islamic law, the man looking at the woman didn't commit a sin. It was always the woman he looked at who was at fault. The woman was responsible for the attention the man had given her since she had obviously not dressed modestly enough. This is the reason that in many Muslim countries, women who have been raped are killed by their relatives. This "honor killing" is forbidden in many places by law, but unfortunately, it is still practiced. This is especially true if a raped woman becomes pregnant. If she were to begin to show, that would disgrace the family honor. The reputation of the family was placed above human life, especially a woman's life.

The regulation that all women had to be fully veiled restricted their freedom considerably. I had a hard time grasping this concept. I asked myself, "If men have a problem with the females, why should women have to pay the price?"

It was difficult for me to accept this way of life! But my respect and esteem for these Arab women were growing. They were forced to live with this discrimination and had very few rights of their own. Still, there was nothing I could do but sit by and watch my female friends accept it since we hadn't come here to find fault or cause trouble, but to serve the people. Our goal was to show them our love and appreciation, especially the women, who were often deprived of both.

---

22 the works and sayings of Mohammed the prophet, passed along from one generation to the next

CHAPTER 4

The Beginnings in our New Home

IT WAS STILL early in the morning. We had been in Sanaa for the past two weeks for training. The taxi dropped us off at our new apartment on the outskirts of Mukalla at around 8 a.m. We were really eager to see how the renovation had come along. When we arrived, the piles of garbage were higher than before the renovation, which was to be expected, I suppose. But the balcony railings and the ceiling fans had been installed, and the plumbing seemed to be working. Everywhere we looked, there were paint cans, wires, and packing materials lying around. Two men with splatters of paint on their overalls were coating the railings with a weird, sickly green. That seemed to be the fashionable color for banisters these days. It would probably take me some time to get used to it, but it wasn't all that important. Most of the other houses in the neighborhood had sickly green railings, or they were left unpainted. Some didn't have any railings at all on their balconies.

We didn't want to wait until the workers got around to cleaning up their mess, "perhaps *Inshallah* next week," if they even came at all.

Their promises were all too suspicious for our taste. So we got to work ourselves clearing the debris out of the apartment. We were eager to move in, and it didn't make any sense to wait around in the office twiddling our thumbs. We didn't want to wait any longer than absolutely necessary.

By the end of March, just in time for Chris' birthday, we were ready to move in.

"We need carpets for the bedroom and the children's room. Then we should get some mattresses, so we don't have to sleep on the floor," I said, prioritizing our needs.

After months of living like vagabonds, we could hardly wait to move into our own home. I realized that Chris would soon be delving into the project and would become absorbed by it. When that happened, we wouldn't have any time to get what we needed to furnish the apartment. It didn't matter to Chris whether the apartment was cozy or not. He just wanted to get going on the developmental work with the locals. What we hadn't realized at the time was that it was impossible for a woman without a man accompanying her to go into a hardware store to buy a hammer or screwdriver. I was only beginning to realize just how much women were dependent on their men around here.

Whenever Chris returned from shopping, usually without the items I sent him out to get, he would say: "I just got caught up in a very interesting conversation. You'll have to learn to be more patient. The way of life here is much more casual than in Europe. These people should be more important to us than our comfort. After all, we are here for them!"

CHAPTER 5

Shariifa,
My Remarkable Friend

FOR QUITE A while, Eva, my team colleague, had been after me to hire someone to help around the house.

"Amiira, why don't you get someone to help you with your household? We all have domestics who are a big help. It's time-consuming to keep the house clean, with all the sand everywhere. And then there's the shopping, cooking, and laundry to take care of. Without our household helpers, we wouldn't have time to pay anyone a visit or even learn Arabic, not to mention help out with the project. Besides, we provide these women with a livelihood. And we use the extra time we gain to visit the neighbors. On top of that, you'll have a private language tutor around to help you learn the dialect."

At first, I wasn't convinced. It felt strange having someone else take care of my household chores. But I finally gave in and agreed to meet Shariifa, a Muslim from Africa who was a friend of Adila, Eva's helper.

We met at the Webers' home. Eva came along, although she and the others would soon be returning to Germany. That way, Shariifa and I could check each other out without it being too awkward. Shariifa was an easygoing and modest woman with a beautiful smile and a chocolaty complexion. I liked her right away. She was a perfect picture of serenity and peace, and we could communicate well from the beginning, even though Arabic was a foreign language for both of us. Shariifa's husband was an impoverished Yemeni nobleman. They lived in a piteous, albeit nicely furnished, tin shack in one of the worst slum areas in Mukalla. Her son was the same age as our son Martin. The two boys were destined to become good friends. All in all, Shariifa made an honest and friendly impression on me.

The three of us talked awhile and finally agreed that Shariifa would come and try it out the following day.

It didn't take long for us to recognize it was a good match. I could use my newly-gained time for writing or taking care of school matters.

Of course, I had to learn to turn a blind eye to some of her quirks. For instance, Shariifa was not very punctual. Sometimes she didn't show up at all, completely without explanation or warning. But her affectionate, friendly demeanor and her trustworthiness balanced it all out.

Shariifa had an unusual way of cleaning house. For example, she would take a large bag or a basket and dump all the toys, books, and tools that were lying around in the children's room into it. Then she would hide it all under the bed or in the closet. Well, everything looked tidy enough, but nobody could ever find anything! It took the children quite a while to realize that the Lego bricks belonged in the Lego box and the Playmobil pieces in their own container.

I told Shariifa time and time again: "Please don't clean up the toys and books in the children's room. The kids have to learn to do that themselves!"

Shariifa usually left the more tedious jobs to me, like scraping off plaster and paint remains from the floor tiles. She also didn't like to wash the dishes, especially new ones.

"These are brand new. Why should I wash them?" she would ask with a puzzled look on her face.

It wasn't long before we were friends. I made sure to treat Shariifa with respect and as an equal. We would often talk with each other while working. Shariifa was swift and efficient, and after a short while, she could do the work on her own. And within that short while, I got so used to her that I couldn't imagine her not being around. In the beginning she came one day a week, then later twice a week for four hours a day. One day, she asked me if we could hire her full-time. She needed more money to support her family, or she'd have to find another job. We agreed. Shariifa had become very dear to my heart and I didn't want to lose a good friend.

By working in our home every day, Shariifa was spared the mistrust of the neighbors, who otherwise would be wondering why she was around all the time. Such is the mindset of the people here—always suspicious and curious. And an added benefit of our daily time together was that I could teach her some handicrafts, as well as reading and writing.

CHAPTER 6

Challenge or Opportunity?

SHORTLY AFTER OUR arrival in Mukalla, the rest of the team took a furlough for several months and left us behind as the only foreigners in this "Valley of Death." We felt as if we had been thrown into the deep end of the pool and would quickly have to learn to swim to keep from drowning.

The projects were just getting started, and we were given the responsibility of implementing the plans that had been worked out. Both Chris and I saw this challenge as an opportunity to immerse ourselves into the oriental culture and learn its colorful language and customs.

During our time alone, our Arab neighbors often paid us a visit. Each week, our family spent several days in the project area, where our team had rented a clay building in a village called Al-Qariyah. We would spend a few nights each week there. It was unfurnished except for a few dusty mattresses covered by mosquito nets. During the summer months, the place remained nice and cool, as long as we kept the windows closed. We didn't even need a refrigerator, which was good since the village didn't have electricity. We moved things around a little so that the house would conform to the traditional design of all clay buildings. It was a two-story building with a stairway leading to the main living area on the upper floor. We used that room either as a living room or a bedroom. Up a few more crooked steps, and we were on the roof, where we had a good overview of the entire neighborhood. That meant, of course, that the neighborhood also had a good view of us, since the houses were built very close together. And since our neighbors were very nosy, that left us with little privacy. On top of that, we could hear every word spoken in the entire neighborhood. The sounds just echoed from the buildings. And that began early in the morning with the cock crowing, the hens clucking, and later on the sheep bleating. Then there were barking dogs, crying babies, braying donkeys, and many other sounds. The village was rudely and noisily awakened every morning, and we were right in the middle of it all. As time passed, we got to know and love the villagers. Our whole family was fascinated by this foreign world, and we soon felt like we had been here our entire lives. Sometimes the language barrier was a challenge, but we were always able to communicate through gestures and antics.

For the Bedouins, it was strange to hear people speak Arabic with accents and a few blunders, but they were very patient with us and always friendly.

"The Germans should be ashamed. When foreigners come to our country, we don't treat them like that," Chris exclaimed.

The first few months were very strenuous, especially because of the high humidity and the summer heat. Chris began to meet with the village men to get certain development projects underway. Of course, he spoke Arabic with them. And occasionally we had to return to the capital of Sanaa to take care of some business.

When we first travelled to the village, we had not known about the widespread political and tribal troubles. So it surprised us that we were made to halt at various military posts and roadblocks. Time and again, we were required to take a couple of soldiers and their machine guns with us for protection through the unstable tribal regions.

After a famous government development organization gave up on a complicated water project, the locals asked us for help. Chris, once again, just couldn't say "no." It was a laborious task. He had to find all the existing water spots, extract samples from each, and take them in for bacterial and chemical testing. Each time, he had to drive back to Mukalla, over 50 miles away. There he stored the samples in the university's refrigerator. He encountered many procedural obstacles and also an occasional bizarre surprise.

For instance, once he had to wait a very long time to get the test results for the samples he had brought in. They kept making excuses and putting him off. After weeks of waiting, he finally found out through the grapevine that the labeled water samples had ended up in the lecturers' refrigerator. Apparently, some very thirsty professors didn't read the labels and drank the samples by accident. It probably didn't taste very good. Nevertheless, it meant more work for Chris. He had to revisit all the water spots, take new samples, label them, and then return once again to Mukalla.

When the results finally arrived, we sat down and decided how we could help the needy in the vicinity most efficiently. We dug new wells and restored old ones, making them functional again. Later, we planned to build a small dam and reservoirs for the Bedouins. The farmers needed irrigation ditches to water their dried-up fields. They planned to grow millet, corn, watermelons, and various types of vegetables.

CHAPTER 7

Love Stories, Oriental Style

WE HAD BEEN in the country only a couple of weeks when we entered a carpet shop. It was shortly after *dhuhr*, and the noonday sun made us sweat profusely. The heat flickered, and I knew that the muezzin would call to prayer soon. Then the local salesman would run off to the mosque without closing our deal. And that would have meant another wasted trip to the city.

Out of the corner of my eye, I saw a good-looking young man getting out of the bus and coming toward us. He was all smiles as he shook Chris's hand.

"I found you at last! I've been waiting for you for months now. I knew you would come to study the book with me!"

Chris greeted the stranger, a bit taken aback.

"Salaam aleikum!"

"Welcome, welcome, my friend! My name is Maliik." The gangly young Yemeni flashed his bright white teeth.

"Thank you! It's nice to meet you, Maliik," Chris replied, then added invitingly, "Why don't you come along with us and see where we live?"

On this particular day, it had not been a waste of our time to go to the city, even if we had come home without a carpet. During our meal, Maliik shared his story. He worked as a waiter in the Tower Hotel and had recently become a Christian. He came from a different Yemeni city and was feeling homesick. He was a stranger here, just like we were.

Maliik was very eager to learn from God's Word. He and Chris would read the various stories in the Bible together. It was like a private Bible study. We were happy to see him whenever he came by our house. We admired him for his courage. Enthusiastically and candidly he shared his newfound faith with all his colleagues and even with strangers. He wasn't concerned about opposition!

A few weeks passed, and Maliik met a young woman. Soon after that, they got engaged. He wanted his darling Tiara to know about his new religion. He tried time and again to convince her.

"You have to go and visit Amiira. She'll tell you about Jesus!"

At first, Tiara and I didn't always see eye to eye, but after a while, this beautiful girl with chocolaty skin began to enjoy her visits. She was proud of me, her newfound friend, because I was a foreigner. Tiara was from the "House of the Nine Girls." At least that's what the neighbors called it since she had eight sisters and no brothers. Her home was located in a slum area of Mukalla. Her father had abandoned the family because his wife had not given him a son. Tiara and her sisters were obviously more privileged than most of the young women in this area. They also were given more freedom than other girls who had been raised in the strict, unrelenting, and legalistic environment typical of the Islamic society.

Tiara's friend, Marissa, came along twice for a visit. She seemed to be more open-minded than Tiara, more interested in the deeper matters of faith. Both she and Tiara worked as police officers, so I had to be careful. Perhaps they were spying on me? But I felt I could trust Marissa. Once, the three of us watched the *Jesus Film* together, and I could tell that Marissa was touched and fascinated by it. One day, she surprised me with a visit. She had come alone and asked me, to my astonishment, "Do I need to tell everyone now that I believe in Jesus?"

My heart leaped for joy for this young woman, who had apparently received Jesus into her heart.

Tiara and Maliik's wedding was a three-day party. Maliik's family came down from Sanaa in the north. They had not yet met Maliik's chosen one and were going to see her for the first time.

During the reception, Maliik's mother and his light-skinned sisters from the city made some very derogatory marks, loud enough for everyone to hear.

"The people here in the southwest are so *aswad*,[23] how ugly!"

I felt my face turning red with embarrassment.

How can someone be so rude and ill-mannered? I thought.

They were nothing like Maliik!

The women from the south had taken extra pains with their makeup, using white powder to cover up their darkish complexion, which they detested themselves. I shuddered. The thought that Maliik's sisters could reject Tiara was devastating. Tiara was such a beautiful, swarthy girl, who was only longing for appreciation and approval.

After the wedding ceremony, the newlyweds moved in with Maliik's mother up north. Unfortunately, Tiara didn't last long in a foreign setting, despite her husband's loving affection and care. She was forced to live in the same house as her spiteful mother-in-law and cruel sisters-in-law. Soon, it began to tear Tiara and Maliik apart. Shortly afterward, Tiara couldn't take it any longer. She returned to her hometown, miserable and unhappy.

Tiara's sister Yasmin worked at a hotel. One day, as we were there for a swim, she confided in me:

"Oh, Amiira, it's so sad! Tiara came home just a few days ago. She left her husband, and she hasn't been the same since the divorce. She never laughs anymore. She just sits around doing nothing. We're worried about her. We've tried everything we know to cheer her up, but nothing has worked!"

I asked Yasmin, "Did she tell you why she left her husband? Did he mistreat her?"

"She still loves him, but her mother-in-law rejected her from the very beginning. Apparently, she stirred Maliik up against her."

---

23 black

I couldn't believe it! The very next day, I went to visit my abandoned friend. Her sisters were happy to see me. But I quickly realized that Tiara was no longer interested in keeping in touch with me. Her face, once so beautiful, was now full of deep wrinkles. She didn't even look at me. Perhaps my presence reminded her of better times. It made me so sad to see her like this. Marissa also stopped coming by to visit me. Losing a friend like this was painful. I racked my brain, trying to figure out if I had done something wrong.

Yasmin kept in touch with me over the years. When we met some time later, she told me:

"Well, guess what. I got divorced, too. My mother-in-law didn't like me because I work as a waitress in a hotel. She wanted me to quit this menial, despicable job because waitresses aren't allowed to wear veils during work. She hated me because all the men could see my face. Many Muslims see that as a sin! But we needed the extra money I earn at the hotel. I didn't want to live in my mother-in-law's house forever. She was taking advantage of me and treating me like a slave!"

Yasmin's mother took care of Yasmin's little daughter when she was at work. Nurseries are not needed in Yemen. Here, the extended family takes care of its own. Very commendable!

Once a month, the hotel Yasmin worked in offered a romantic candlelight dinner by the pool. On our wedding anniversary, Chris and I went there. From where I was sitting, I observed a passionate young Yemeni couple. They were flirting, oblivious to everything around them—and despite the girl's black veil! They sat just a few tables over. In this strongly traditional region, we rarely got a chance to see a young woman, modestly wearing a veil and headscarf and gloves—all in black, of course—being coy with a man. She didn't reveal an inch of skin! The man was captivated still the same. He just stared into her undetectable eyes. It touched me and fascinated me deeply, and I sighed:

"How romantic! Isn't love just beautiful?"

Suddenly, I saw the mysterious woman in black wave at me. Had she noticed me staring at them? I had been caught, so I sheepishly waved back. I suppose I should have been used to sticking out in the crowd by now, especially since I wasn't wearing a veil. I wasn't wearing a *balto* either, and my blonde hair was uncovered. Perhaps I should have been more cautious about staring indiscreetly at others. At the hotel, I could wear elegant, colored clothing without breaking any rules of etiquette, as long as the dress covered my knees and shoulders. Today, on our anniversary, I wore a floor-length, dark-blue gown with silver stitching on the neck and the hem. It highlighted my curly blonde hair.

While I was at the dessert bar, this mysterious, black stranger approached me. She stood there inconspicuously and whispered without looking at me directly: "Don't you recognize me?"

I could tell by her voice that it was Yasmin! I had never seen her with her face veiled. As a waitress at the hotel, she usually wore a dark skirt, light blouse, and colorful scarf around her head.

I was completely blindsided. "What are you doing here? Did you get remarried?" I asked.

"Just for one night with this Saudi Arabian fellow. I want to get back together with my husband. But to do that, I have to marry someone else, at least for one night."

She returned to her seat without saying another word. She immediately went on flirting unabashedly with the stranger while somehow enjoying her meal despite her veil.

Life didn't make sense anymore. I just stared at her and couldn't believe what she had told me. I staggered back to my table, totally dismayed. What was she talking about? How could she be married to a man from Saudi Arabia for just one night?

My husband noticed something was wrong. "What happened? You look so pale? Did you eat something bad?"

I had to calm myself down before I could tell Chris what Yasmin had just shared with me. I could barely get the words out. Then Chris told me everything he knew about marriage and divorce traditions in Arab culture. This was all about a "short-term marriage," also called "pleasure marriage."

"Islam allows a marriage to be consummated for only a few hours to make an affair or act of prostitution within the marriage legal. A man can have many wives at a time. It is agreed upon in advance how long the marriage is to last. It can be anywhere from one hour to ninety-nine years. This 'short-term marriage' is especially common among the

Shiites. But the Sunnis here in Yemen use this rule to allow divorcées to remarry each other!"

I sighed. "How complicated! If the two love each other, why does the woman have to marry someone else to get her first husband back?"

Chris just smiled and softly squeezed my hand. He felt just as helpless and frustrated as I did. He knew that my heart was bleeding for my Yemeni girlfriend.

CHAPTER 8

Everyday School Life

SEPTEMBER 2000. THE sun bore down relent-lessly, and it was still very hot and humid. I had mixed feelings about our first autumn here in the new surroundings. Our eldest son, David, was to enter first grade. During his first year, Papa would take him along to the office. He was excited about that! The building that housed the ground-floor office, in which we had stayed for a few weeks directly after our arrival, also accommodated the two other German families in our team who lived in the apartments upstairs. Our team leader, Sebastian Becker, lived with his wife, Larissa, and their two daughters, Mia and Lea, on the third floor. The second floor belonged to the Weber family with their four boys and one girl. There was a terrace at the very top of the building where the kids could play. It was a nice place to relax and spacious enough to hang the laundry out to dry.

The Weber family had turned one of their rooms into a classroom. This is where Ruth, the tutor, taught the four schoolchildren. David truly enjoyed school, since he liked all the Weber children.

Ruth was here to do a year of volunteer work. She was 20 years old and had just finished high school. She lived down the road in the "house of the single women," together with Heidi, the midwife, and Mina, a German nurse. Ruth was an artist, very creative and full of ideas. During her year with us, she organized a sports festival and taught the kids circus acts. Later, she secretly had the children rehearse a musical about the blind beggar Bartholomew. It was a big surprise for us all, when one afternoon, the four of them put on the show! The audience included Udo and Eva with their two small children, Sebastian and Larissa, Mia and Lea, Chris and me with Martin, and Heidi and Mina, the other two single women.

I was very surprised and moved by their performance. David played the lead role. He had been practicing his solos without our noticing. He was really good! Samuel and Benedikt, the two older students, were a little envious of David for getting to be Bartholomew. Chris portrayed Jesus, and with his beautiful baritone voice, he proclaimed to the beggar: "Be healed!"

The premiere of the musical in Yemen was a big success and was greeted with much applause.

During the Christmas season, the children did a play about the birth of Jesus, and in the summer there was a school fair. In addition to all these special events, Ruth put particular effort into making her lessons interesting and informative for each child. She was very creative!

The four children were in three different grades, and Ruth had to teach them all in one room! But she was good at what she did and managed splendidly. David and Tabea Weber were in first grade while Samuel and Benedikt, Tabea's two older brothers, were in third and fourth grade respectively. Ruth was a real blessing for the children, as well as for us parents. She was still very young, but she had an extraordinary talent for teaching and a special love and compassion for each of the children placed under her care. She played violin and piano and had a wonderful singing voice. On top of that, she was very athletic. She exuded a special zest for life and had a wonderful impact on our children.

The Weber family found a "real" teacher for the following year. His name was Peter, a young man from Switzerland, who had taught for a year in a secondary school in Switzerland before joining us.

* * *

The owner of our house came by one day and dropped a bombshell: "I have to rent out the apartment below you. I need the money! A local family is interested. But if you want to rent this apartment, too, I'll make you a good deal. I just can't let it stay empty any longer."

"We need some time to think about it," Chris answered.

"I'll give you until Saturday. Then I'm going to have to rent it out!"

He finished his coffee, got up, nodded in Chris's direction, and then left the house without once looking back. He knew he had the upper hand!

Chris said, "There are advantages and disadvantages to a Yemeni family moving in. One thing's for sure, though: If they do, you'll have to wear a headscarf and long dresses when you're in the yard."

"I've had to sacrifice so much already. I can't even be myself anymore. At home, I could at least dress like I wanted to. By the way, I heard that wearing a headscarf can cause your hair to fall out. That's too much to ask! Besides, if we had the downstairs apartment, the kids would have more room to play, and we'd have an extra guest room. Our apartment is big, but the floor plan isn't ideal: There's the bedroom, the office, the large den, the terrace, the men's living room, and our spacious kitchen and dining area. But the kids have to share a room. Maybe we could set up the school classroom in the extra apartment. I'm sure the Webers would be happy about that. They'd have their room back, and with five children, they can use every inch of space they can get."

At our next team meeting, we brought up the matter for discussion. Surprisingly, the others thought it was a good idea. They even suggested using the apartment for overnight team guests. And so it was decided: We would go ahead and rent the apartment.

Mr. Chalil, the landlord, came by to let us into the apartment so that we could check it out. When we went in, we realized it was high time for this place to be occupied! There was a layer of sand everywhere! And just like the apartments we had seen during the previous months, the place was covered with building rubble and garbage. In one of the rooms, we discovered that it was already occupied: A snake had settled in, only to die of starvation.

I enjoy arranging furniture and decorating rooms, so I enthusiastically jumped at this opportunity. The tedious part came first: getting all the rubbish and rubble cleaned out and ridding the floors of all the dust and paint residue. Then the fun began: choosing the furniture, decorating the rooms, and picking some nice material for the drapes. We set up two of the rooms as guest rooms. A large living area was later used as a classroom. The small room became a storage area for Christian literature.

Soon afterward, the first guests began arriving. Since the kitchen wasn't finished yet, Chris and I invited the visitors to eat their meals with our family.

I didn't realize at the time how much additional work this all would mean for me! Being in charge of a hotel, a restaurant, and later on, a school was much more time-consuming and demanding than I could have imagined. I would have liked to spend more time with the locals. But I ended up spending more time with the laundry. That in itself posed quite a challenge, since we didn't have a washer, and there was always a water shortage. On top of that, I took care of the guests, cooking for them and driving them to and from the airport. Even if we just wanted to book a flight, we had to drive all the way into the city to the travel agency, since we had no Internet connection.

CHAPTER 9

Socotra

AFTER THE OTHER team members arrived back from their furlough in September 2000, Chris could take a few days off. The first few months had been rather strenuous with all the new beginnings, changes, and adjustments we had to make. Everything was new: the country, the people, the language, the work. We were all in need of a holiday!

A couple of weeks earlier, friends of ours visited us for a few days in Mukalla. Just before they left, they extended us a friendly invitation: "We'd love to have you visit us on the island of Socotra. Our kids would enjoy seeing David and Martin again. You're welcome to come anytime!"

Chris knew how much I loved the ocean, and that I had always dreamed of making a voyage. So one day, he surprised me with a brilliant idea:

"Sweetheart, you look so tired. How would you like to take a trip on an Indian sambuca to Socotra? It would take us several days out on the open Indian Ocean to get there. But there's a catch. These simple wooden ships don't have any cabins. They don't even have a bathroom! We'd have to take care of our 'business' like the sailors of old did: overboard! You just need to hold on tight!"

I was thrilled, even though sambucas weren't passenger ships.

"Cargo vessels are probably a lot cheaper, anyway. And who doesn't love an adventure?" I was all in!

Early the next morning, Chris took the boys down to the seaport. The place was bustling with noise and activity! The well-tanned fishermen had just come back from a night of fishing. Barefooted and bare-chested, they were cleaning their nets. The men worked closely together, all the while belting out their sea chanteys. Their colorfully painted boats swayed back and forth on the waves and shimmered in the sun. They had already taken their night's yield to the fish market, where traders were competing at the top of their lungs for the buyers' attention. The pungent smell of dried blood still lingered in the air. It was almost unbearable! In the distance, huge merchant vessels from all around the world had cast their anchors. Even two white yachts were docked here. Despite the hubbub at the port, the atmosphere was quite calm and laid-back.

Chris soon discovered that it wasn't going to be easy to book a ship to Socotra. Timetables didn't exist. A common saying here was: "If I don't show up today, I might show up tomorrow." While the vessels lay at anchor, the sailors dozed in the shade. The skippers waited for a lucrative offer. One could never know when a cargo ship would be sailing out, what freight it would be carrying, or where it would be heading. But as soon as negotiations were completed, the sailors loaded the cargo and set sail,

For the next few days, Chris hung around the dock with our boys, waiting. He had gotten to know a number of the sailors by now and was no longer so easily tricked into believing every word they said.

He kept hoping he would find a sambuca that would take us to the destination of our dreams.

It was unlikely, though, that such a ship would be sailing out anytime soon. Every year during the monsoon season, the island of Socotra is completely cut off from the rest of the world. For safety reasons, shipping traffic across the ocean comes to a standstill. But now, the monsoon season had ended, and some sailors were daring to set sail again. The islanders were in desperate need of provisions. During the stormy months, most of their resources had been depleted, and the cost of living had exploded.

The days at the dock were interesting enough for Chris and the boys, but after a week, we decided not to wait any longer. Chris had important meetings to attend and would have to be back in time for them.

So we just took it in stride and booked air passages to the legend-ary island of Socotra—and then we were off! On Saturday at 2:30 p.m., after only an hour's flight, we landed on the steppe-like runway of the island's little airfield. We were in the middle of nowhere. No streets or buildings anywhere to be seen! No taxis, no buses, only a few grazing goats and three soldiers. And of course piles of rubbish everywhere. We felt like we had reached the end of the world. Soldiers stood under a makeshift shelter—just a couple of posts holding up a thatched roof— to protect themselves from the scorching sun. Bags and suitcases were dumped onto a big pile, and one of the soldiers mindlessly circled it and pretended to guard them. The other soldiers rather crudely inspected the luggage, rummaging through the contents with their filthy hands. On their orders, small bottles of shampoo and other toiletries had to be opened for inspection. Sometimes they just emptied the contents onto the ground, allegedly checking for illegal substances. Our "souvenir" from this memorable customs experience was a bent latch on one of our suitcases, which kept us from closing it properly. Chris's travel bag was also slightly damaged.

"Oh well," Chris sighed. "At least we're on vacation now. Here we are on this beautiful desert island!"

After a while, we saw a Land Cruiser racing toward us along the runway at high speed, leaving clouds of dust in its trail. We were relieved to see our friend Jan at the wheel. After a warm greeting, he loaded all our things into his car and drove us over a bumpy gravel road to his home in Hadibu, the capital of Socotra.

On the way, he told us about the island and its inhabitants.

"The trade wind clouds lodge among the mountainsides of Socotra at over thirteen hundred feet. Sometimes a heavy fog extends like gray autumn drapery along the *wadi*.[24] Whenever it rains, it pours! Gale force winds whip the people with rain, and just being outside can be quite a soppy, nerve-racking experience. But usually, within an hour, it's all over."

When we arrived, Jan's children were delighted to see us! Aaron, Joel, Sabine, and Jeremias were about the same age as David and Martin. The kids always got along well and had a lot of fun together.

The houses in Socotra were all L-shaped. The exteriors were built up against a wall, and together they formed a rectangle with a courtyard at the center. All the rooms, including the kitchen and the bathroom, were lined up next to one another and were accessible from the courtyard through low-framed doors. Part of the courtyard had a canopy and was outfitted with comfortable mattresses, a table, and benches. Bianca had planted some vegetables on the far side, and in the middle, there was plenty of gravel and sand for the kids to play in. It was almost always warm and sunny here in Hadibu, so tenants spent most of their time in the courtyards, where the pleasant breeze kept them cool. In the house, it was stuffy and hard to breathe, and swarms of flies were constantly making their rounds.

We all extremely enjoyed our vacation on the island. Since we were of the adventurous sort, we didn't want to spend the whole time at our friends' home. We decided to rent a car for an exploration tour of the island.

Jan warned us: "We've got a shortage of gasoline right now since ships haven't been arriving for quite a while due to the monsoon season."

But we were confident we'd be able to find fuel somewhere, so we rented a car and a chauffeur. Then we loaded up the drinking water, enough provisions for several days, and our camping gear.

"We'll be fine!" we told ourselves and tried to convince our friends not to worry.

Perhaps we should have listened to them. Our chauffeur ran out of gas after only 12 miles. That left us stranded on a rugged plateau in the middle of the desert, the breaking waves roaring at us from underneath the steep decline. It was noon, and the sun had reached its peak. Our

---

24 river valley (mostly dried up)

driver knew, of course, that nobody in his right mind would be out and about in these parts at this time of the day. I was almost envious of his oriental mentality: He just lay down comfortably in the shadow of the car and took a nap.

This was just another opportunity for us to practice patience. We hoped and prayed in defiance of all Arab logic that God would send somebody our way. And sure enough, after about two hours, a fishing boat came chugging around the cliff.

Chris dashed down the rugged slope, jumping over stones and branches, and waved at the fisherman to pull his cutter over.

He pleaded: "Do you think you could get us to the beautiful Errehä beach before sundown?"

A discussion ensued, with hands and feet flying everywhere, but in the end, the skipper remained unmoved:

"We can either take you and your family or the luggage, not both!"

Chris tried to change the fisherman's mind, to no avail. He had no chance!

Chris gave up and climbed the steep slope again.

"If only we hadn't brought so much stuff along!"

We decided right then and there that we could do without some of our camping luxuries the next time around. So there we were, waiting again for someone to come along and rescue us. The time just dragged on and on.

"Did you hear that? A motor!"

And sure enough, another boat was coming around the cliff. Chris rushed back down to the shore. He was sweating so hard; it looked like he had just taken a bath. This time Chris was able to negotiate a deal. The fishermen agreed to take us and our belongings for just a couple of Socotra rials. We didn't have to think twice about that!

Chris took some of the heavier things down the slope. Our driver woke up, and when he realized we were leaving him, he was relieved. We had paid him in advance, so he made some easy money that day! He just smiled and waved us off.

David, Martin, and I began our tedious trek down the side of the plateau. Each of us took as much as we could carry. We had to be careful not to cause a landslide. As soon as we evenly distributed our things on the boat, we set out to sea, into the golden sunset. The boat skimmed over the shimmering waves, which rocked it back and forth with frightening intensity. We felt the sea spray splash in our faces. It was a wild ride, but it was fun. Our boys just laughed and held on tight to the side of the boat.

Martin asked, "Can I drive it for a while?"

But we were already in the middle of the ocean, and the waves were getting stronger. It would have been too dangerous to get up and exchange seats.

It was dark when we got to the shore. We unloaded all our belongings and quickly set up sleeping quarters. I hung the mosquito nets. Before the fishermen left, they promised to return a couple of days later to pick us up, after they were done fishing.

The kids were tired and hungry. While I was getting some tomato sandwiches ready, I asked: "Do you think there are snakes out here?"

Chris just kept his cool, as usual. He reassured me it would be okay, and soon our peaceful campsite was flooded with light from the clear full moon. Chris and the boys built a crackling campfire, boiled some water for tea, and roasted fish on it—fish the men had sold us for a rather shameful amount of money! But it sure did smell good, and it tasted delicious!

From our campsite, we could see the small lights on the fishing boat. The men stayed close to the shore to fish. They cast their nets all night long, and we could hear them singing their little chanteys.

The sun rose around 5:30 a.m., the warm rays rousing us from our sleep. Now that it was bright outside, we could appreciate the fascinating beauty of our little island of paradise. A fresh water spring ran down from the cliff into the ocean, creating a little stream on the white beach. Behind us, dark mountains rose high into the sky. A little farther up from our camp was a dune, about 350 feet tall. Chris and the boys climbed the mountain to the dune and played around in the sand, while I enjoyed a bit of peace and quiet. We were all truly enjoying our vacation here on this beautiful, secluded island! During lunch, we watched the dolphins play. They swam so close to shore that we could almost touch them! Time and time again, baby dolphins jumped out of the water in high arches. Apparently, they were enjoying all the attention they were getting. Once, David ran out into the water and challenged the porpoises to a race. It was a delight to watch!

It was on this romantic vacation that our hopeful suspicions were confirmed: We were going to have another baby! It had been hard to discern because I was already sick from amebic dysentery. During this season of my life. I struggled with weight loss and weakness.

Our water and food rations were beginning to run out. We waited and hoped the fishermen would keep their promise. They were to return to our camp after four days. Martin contracted a painful ear infection from his constant exposure to the brackish moisture.

The fourth day came, and with it, thick, dark clouds. The children were beginning to get fidgety. I had a hard time hiding my strained nerves. Chris stowed all the toys, clothes, and sleeping bags into the backpacks and an aluminum crate. We were all set for departure. And then the fishermen showed up, just as promised and right on time! They helped us put our things on board. Our load was lighter now. The men pointed to a dark bank of clouds rapidly coming our way and hurried us into the boat. The sky was indeed getting very dark, very fast.

I remembered what Jan had told us in the car on the way back from the airport.

Our turbulent ride in that tiny fishing boat was something we will never forget. The tumultuous ocean became more unpredictable by the minute, and the waves rose higher and higher and began to fill our little motorboat with their spray. A cloud burst, and the boys and I scooped the water out as quickly as we could. But we weren't fast enough. Chris and the men were busy rowing, since the motor wasn't any match for the storm and the heavy load of cargo.

I was worried. "Are we going to reach the shore?"

After fighting the thunderous storm for several miles, we finally caught sight of the shore of Hadibu and landed the battered vessel safely.

"How do we go on from here?" Martin asked Chris, who was thanking the fishermen and paying them a handsome fee. These brave men had just saved our lives!

But help was already on its way! Out of the blue, a car drove up and stopped. The driver had just gassed up at a station close by and offered us a ride. He helped get us and our belongings—soaked as we were—into the car and drove us all the way to the front gate of our friends' house.

The stranger helped us unload our things and was gone before we could even thank him. And so we stood there on the street in front of our friends' house, with all our things being soaked by the pounding rain. We had reached our destination—almost. We were relieved and hoped that somebody would open the door soon. Meanwhile, the four of us were drenched to the bone and shivering in the cold. Chris knocked on the door again. Nobody answered. He knocked again, this time louder. Nobody could hear us knocking. The rain was pounding too loudly on the tin roof, and the storm had no intention of letting up.

Nobody noticed the tears running down my face as they blended in with the raindrops. An additional 45 minutes in the rain shouldn't have made any difference since we were already sopping wet. In front of the neighbor's house, we found a car that was unlocked and placed our things inside it for protection. After a while, the rain stopped, and the sun came out. And then, finally, the heavy front gate began to open.

A child's voice asked, "Where did you come from? We thought you were lost. The rain pounding on the roof was so loud that we couldn't hear you knock."

Aaron quickly opened the gate all the way, and we stumbled inside.

I told my family, "We need to hang everything up. The wind and the sun will dry it all off. We don't want anything to get moldy."

It was fun to lay our wet things on the wall, over the branches and trees, on the chairs, or simply on the grass. There weren't enough clotheslines for all the soaked items.

By the evening, we were all exhausted. There was a power outage, and it would soon be pitch-dark. I was happy to be able to get the kids to bed early that night.

The children brushed their teeth and took a shower, and then put on their pajamas and crawled in under the huge mosquito net which covered both their beds. I tucked the net under their mattresses as I always did and then snuggled up next to my husband in our own net-covered bed. It was dark and completely quiet, except for the buzzing of the insects. But it was also very hot and sticky. The fans didn't work without electricity, and the air stood unbearably still.

Just as I was about to place my head on my soft pillow, Martin began to cry loudly. It was dark and I was tired, so I tried to comfort him without having to get out of bed.

"It's okay. Mommy's right here. Now turn over and go to sleep. We're all just tired!"

But it didn't work. He just cried even louder and worked himself up as only a 4-year-old can. I broke out into a cold sweat. What would the others think? After all, we were guests here. Our room was only a few yards away from our hosts, and we had left all the doors and windows on the courtyard side open because of the heat. I didn't want them to be disturbed by Martin's loud screaming, so I grabbed the flashlight Chris and I kept between our pillows and slipped out from under the mosquito net into the darkness. Quickly tucking the net back in, I crawled over to Martin, whose bed was not far away.

"What's wrong? Does something hurt?" I asked as I tenderly stroked his forehead.

I made sure I didn't let any mosquitoes in. He calmed down right away and then smiled when I turned my flashlight on to check for insects. Everything was all right again, and I went back to my own bed. Just as I was going to turn the flashlight off, I saw something dark on my pillow. I gave a short screech when I realized what it was. That startled Chris, and he quickly sat up. He had almost fallen asleep when I screamed. Now he was wide awake.

"A scorpion!" he whispered.

I grabbed a flip-flop that was lying nearby and beat the mosquito net and the venomous creature underneath until it was dead. Chris was scared stiff. My heart was pounding wildly. That was close!

Before getting back into bed, I smiled over at Martin and whispered to him: "Thank you. You saved my life. If you hadn't cried, I would have placed my head right on that beast!"

Martin was all smiles! And I vowed to check the net more closely from this point on before going to bed.

Although I was very tired, I had difficulty falling asleep. The excitement of the day and the spook of the night kept me awake. Chris realized that and gently rubbed my back until I finally dozed off.

Our vacation was quickly coming to an end. Chris spent the final two days with Jan on a hike around the island. He wanted to go up to the mountains to inspect the unique dragon trees. Unfortunately, I was too weak from dysentery and my pregnancy to join them. I preferred to get some rest before setting out on our adventurous return trip to Mukalla.

CHAPTER 10

A Dead Giant Lizard

AFTER RETURNING TO Mukalla, we took up our responsibilities again. Ever since Shariifa started coming two mornings a week, I could help out with the development project or teach the schoolchildren English, French, and German.

Meanwhile, I was truly grateful that I had help around the house. At the same time, I realized that she was watching our family closely to see how we conducted ourselves.

On one occasion, Chris and I were out of town, taking part in a conference at the university. The medical school had asked me to evaluate students who were presenting their dissertations.

That was to be a day Shariifa would never forget. She told me later what had happened:

"David was quite upset and was crying his heart out. He hardly ever cries! But he was inconsolable because his pet lizard had died. Shortly after you and Chris left, he found it lying in the yard. He picked it up and carried it around with him everywhere he went, grieving his loss. I tried to comfort him the best I could. I couldn't understand how someone can be so upset about an animal! When I couldn't think of anything else, I asked him if he would like to pray."

Her eyes began to water as she continued:

"He folded his hands, bowed his head, and moved his lips as if he were talking to Somebody. Then he got real quiet, dug a hole, and buried the dead lizard in it. After that, he just went on playing as if nothing had happened. He was happy again!"

A few weeks later, Shariifa revealed to me with a smile: "I love this boy as if he were my own. When he said that prayer and was changed in an instant, I figured he must have a really strong faith or a really strong, personal God!"

Shariifa was interested in both. But she had no idea at this point what this encounter with David was getting her ready for.

I never did have a sister, but I always wanted one. Shariifa was like a sister to me. And although we were very different, by now we were very close.

CHAPTER 11

Christmas

December 2000

DURING THE WEEKS leading up to Christmas, we decorated our home. It was hot and humid outside. The sand made a crunching noise under our feet, and the tiny individual grains shone like jewels in the sun. Chris made an Advent wreath with candles, using branches from acacia bushes, which grew right next to our home On Christmas Eve, he hung a few of the branches on the wall as a substitute for a Christmas tree, and we all attached candles to them, along with a few apples and stars made of straw. On a table next to our improvised Christmas tree, we placed a simple Nativity scene with homemade clay figurines. We hung a gigantic wreath with red bows over the threshold of the living room.

Every evening during Advent, we lit the candles on the wreath and sang traditional hymns.

We were trying to help our children appreciate German traditions, which were a part of their heritage. We didn't miss the overly decorated pre-Christmas season in Germany, with all its excessive gloss and glitter, but we did get a bit homesick as we sang these Christmas songs.

The decorative lights and our singing, which could be heard through our open windows, aroused the curiosity of many locals and drew them to our house, like bees being attracted to flowers.

"What are you celebrating? Is this your New Year's celebration?" they would ask.

Chris and I used these wonderful opportunities to share the Christmas message with our visitors. We told them the story and used the symbols around our house to explain it. A man from India named Ranjad, who worked in our town's hospital, came by. As he entered our house, it touched me to see his attention turn directly to the Nativity scene. His face lit up, and he went straight over and knelt before it reverently, without saying a word. It was as if he didn't even notice us or the others in the room. Then he began crying. Later on, he told us what had happened.

"I was raised a Catholic, but I never had a personal relationship with God. Religion had always seemed empty and shallow to me. But when I saw that simple presentation of Jesus in the manger today, I just had to kneel down and give my life to Him."

Our whole family was amazed to have witnessed that life-changing moment. Chris and I looked at each other and were at a loss for words. David hit the nail on the head when he smiled at Ranjad and told him: "Now there's joy in heaven. The angels are dancing and rejoicing, and we're rejoicing, too, because you are a part of God's family."

From that day on, Ranjad came to visit us often, and we welcomed him warmly.

One Friday afternoon, I was drinking tea with the other three women members of our team, when Heidi announced: "Christmas is just around the corner, even though it's hard to get into the Christmas mood when it's 90 degrees outside, and there are no decorations to be seen anywhere! But a birthday party for Jesus would be a good opportunity to invite friends and neighbors over and share the Good News with them!"

Larissa picked up the thought: "Maybe our husbands could organize a 'business Christmas celebration' for the men up on the roof of the office. What do you think?"

We just looked at one another and smiled. The suggestion was enthusiastically and unanimously approved. During the following weeks, we were like little children as we eagerly made all the preparations. The joy of anticipation grew and grew. We decorated the house, where the two single team members lived and where the party would take place. Then we baked tons of cookies and cake. It was very important to have enough to eat and drink at a party to which Arabs were invited.

Eva suggested: "Why don't we do a Christmas play about when Mary returned home after Jesus was born."

We agreed to enact the story of how the young virgin was despised and rejected. The Arab audience could greatly identify with Mary's situation. Their culture is very similar to the culture in the Bible. Eva played the part of Mary, who was returning to Nazareth with a newborn baby, thought by everyone to be an illegitimate child. The rest of us portrayed the neighbors, who reacted in a typical Arab manner, gossiping about Mary and questioning her reputation, which was as good as ruined. Everybody despised and ridiculed her. Poor Mary was treated with contempt because she hadn't kept the social norms. She was lonely. And yet, she radiated a deep peace, because she knew that she was special in God's eyes.

The whole evening was a noisy but cheerful celebration. Many women from the neighborhood and the Bedouin villages came and brought their friends and relatives along with them. Children were everywhere, and the women talked and talked, even as they ate vast amounts of homemade baked goods. These women weren't used to just sitting around quietly and listening. Most of them had not even attended school. Usually, in their homes the television was on all the time while they were talking, assuming the electricity hadn't been shut off.

So when the first act began, they just kept on talking. But when they realized what was happening, they shushed one another up.

"Sshhh, *uskutuu!*"[25]

Some were listening very closely to the unfamiliar story. My household helper, Shariifa, for instance, was so intrigued, that she forgot to continue eating. I could see her becoming more engrossed by the minute. It didn't even distract her when others began talking loudly again.

---

25 Be quiet!

Shariifa was illiterate, but she understood the message of the Good News and soaked it in like a dry sponge soaks up water. In her gleaming eyes, I could see that she was quite moved.

And then, suddenly, everyone began to leave. All the women simultaneously put their *baltos* and veils back on, wrapped a few cookies in a napkin, and stuffed them in their handbags, and left the party. It was as if somebody had blown a whistle. It amazed me to see these women find their own overcoats from the huge pile of black material. While standing at the front door saying good-bye to the women, I realized that the sun was setting. Apparently, somebody had indeed "blown a whistle"—the *muezzin* had begun reciting verses from the Quran and had called to evening prayer. I had not heard it through the din of the party, but these women seemed to have an internal alarm clock that told them when it was time to hold their ritual cleansings and begin the obligatory time of prayer.

We were thankful and full of energy as we began to clean up. There were scraps of paper, crumbs, and food remains everywhere, and the toilet was clogged. Then the lights went out, which happens in this part of the city regularly. The power had been shut off—again.

"At least we had electricity during the party," we sighed, as we lit some candles.

We stretched out on the *mafraj*,[26] leaned back, and put our feet up. In the candlelight, we couldn't see the dirt very well, and vacuuming wasn't possible without electricity anyway. So we just sat there a while longer and chatted about the events of the evening.

The men also had a successful evening. They met with their guests on the roof of our office building about 350 feet down the road. The Bedouin co-workers and many from the villages in the project area came and brought other men. Chris and his colleagues played a role-playing game with the locals. It was about the meaning of Christmas and was great fun for all those involved. Faisal, a sheik from a mosque in our project area, was especially amusing. They had many good talks, even though the guests watched each other closely, suspicious that there might be "apostates" among them.

---

26 a sofa without legs; mattresses that lie on the floor near the walls of the living area and have backrests and armrests

It was quite an eventful evening that brought us closer together as co-workers and deepened our relationships with the locals, as well.

Several days later, our children performed the Nativity play they had rehearsed with their teacher, Ruth. Our team celebrated the birth of Jesus up on the roof, singing Christmas hymns to keyboard and guitar. Under the oriental sky, full of stars, we felt like the shepherds in the fields in the New Testament account, except for the sheep. This time of the year, it cools off in the evening, so we had a mild 75 degrees. We set up a buffet with delicious sausages, pasta, finger food, salads, desserts, and homemade Christmas cookies. Everybody brought something to share. This was our first Christmas away from Germany, but we didn't feel homesick. We got along so well with the other team members here, and in this new home of ours, we were grateful to leave the typical German Christmas bustle behind.

CHAPTER 12

A Bloodcurdling Explosion

AROUND CHRISTMASTIME, I invited my friend, Shariifa, over for a visit.

"Come on over, and we'll watch the *Jesus Film* together. It shows the events around the birth of Jesus, and that will help you understand why we celebrate Christmas!"

Ever since we had celebrated Christmas with the women from the village, Shariifa had been asking all sorts of questions about religion and faith. The play about Mary also deeply touched her. She was honestly searching for the truth.

Now she was watching the screen in silence, her mouth wide open. She was so fascinated by the life and miracles of Jesus that she watched the entire three-hour movie from start to finish. The message obviously moved her greatly. The following day, she had quite a dramatic experience.

It was Sunday, in this part of the world a normal workday, and I was out with the children and Ruth, their teacher. Shariifa was at our home in the kitchen and went to the refrigerator to get something to drink. She was absorbed in thought, her mind wandering to the touching stories about Jesus that she had seen in the movie the day before.

"The man in that movie had such soft eyes! And he performed so many miracles and helped so many people. I want to know more about him. I'd like to get to know him personally," Shariifa sighed.

Chris was working in his office in the front part of the house when a bloodcurdling explosion tore through the silence. He was quite shocked.

"What was that? An earthquake?" he yelled terrified, as he stormed out of the office and into the kitchen, where the thunderous noise had originated. Dust filled the air.

He was shocked to see chaos everywhere, and Shariifa standing horrified in the corner of the kitchen. She was speechless and covered in dust.

In some mysterious way, the explosion had broken the light-colored floor tiles at the entrance to the kitchen and along the walls. The floor was left with a wide opening, and there was debris and rubble everywhere—on the floor, the stove, and the counters. It looked as if someone had covered the entire kitchen with sand.

The kids and I arrived shortly after that. Chris met us at the door. He was white as a sheet.

"Don't freak out, sweetheart! There's a hole in the floor across the entire kitchen. I put a couple of boards at the doorway to cover up the opening. I don't know how deep it is. You'd better use the backdoor and enter through the balcony. I don't want to risk anybody falling through and ending up downstairs."

He quickly related what had happened.

"I heard a loud detonation. At first, I thought somebody was attacking our house. I ran to the kitchen, where the noise had come from. Shariifa stood there completely motionless with her hands in front of her mouth. I think she was in shock. She didn't say a word."

David and Martin ran upstairs to check it out.

Martin moaned, "Papa, why didn't you leave it the way it was? We could have used our steam shovels to haul the dirt away!" He was always eager to help.

I went over to Shariifa and put my arms around her. "How are you doing?" I asked, concerned. "Are you okay? Did you get hurt?"

Shariifa shook her head. Then she put on a brave smile and began picking up the larger pieces of rubble and sweeping the dust into a pile in the corner.

"I don't know what happened. I was over there next to the refrigerator when everything just exploded," she whispered, still a bit taken aback.

"I know it wasn't your fault, Shariifa. Do you know why this happened?"

"I believe it's because I was thinking about the movie we saw yesterday," Shariifa answered right away. I realized she had already asked herself the same question.

"Right. You want to know the truth about God. Your heart is longing and searching. But the enemy of *Isa al-Masih*[27] is *Schaitaan*,[28] the devil, also called 'the one who confuses.' He doesn't want you to know the truth. He wants to deceive people and keep them blind to the truth."

"That's all the more reason for me to discover the truth," Shariifa answered.

"I'd like to stay longer after lunch and watch the movie again," she added. "Did you get it for me in my native language?"

I nodded.

Although our children and I didn't understand Somali, we sensed that my dark-skinned friend was deeply touched by watching the movie in her mother tongue. She hung on the actors' words, and tears flowed down her cheeks.

After she had gone home, we began the sobering task of trying to figure out how we were going to get the floor fixed.

"We have to inform the landlord!" Chris said decisively.

The landlord sent over a specialist, who took several days trying to figure out what had caused the explosion.

After thoroughly examining the damage, the expert shrewdly reported: "There is no distinct or obvious reason for this absurd incident. It was simply the will of Allah!"

27 Jesus, the Messiah
28 Satan

The repairs claimed another few weeks. Unfortunately, we weren't able to find the same light-colored tiles anywhere. The workmen spent three days replacing the tiles with less attractive, yellowish tiles. It took them an unusually long time to get the job done. Apparently, they enjoyed hanging around our house and being able to catch an occasional glimpse of me, the exotic foreign woman. I decided to hide in my own house as best I could.

After the renovation was complete, the darker tiles always reminded us of what can happen when somebody opens his heart for Jesus.

During the following weeks, we were amazed to see the change taking place right before our eyes. Shariifa's life was turning around completely. It seemed that a light had been turned on inside her heart. We knew that it was God who had prepared Shariifa and drawn her to himself. That filled us with awe and wonder. It was obvious to us that God wasn't interested in someone's education or knowledge. Shariifa was illiterate, but she could grasp spiritual things. I just marveled at God's ability to do such a miracle.

Shariifa's enthusiasm for Jesus was dynamic and contagious. That made it just a matter of time before she would receive backlash for her faith.

"I have to tell all my friends and neighbors about *Isa al-Masih!* I can't keep that from them. He is the answer to all their questions!"

It wasn't long before the Imam, the head of the mosque, started calling on Shariifa unannounced on a daily basis. He began giving her private lessons on the teachings of the Quran. In the end, this strengthened her faith, because she would always come to me with the questions she had from her lessons with the Imam.

"Islam teaches this. What does your Christian book have to say about that?"

Since she couldn't read, I would share the appropriate biblical stories with her or relate what I was personally learning from God's Word. In addition to that, we got some audio CDs of the Bible, which she could listen to while she worked.

But sometimes I was concerned for my friend's well-being.

I wondered, "If she is persecuted for her newfound faith, how will I deal with it?"

I wrestled with that problem for a long time. And not without reason. Shariifa received many death threats over time. Even in the bus on her way to work, people would pressure her and mob her. Shariifa was aware that immigrants like her didn't have many opportunities and that her newfound faith could easily cost her life. Her husband, Sultan, who was not a very religious man, apparently had no problem with her new convictions. He gave her a lot of leeway, trusted her, and allowed her to continue to come and work with us Germans. He even watched the *Jesus Film* with us. He had the education of a Yemeni nobleman and could read tracts and other literature. Sultan got along very well with Chris, and they had serious discussions about faith.

It was Shariifa herself who provided the answer to the question that had tormented me. "What do I have from life, if I have to live it without Jesus? Life is not worth living without him. And if I die, I'll go straight to him in paradise. Other religions don't offer that security, no matter how hard you work to attain it! I have finally found peace, and my heart is at rest. So don't you worry about me!"

CHAPTER 13

Everyday Life and the Project Operations

WHEN WE FIRST came to Mukalla, everything was new and exciting. Nothing was predictable. It was just one surprise after the other. I felt like one of these transparent snow globes, where the multicolored snowflakes twirl around and around inside. As soon as one of our life's "snowstorms" began to settle down, the next event came along and swirled the flakes up again. Everything was spinning around inside me like a whirlwind. There was no way to process all that was going on. But maybe that was just me. I was sensitive and was often overwhelmed by all the signals I received from people around me.

But after we had been in our new "home away from home" for a few months, the snowstorm inside me calmed down, and only a few flakes swirled around at any given time. Our everyday life started to develop a certain rhythm. The daily routine with the kids became predictable. Shariifa was a welcome companion, and I depended on her support and appreciated her friendship. We all began to feel less foreign in our new homeland. We finally felt like this was our home.

The other women on the team and I kept very busy. Reaching out to the neighbors took time, and on top of that were the household chores, which were a lot more time-consuming than we had been used to. We would also spend quite a bit of time bargaining with the merchants in the marketplace. Then there was the time involved getting the school up and running. There was never a moment I can remember during our entire stay in Yemen when I could sit around with my hands on my lap. Unpredictability was something we could count on: the electricity broke down; without warning visitors came by anywhere from 6 a.m. to midnight; the plumbing clogged up, and we were without water, again. Without running water, we couldn't brush our teeth, wash our hands, flush the toilets, or even rinse the lettuce for a salad. Creativity and flexibility were constantly required. For example, the water pressure was highest in the middle of the night when others were sleeping, but still too low to pump it to the roof to fill the tanks. So I would put a bucket under the tap where it would fill slowly drop by drop. Back to bed I would go until it was full. Then up to put another under the tap. Throughout the night I would babysit those buckets for precious water.

There was never a dull moment. One day, Shariifa decided not to show up, without letting me know in advance, of course. The next day, one of the children got sick and had to be taken to the hospital, since there weren't any doctors' offices in town. And so it went.

But for the most part, we had adjusted well. Our motto was, "Make the best of everyday life, and embrace the unexpected with a smile and a song!"

Often, I would interrupt my daily household chores to visit my neighbors or help out in one of the project areas.

I quickly got used to wrapping a colorful scarf around my head whenever I left home. Sometimes my hairdo was the worse for wear because of it, but the other women on the team and I wanted to fit into this conservative Islamic society, so that wasn't very important. While in the house, I usually wore the same colorful, flowing robes that the Yemeni women liked to wear. They were made of silk and reached all the way down to the floor. Jeans or close-fitting clothes would have been very uncomfortable in this hot and humid desert climate.

On more than one occasion, women who were perfect strangers came up to me and pulled my veil farther down into my face or shoved a rebellious strand of hair back under my headscarf. These very intimate intrusions were something I had a hard time getting used to.

The city women, elegantly dressed in black, would scold, "Why aren't you wearing a black veil? Only country women and the Bedouins wear such colorful headscarves!"

But I wasn't going to allow them to dictate my taste in color! These women learned at their mother's knee that the color black was chic and elegant. I thought black was a depressing color and didn't like the way I looked in it.

I complained to Chris, "It's bad enough that I have to cover my head and wear that black *balto*." But I did it for the sake of the local women here.

Sometimes talking with the women about veils and the like afforded me an opportunity to reach deeper. If the women noticed that I was taking a genuine interest in them and sincerely listening, they were willing to let me share my faith with them.

As Chris personal secretary I helped with the office work and prepared reports, applications, and other paperwork. He spent most of his time with the development projects, which reached into several of the poorest villages in Hadhramaut. Child mortality was very high among this destitute rural population, even by Yemeni standards about 90 deaths per thousand births.. The hygienic conditions were very poor, and there just wasn't enough clean water.

Our team's goal was to help improve the medical care and general living conditions in the rural areas and villages. That involved passing on information about how to prevent disease, holding vaccine drives, and offering basic hygiene instructions. We concentrated specifically on helping underprivileged groups of people—the poor, the women, and the children—by holding campaigns to "help people help themselves." We also encouraged them to accept more personal responsibility for their health and environment.

Training local health teachers was one of our priorities. They, in turn, could teach the villagers what they had learned. By having the locals help out, we hoped to create a positive snowball effect, with each one passing their knowledge on to the next ones. Our goal was to make life easier for them and reduce child mortality significantly.

We came to Yemen with a big heart for the people here. That helped us endure all the opposition, hardships, and dangers we experienced. We all knew for sure that God had called us to this place, and we wanted to show his love for these poor people by offering practical humanitarian aid.

By the way, the idea to settle here in Hadhramaut was not ours. The Yemeni government had suggested it. They were grateful for the humanitarian support we had to offer since they had not been able to deal with the poverty and widespread diseases in this area. The men from our team spent much time with the underprivileged, abandoned tribes, trying to gain villagers' trust and convince the skeptics. These simple people tended to believe every horror story told to them about us foreigners. Soon after we moved here, the Islamists felt threatened and began sowing seeds of distrust among the residents, telling lies and half-truths about us and our intentions.

"These light-skinned foreigners don't want to help you. They want to make you turn your back on your religion and become heretics. They get money for every Muslim they convert to Christianity. Beware of these people!"

It took time and patience to win the people's trust. Our men visited individual villages, established contacts, talked with the elders of the village over a cup of tea, and shared our ideas with them:

"We'd like to hold a vaccination drive in your village. And we'd like to check your schoolchildren to find out which diseases are most common. Is it diarrhea, typhoid, malaria, or maybe ear disorders or skin problems? That will allow us to help you more efficiently."

We met and talked for hours on end. And finally, the elders of the villages were amazed and convinced that these "dangerous foreigners" were obviously not as bad as some would have made them out to be. They started to trust us.

As soon as the people of a village agreed to work with us, we sent in a team and started to work, setting up various projects in 11 of the poorest villages in Hadhramaut and four of the Bedouin settlements. In the main village, we built a health care center and a dental clinic. From there we conducted the vaccination drive. We had local medical personnel available to do health checkups or administer vaccinations to the underprivileged free of charge (the government helped to pay for it). A second building was constructed to set an example for the locals in methods of personal hygiene and show them how to lead a healthy lifestyle in their home settings. We had an exemplary "hand washing unit" on display, which anyone could easily build from readily available materials: We tied a cord to the handle of a simple salad oil can and filled it with clean water. By tipping the can, a "running water faucet" could be simulated, something we called a "tipi tap." This was a first step toward improving the hygiene at home and reducing diarrhea.

With the help of locals, we could construct beautiful, cement-block school buildings in several of the poorest villages. The straw shacks previously used as schoolrooms didn't offer the children protection from the scorching heat. The pupils had to sit on the ground, and every summer, the huts would be destroyed by the strong desert wind called *qauzz*.

Our new, white school buildings drastically improved the reputation of the villagers, who were otherwise despised because of their illiteracy. After school hours, the buildings were used to offer sewing classes and literacy courses to the women.

We offered these sewing classes free of charge to women who could not afford it, so they could learn to make their own clothes. With the help of local teachers, we provided reading and writing courses for illiterate women and children. They could also learn to weave using a loom. These courses not only increased the women's self-esteem but also supplied them with a source of income through the sale of their self-made products. Our desire was to help these "poorest of the poor" get out of poverty's downward spiral by becoming self-sufficient.

We also dug wells, so that the women didn't have to fetch water from the distant river and carry it back on their heads to the village. They would wash their clothes in that river, as well.

Chris set up a co-op cement factory for the locals at which they produced cement blocks for private and public building projects. That created jobs and revenue. A nice side effect was that the cement blocks they made were less expensive than those from other factories since transport costs were negligible. The villagers and the local development projects profited directly from the factory's earnings.

"As soon as we get more helpers, we can accomplish a lot more!" Chris was always full of ideas, constantly thinking up new projects. "We could offer trade courses for the men, and then…"

We had many projects on paper and could implement most of them over time. There were irrigation and farm projects for the farmers; various fishing projects, for instance, fair-trade initiatives for the local fishermen's merchandise; projects for establishing democratic associations to give the poor a voice and representation in society; training projects for the unemployed young people; projects for the handicapped; continuing education courses for county and state councilmen; small loans for families wanting to start up their own businesses; drinking water projects for the Bedouin population; and many, many more.

My hard-working husband was always quite involved in these projects. Even when he was at his office in Mukalla, he would often be reaching out to various government departments and agencies. The best part about him working in the office was that he could take his lunch break at home. Chris would sometimes spend the lunch hour making Lego brick buildings with the boys or reading to them. The children loved playing with their father, exploring the Playmobil knight's castle, or building towers from the sofa cushions and hiding behind them. Sometimes Chris would just fall asleep on one of the cushions, fully exhausted. But the boys wouldn't let him sleep very long. Other times, though, the children were disappointed. They had so looked forward to spending time with their father, only to find out that someone had come by unexpectedly and had "stolen" him away from them. Or Chris had something to take care of on the computer that just couldn't wait. But he always found time for them in the evening. He would read them exciting stories from the Bible or share some of his own. After a while, the boys knew all the biblical accounts by heart and could recite most of them word for word.

Martin and David admired their father greatly and couldn't get enough of his stories. When he stopped reading, they would make a contest out of who could ask the most questions to keep him going. That way, they could postpone bedtime almost indefinitely. After this "delay tactic," as we affectionately called it, was finally over, Chris and I usually sat down with our guitar and keyboard and sang some worship songs together. Our boys enjoyed that just as much as we did. We pretended not to notice them hiding behind the sliding door, secretly listening.

CHAPTER 14

Free Advertising
from the Mosques

AFTER OUR CHRISTMAS and New Year's cel-
ebrations were over, and we reopened the office in Mukalla in January 2001, Walid, the office secretary, came in all worked up. We were
expecting the worst. He handed a note to Chris, and I noticed that
Chris looked concerned. Walid was upset:

"This pamphlet is hanging in every mosque in Hadhramaut within
a one hundred and fifty mile radius."

He wiped the sweat from his brow and, after a short pause, continued his rant. "Yesterday at the Friday services all the sheiks and the
mullahs in the entire district preached from this hostile brochure. They
are shouting warnings from the minarets, warnings about you. They
claim that you came to Christianize the God-fearing Muslims here in
the 'Valley of Death!'

"They decried the Christmas celebration you held in December for
the men of the community. They claimed that you allowed women to
dance with men! That's a lie, of course. I was there myself and can attest

to the fact that the men were off to themselves and that nothing objectionable at all took place!"

He sighed and continued: "The Arab news media reported about the New Year's Eve celebrations in Western Europe. They showed fireworks, drinking binges, and dance events, where men danced with women! That's quite inappropriate in the eyes of Muslims! They probably got something mixed up and thought you were doing those things, too.

"You are being unjustly accused! People here often confuse Christmas with the New Year's celebration, since most of them don't know when Christmas is actually celebrated. The leaders of the mosques denounce you Christians for trying to lead Muslims away from the true faith and getting them to participate in your immoral behavior. This defamation campaign could become threatening. The pamphlet even calls on the pious Muslims to do something to stop the Christians!"

Of course, the men in our team had noticed that something was wrong during the past Friday's noontime prayer. The agitation in the mullah's voice couldn't be missed. We all spoke enough Arabic to understand that they were villainizing us. We were alarmed and discussed what we should do. We asked our native co-workers how they would deal with this denunciation. While we were still talking, the phone rang. The health minister, one of the main sponsors of our development projects, was on the line.

"Please come right away to the ministry building and bring your project director with you. We need to speak with you immediately." His voice, accustomed to giving orders, had an urgent ring to it.

Chris and Udo quickly finished their tea and left. What should they make of this summons to the health department? I stayed behind with the children and prayed. Later, Chris told me what happened at the meeting.

As soon as Chris and Udo arrived, Ahmed Ibn Saiid, the government official, sent all the people in the waiting room home. After they had all left, he warmly greeted the two Germans.

"I want to let you know that I am very pleased with the work you are doing, and I am sorry that fundamentalists are trying to disqualify you and cause you trouble! Yesterday they shouted it from the mosques for everybody to hear. They even called upon the Muslims to revolt against you. This is a very serious matter and something we do not take lightly!

"I have talked with the chief of our secret service, and we have come to the following conclusion: These accusations are completely unfounded, but this malicious campaign against you is very dangerous. That is why I would like to give you some advice. First of all, the government wants you to continue your work. We feel that it is highly productive and helpful. But there are some people who would like to see you deported. So please regard what I am saying very carefully: Continue your work as usual, but in the project area, try to concentrate on what's most important. You have been accused of owning Bibles. If that is true, please don't pass them out in the project area or on the streets. We don't want to give your opponents more grounds for criticism!" He sighed:

"I personally don't have anything against you owning Bibles. What you do in private is none of my business, anyway. But please don't give your adversaries ammunition to fire at you. Otherwise, we won't be able to protect you."

With a mischievous grin on his face, he waved his hand as if making light of it all and suggested: "If you leave a Bible lying around at home and somebody picks it up, no problem! But please don't actively distribute them, okay?"

Chris and Udo smiled and nodded. They were relieved how the conversation had gone. Our men were dismissed with a friendly, supportive smile, and after only a few short days, the crisis had been resolved.

Interesting enough, the denunciation had a pleasant side effect: It was free advertising for us! Yemenis interested in Christianity now knew where to find us and get their questions answered!

But the fundamentalists didn't give up so easily. They tried time and time again to discredit our work and rile the crowd up against us. Wherever we began a new project, new mosques would spring up, paid for by Saudi Arabia. Next to our infirmary in the main village of Al Qariyah, they built a large, new mosque with a green minaret. That was quite a setback for the friendly Imam, the head of the existing mosque.

After we had finished building the school in Sherj, this scorned, despised little village was suddenly worthy of a white, oversized mosque with a green minaret.

In our immediate neighborhood, we already had five mosques. Within a short period, three more were built in our vicinity, giving us a total of eight mosques near our house. After that, we were blasted every day from all sides during each of the five times of prayer.

The poor also noticed this building boom. Ali, a Bedouin friend of ours, told Chris: "I don't get it. You people came from far away to help us, even though you aren't Muslims. And all the while, our rich Muslim neighbors from the Gulf States come over and build new mosques, but they leave us to die of starvation!"

CHAPTER 15

Foiled Plans

"TOMORROW MASEJA IS coming to work in your home. She will be my substitute for a week or two since I am going away for a while."

I was shocked, when Shariifa announced that out of the blue. But it was only when she was away that I realized what a gem she was. I waited every day for her return until I thought she would never come back. The long and lonely months seemed like eternity and I really missed my friend and companion.

A difficult time began.

Maseja had two small children, and sometimes she brought them along with her. I ended up watching them while Maseja worked, trying to keep them from turning the house upside down. Maseja had some trouble doing the household chores properly. For instance, she just couldn't understand why she shouldn't use the toilet rag to wash the kitchen dishes. But at least she had mastered the art of wasting water. She poured it onto the floor by the bucketful when she was mopping.

More than once she would break some household item. She came only one day a week for four hours. I let her decide which day she wanted to work. But since I never knew in advance when she was coming, I usually had the house cleaned by the time she showed up, which was often right before noon.

She was always begging me for more money. "Please, can't you pay me more? My children need clothing. Oh, Martin's trousers and T-shirt are so pretty! My child is sick, and I need to get some medicine for him."

But the more I gave her, the more she demanded. It was never enough. She was like a bottomless pit. Actually, she was more of a burden than a help. If I hadn't felt so sorry for her, I would have fired her for good.

Meanwhile, I was five months pregnant, and my tummy was already bulging beneath my dress. One day I was in the kitchen shaving Swabian noodles, and my legs were tired. Our most recent guest had gone home just that morning after having stayed with us for the last three weeks. She had been quite demanding, always wanting special attention. Chris had just left to pick our next visitor up from the airport.

Suddenly, I felt horrible stomach cramps and had trouble staying on my feet. Why wasn't Maseja here when I needed her the most? I had already spent the entire morning teaching the schoolchildren and preparing the guest room for our new visitor. Shariifa had been gone for months. Oh, how I missed her right now! But it was no use complaining. I had to keep going and get dinner ready before our guest arrived.

While dining with our guest, I began to bleed profusely. I ran to the bathroom. I felt faint, and my head was spinning, so I decided to lie down and rest for a bit. I was in no condition to entertain guests anyway. My thoughts were with the baby, and I was very worried. My husband and our guest were sitting in the living room, drinking a cup of tea. They were immersed in an important conversation.

It was quite a while before Chris noticed that something was wrong with me. He called Heidi, the midwife on our team, who had previously helped me with the birth of our elder son in Jordan.

"Please come quickly," Chris pleaded. "I think Amiira is having problems with the baby."

She came at once and examined me.

"We have to go to the hospital immediately!" she ordered.

Chris rushed the two of us to the nearest hospital, the Mustashfa-Hadhramaut. The doctor tapped at my abdomen, then followed up with an ultrasound. She said soberly:

"Your child is dead. But there is still some tissue in your uterus. We'll have to perform a scraping to remove it. Do you want to do that now or later?"

Although I had suspected something like this, the initial shock was overwhelming. I said I'd prefer to go home and be with our children. But Heidi objected: "Amiira, be reasonable! The bleeding and pain won't stop until you have it done." She insisted that I go straight to the operating room.

"Take care of it now. Otherwise the bleeding will continue!" The blood loss had weakened me, and I finally agreed. Chris went home to put the kids to bed.

Heidi promised to stay behind and help me. It was a comfort to have a good friend and trained midwife by my side, especially when I realized that I was about to be anesthetized in a foreign country.

Afterward, Heidi told me that the doctor had given me a fairly heavy dose of anesthesia, one strong enough to knock out a 170-pound man. I weighed only about 95 pounds due to the amebic dysentery I had just recovered from, so that was quite a doozie of a shot! While I was going under, I murmured, "No, please don't take my child away from me!" That prompted the doctor to give me a second dose of the narcotics, which left me completely unaware of anything that happened during the hours that followed. I was sound asleep!

Heidi told me later, "Even then, right after the scraping you tried to open your eyes. You were so stubborn and just blurted out: 'I'm awake! Let me go home!'"

I didn't remember that, either. I apparently fell back to sleep with those words on my lips.

Chris and Heidi took me home, still out cold. They tried to break the news to the boys as gently as they could.

Chris explained to them what had happened. "Jesus took your little sister to heaven and is holding her in his arms right now."

Martin was very upset. "I wanted to hold my little sister in my arms, too. Why did he take her away from me? That's not fair!"

We couldn't have anticipated how much our sons would suffer from the loss of their sister. I remained asleep and was oblivious for hours. Somehow I was glad to be able to forget everything for a while.

Letting go was hard for Chris and me. But many friends showered us with love and compassion, especially our team. It was hard for the two of us to talk to each other about our daughter's death since each of us mourned in our own way. Like most men, Chris retreated and got lost in his work. We both felt isolated and alone, yet somehow this painful episode bonded us together.

During this time, a call from my twin brother in Germany comforted me greatly. He couldn't even speak but just sobbed. He cried the tears that I could not because they had been locked up in my heart. I blamed myself for what had happened.

Was the culprit the Lyme disease that I had caught 2 years before, weakening my body or was it the amebic dysentery I caught in Socotra? Had I overexerted myself during the last few days? What had caused our baby's death?

We had experienced disappointments before and knew that Christians sometimes must endure difficult times. But we didn't know how to cope with the monster called "despair." Some time later, I finally let go of the torturous, piercing questions, to which I had no answers. It was no use! I just had to stop racking my brain about it. So I decided to return our little girl into God's loving arms.

Slowly but surely, I regained my sense of peace, and it gave me great comfort to know up in heaven our baby was well taken care of.

CHAPTER 16

Dinner with Bin Laden

A YEMENI PRIVATE school had just opened, and we decided to enroll David in their second-grade class in the morning. In the afternoon he would continue with German and English in our homeschool. We spoke with the school principal to make sure David wouldn't have to participate in the Islamic religion classes. We only found out later that he actually was required to take part in those classes. He even had to memorize the Quran. Altogether, the Islamic lessons took up more than half of the entire schooling period.

David told us what went on in the school behind closed doors. All the pupils had to wear green school uniforms. Each morning at 7:25, he went with his fellow Yemeni students to the front of the school building and stood at attention during the hoisting of the flag. Then they marched two by two into the school building, each grade separately. The classrooms were small and cramped and seated up to 68 children in pairs at tiny desks. The students were to sit there quietly until the teacher arrived. Then they all jumped to their feet, stood straight as a ramrod, and greeted the teacher with the appropriate respect. Order and discipline reigned in this school, and disobedient pupils made the acquaintance of the paddle.

Lessons went on without a recess until 1:00 p.m. When school finished, the children ran home in swarms, still dressed in their uniforms. They could be heard a mile away, running and yelling at the top of their lungs, releasing all the energy they had been required to hold in during school hours. From a distance, I recognized my son's voice, even though he was speaking Arabic. Then on September 11, 2001 two planes crashed into the World Trade Center and the political situation here escalated. The atmosphere became more and more anti-American. It made me nervous to see the students wearing black headbands with slogans from malicious Islamist anti-Hamas and anti-West campaigns.

Shortly before the holy month of Ramadan began, David's teachers asked us to come in for a talk. Though embarrassed, they strongly recommended that we should accompany our son on his way to school. They told us that several difficulties had already been reported. For instance, a student had stabbed a sharpened pencil into David's back, just because he was the *ajnabee*.[29] It didn't make any difference to the local children whether we were Americans or Germans, because the Arab television networks broadcasted defaming language against the West in general.

For months David had often complained about stomach cramps and headaches. I was worried since sometimes he had also a fever and other symptoms Was he seriously sick, or did he hide things so we wouldn't worry?

But one day, it was as if scales fell from my eyes. I suddenly intuitively knew that the situation at school was getting unbearable. I desperately tried to convince Chris that we should take David out of the school as soon as possible. That was rather difficult since I couldn't base my intuition on any evidence. But I was totally sure what we were supposed to do. It was almost as if I had heard a voice telling me: "Enough is enough!" I convinced my husband that we should talk to the teacher the next day and take our son out of the Yemeni school. To our surprise, the headmaster started the conversation after greeting us friendly, "I am sorry to tell you that there were problems with some older kids.

---

29 foreigner

They harassed David, because they see the campaigns in TV against the West. We as teachers think, that it is better to take him out of school for some time. But we all hope, that things will calm down soon. Oh, what a shame! He's such a gifted student.

"*Inshallah* you can send David back to our *madrassa*[30] soon. He is very smart and has good comprehension skills. He would be able to catch up quickly!"

David was relieved that he no longer had to attend the Arab school. Later, we got the story out in bits and pieces of how badly he was harassed by some older boys. Silence filled the room, and I held my breath, not knowing what to say. We had definitely made the right decision in taking him out of this school! He had suffered enough!

I blamed myself. "If only I had realized earlier what he was going through!"

I had been distracted by the pregnancy during David's enrollment. We had signed him up for classes along with Tobi Weber, who was David's age. During the past few weeks, I had also been very busy setting up the new classroom in the basement of our house.

I decided then and there to pay more attention to my intuitions. I began to believe that the Holy Spirit had given me a special gift of discernment. And it was important for me to learn to use that gift instead of putting it on a shelf.

* * *

Now we knew without a doubt that our life here in Yemen was being affected by the attacks in America. The whole world was in an uproar, and on the Arab peninsula, the guest workers and foreigners had to suffer. We couldn't deny it any longer.

* * *

A few weeks later, we received an invitation to the opening ceremony of a new Holiday Inn Hotel. A renowned wealthy businessman had built a luxurious hotel just outside of Mukalla.

---

30 school

We got dressed up and drove that Friday afternoon to Khalf, a suburb of Mukalla. We were very excited as we moved along the seafront and admired the beauty of the ocean, shimmering brightly in various shades of emerald green and sapphire blue.

As we got out of the car, we noticed that not many other guests had arrived yet.

Upon entering the reception area, we met an elegantly-dressed waiter with a tray full of ice-cold beverages. He served us more than once, and we were grateful for the sweetened drinks. After that, he led us into the beautiful dining area. From our table we had a wonderful view of the newly landscaped palm-tree garden and the wide-open sea.

A distinguished Yemeni gentleman, dressed in European clothing, sat at the table next to ours, while we waited for dinner. He gave us a friendly nod, then he stood up and turned to my husband, shaking his hand.

"Welcome, sir! Thank you for coming!" he said. "We are very sorry that we had to postpone the celebration for two weeks The construction workers just weren't able to finish in time. But since you obviously weren't aware of the delay and came here to celebrate with us, allow me to welcome you as our very special guests! The bill will be on the house, so please enjoy your meal!"

Of course, we enjoyed being the only guests!

After we finished the delicious dinner and dessert, the hotel manager, Mansur from Syria, gave us a guided tour of the hotel. He mentioned that he lived with his family fairly close to our home and that his children were about the same age as ours. His wife Samantha became a good friend of mine and the kids would enjoy playing together with their new Syrian friends in the following weeks.

"Oh, by the way, that friendly gentleman in the dining room, who sat at the table beside you and paid your bills, he is my boss and the owner of the hotel—Mr. Bin Laden from Saudi Arabia!" Mansur explained. "He is partner of the hotel chain Holiday Inn and wanted to build a outstanding beautiful hotel here in Hadhramaut, where his family comes from. He had all the building materials imported directly from Saudi Arabia, even the mirrored balcony doors, and all the flooring!"

Tim was just finishing his ice cream and remarked: "How can this nice man be Mr Bin Laden? He gave me Coca Cola and ice cream!"

Chris laughed, "That's Osama Bin Laden's brother. The Bin Laden family is very rich!"

There was not much going on in this beautiful hotel, and since we were the only guests, we took advantage of the nice pool and the beach, which we had all to ourselves.

Osama Bin Laden's activities, unfortunately, didn't do his brother's hotel any good. On the contrary, the hotel suffered a great financial loss.

CHAPTER 17

The Risk

SHORTLY FOLLOWING THE miscarriage, I became pregnant again. It was a big surprise since we hadn't planned it, but we were both very happy. Of course, I worried just like all expectant mothers do. The doctors told us we shouldn't have another baby. There were still bacteria from the Lyme disease in my body, which could have negative effects on me and the baby. And my body was still very weak from the miscarriage.

During the seventh week of my pregnancy, we were on our way to Germany for a visit. The timing wasn't ideal. I wasn't well at all—I had a bad cough, morning sickness, and was just feeling miserable all over. I spent most of the time in the plane's lavatory throwing up. When we finally arrived at the airport, I was completely exhausted. The doctors diagnosed me with pneumonia.

For a while, we stayed with friends and then moved into our employer's headquarters. I found a gynecologist and went in for regular checkups. When the blood test results came back from the lab, the doctor called and said that I should see him as soon as possible.

"You have to come right away. We found acute and chronic Lyme disease bacteria in your blood. That means your life and your baby's life are endangered. We can't guarantee you'd survive the birth. You might bleed to death!"

I tried to reassure the young doctor. "I got Lyme disease a few years ago, but I don't have any symptoms now."

The doctor almost became hysterical. "You knew that you had this disease and didn't say anything? Well, unfortunately, a new acute infection has set in. Come to my office the first thing tomorrow morning, and we'll talk about what to do next."

I didn't sleep well that night. I just prayed and wept. Slowly but surely, a deep, supernatural peace came over me, and I started to calm down. I knew without a doubt that Jesus was in control. He told me, "If I want to give you another child, then you have no reason to worry. Nothing can happen to your child. I can do the impossible. Don't look at your circumstances. Just trust me!"

"OK. I'm going to decide right now that I won't worry anymore," I said to myself.

I was surprisingly calm at the doctor's office the next morning. The doctor across from me, however, was upset. Chris couldn't come along since he was on the road lecturing. The doctor got right down to business.

"I want to send you to the clinic to abort the child. The embryo can't survive anyway, so it's best we do it right away. It's for your own protection!"

I interrupted the doctor before he could continue. Calmly but resolutely, I told him: "I appreciate your professional opinion. I know you only want what's best for me. Thank you for your concern. But my husband and I need time to talk about such an important decision as an abortion. I can assure you that we are not naïve, but we believe in miracles, and we would like to..."

Now the doctor interrupted me. "Please listen to me. This is a very serious matter. It's a high-risk pregnancy. If your immune system overreacts, it could poison you. Then it will be too late for antibiotics or other countermeasures. You have a damaged blood clotting mechanism, and you are at great risk of bleeding to death!"

I just nodded. I figured I wouldn't be able to convince the doctor, no matter what I said. But I wasn't about to let his well-meant advice rob my peace.

The gynecologist got impatient and ended the consultation.

"Have the assistant at the desk give you a new appointment. Good-bye."

I didn't stop at the desk. I went straight to the door. I never intended to return to this office again! Right then and there, I decided to place my trust fully in God.

Chris wrestled with my decision at first. He felt responsible for me and was worried. We agreed I would consult another gynecologist and get a second opinion. This doctor was less pessimistic, and so after much prayer and reflection, Chris and I made a decision: We were going to believe our heavenly Father. He promised that he has a solution for every problem, ours included. We decided to keep the child. No abortion! We were full of faith and determined to return to Mukalla with Martin and David as planned. Some of our friends had difficulty accepting our decision. It was painful to see them turn away from us just because they couldn't understand our desire to trust and obey God.

* * *

We all had been eager to return to the country we loved. And now we were finally home again in Mukalla! We had been away for three months, and a lot of dust had accumulated in the apartment. Our windows weren't airtight. I had plugged up the holes and crevices with towels, but the desert wind had just been too strong.

Shortly before Christmas 2001, Shariifa suddenly came back.

"What a wonderful surprise!" I ran up and hugged her, tears streaming down my cheeks. My round tummy got in the way, but Shariifa just stroked it tenderly, her big dark eyes smiling at me.

"You came back just in time for the last few weeks of my pregnancy. The baby is due in one month," I said with a big smile.

She ran her finger over the dusty shelves in the kitchen, then turned and scolded Maseja, "What is this? You have to take the spices off the shelf before you dust it!"

She grabbed the rag out of Maseja's hand and promptly dusted the shelf. Maseja would never have done it like that.

"Go home! From now on, I'll be helping Amiira again!"

Saying good-bye to Maseja was short and sweet. I paid her well, filled up some plastic bags with food, toys, and clothing for her children, and was glad that my friend Shariifa would be taking over.

Shariifa and I sat down in the living room with a cup of coffee, and she told me all about her adventures. She had walked through the middle of the desert, along with many others, looking for work. Some of them didn't make it out alive They died of thirst or fatigue while trying to make it by foot to the border of Dubai. I had missed Shariifa, but I'm sure her husband and her son, Fuad, whom she had left behind, had missed her more. They waited for months without ever hearing from her.

Now that she was back, Shariifa was more like a sister to me than ever before. She really pitched in and helped around the house. I guess her conscience hurt her for not staying in touch.

Unlike Maseja, I could depend on Shariifa. I could also trust her when it came to money matters. In this country, cash was comprised mostly of banknotes. Coins were very rare. The men didn't keep the bills in their wallet, but rather folded them into a wad and stuffed them into their shirt's breast pocket.

The largest denomination was a 1000 rial bill, which amounted to about $15. My absentminded professor, Chris, sometimes had bundles of folded bills in his shirt or pants pockets which he occasionally forgot to remove when he changed clothes. Shariifa was an honest person, and if she found money while she was doing Chris's laundry, she would just place it on the chest of drawers. She also knew, not to touch any documents she found lying around. She couldn't read them anyway since she had never gone to school.

Later, I taught Shariifa the Arabic and English alphabets. She was very eager to learn and thankful for everything I taught her. We also knitted and crocheted together and always had a lot of fun.

Shariifa was very aware of what went on in our family. She especially enjoyed the times when we got the guitar and keyboard out and sang worship songs together. She would always manage to find some chore to do nearby, so that she could listen.

* * *

The time finally came. During the past few days, I had been experiencing some pain, and was becoming more restless by the day. My belly was getting rounder and bigger, and my movements slower and more cumbersome. It was the evening of January 22, and I could see the muscles constricting on my abdomen. I was glad that Chris was not away in the project area.

"It's time, Chris. The contractions are starting. Please put the kids to bed, but don't tell them what's happening. I don't want them to know just yet."

"I'll call the midwife!" Chris exclaimed.

I sighed wearily. "You can't. She's down in one of the project villages. You know it's impossible to reach her there!"

"Right, with all this excitement, I totally forgot. Well, at least Joy is here. She can help!"

Joy was a friend who worked as a midwife in one of the neighboring Arab countries.

"And it's not like we don't have any experience when it comes to having a baby!"

Chris stroked my arm affectionately and gave me a little smile. Then he shoved David and Martin into the bathroom to brush their teeth. He told them to be quick about washing their faces and then got them ready for bed. He read them a short bedtime story and tried to hide his impatience. He managed to ignore their "delay tactics" this time and didn't even let them give their mother a good-night kiss.

David had often been sick recently, and Chris and I were worried about him. Even now, he had a high fever and a bad cough. He and Martin slept in the same room. The air conditioning was so loud that they couldn't hear any sounds from other parts of the apartment. That was good because, on this particular night, our bedroom—which was separated from the kids' room by a large reception area—would become a delivery room.

Joy was getting everything ready for the delivery, boiling water and clean towels. I tried to relax between the contractions. My first two births had gone fairly quickly. But it had been only ten months before that I had lost a child, and my body was still very weak due to the third stage Lyme disease I had been dealing with for years. Nevertheless, both Chris and I trusted God to help us through, and we were really looking forward to having another baby!

Chris finished his bedtime story in record time and rushed into the bedroom. He didn't want to miss out on anything! And as if that was my cue, the labor pains suddenly became more intense and frequent. Joy tried to slow things down.

"Breathe now, breathe! We have to wait for Heidi. I've never done a home delivery!"

But our baby didn't want to wait. His mother didn't either! I felt a supernatural peace in the room, and all worry and fear faded away. Even before Joy could get her gloves on, Tim had entered the world. Joy was calm and collected and intuitively did all the right things. Her actions and words reflected her many years of experience. It was an overwhelming moment when Chris cut the umbilical cord. He held our newborn son in his arms, blessed him, and then handed him over to me. Joy was overwhelmed, and tears of thankfulness streamed down her cheeks. She had delivered so many babies before, but this one touched her heart.

"That was the most beautiful thing I've ever experienced!" she told us later.

We were filled with awe and gratitude as we stared at our beautiful baby boy lying there on my tummy. His perfect little fingers clasped mine, and he was completely content. He closed his eyes, and we cuddled up. Chris joined us on the bed and began stroking our son's tiny cheeks.

It wasn't long before our baby could drink. He was a natural and had no problem finding the source of the milk to satisfy his hunger!

When Heidi, the team midwife, arrived two hours later, she was a little disappointed. She had just returned from the project area and had come too late to help with the delivery.

"Why didn't you tell me the baby was coming today? I would have stuck around," she said jokingly.

She washed her hands, and when she picked up our newborn baby and held him in her arms, it was love at first sight.

Tim won over everyone's heart with his innocent little face, huge dark eyes, and long black eyelashes. His delicate eyebrows looked like someone had drawn two thin lines on his forehead.

The following morning, Chris went to wake up the boys. "Come on, boys. I've got a big surprise for you!"

He brought them into the bedroom, and at that very moment, the baby smacked his lips from behind the mosquito net. The boys couldn't see him because of the wardrobe we used to partition off the room.

"A frog! It's a frog!" one of them screamed, and then they both ran over and jumped into bed with me. That's when they realized that this creature wasn't a frog, after all. Boy, were they surprised! Curious and full of awe, they gently touched and stroked the newborn child.

The children couldn't believe it was a real baby! They had a little brother!

"He's alive! Just look at those tiny fingers! He's so cute!"

They admired his curly brown hair and soft, tender skin. They just couldn't get enough of this little miracle and kept caressing him.

"May I hold him, please?"

"No, me first!"

They were both incredibly proud of their baby brother, and their protective instincts kicked right in. It was only now that I realized they had secretly feared they wouldn't get to see the baby, since they hadn't seen the sister they lost. Following the miscarriage, I had been laid up in bed with an infusion for several days and hadn't had the strength to deal with the boys. But now their sorrow and hurt could finally heal.

Shariifa was just as thrilled as the boys were. When she first held the baby tenderly in her arms, she thanked God for the gift he had given us. She loved our little Tim as if he was her own child.

Soon the boys were fighting over who got to hold the baby and play with him. Unfortunately, David was still contagious, so it was a challenge for us to keep the two brothers busy and occupied.

The whole family gathered together in the bathroom for the baby's first bath. Nobody wanted to miss out on that event! Tim seemed to enjoy the sink full of warm water. Later, we discovered that he was indeed quite a water rat!

"Maybe he wants to dive? Let him try," our five-year old suggested, because he was loved to dive.

Chris and I and the two midwives wished we could just spend time with the baby and forget about everything else. Joy's visit was coming to an end. I had known her since my youth and would be sorry to see her go. We tried to make the most of the few remaining days before she had to leave.

CHAPTER 18

An Unforgettable Birthday

IT WAS TO be a special, unforgettable day—my birthday! Unfortunately, my twin brother and I would not be able to celebrate it together, since he lived so far away. It was on special occasions like this that I missed him the most. My brother was my best friend. Chris couldn't understand why I was sad when my birthday came around. It was because I missed my brother so badly. We had always been close growing up and had always celebrated our birthday together.

Chris had already set the breakfast table. He had decorated it and made me a beautiful birthday card.

Tim, our newborn baby, was now 20 days old. The entire family was really enjoying our little curly head. He was a ray of sunlight and always managed to make us all laugh.

However, the baby was not currently the center of attention. His older brother, David, had been sick for weeks and his illness had kept us busy and worried.

His condition had become worse, and I couldn't take it any longer. "Chris, I think Dr. Garzias is returning from Cuba today. Please call him and have him take a look at David."

Chris protested, "But today is your birthday! We've got to celebrate that. It would take hours to get to the clinic, and I made sure I got off work for your birthday party."

"The best present for me would be to find out what is wrong with David and have him treated!" I said.

Chris was puzzled and just stared at me. The most important part of a birthday was the party—with coffee, cake, and the works!

When Chris realized I was serious, he agreed. "All right, let's take him to Mustashfa Hadhramaut for a checkup. We'll have to do it today. The next few days I have important appointments I can't miss."

"I don't want to wake the baby. Besides, there are all sorts of germs and bacteria in the hospital. If it's all right with you, I'll let you take David while I stay home with the other two."

Chris nodded. He conceded that this was the best idea, although he didn't feel right about leaving me on my birthday.

But David wasn't enthusiastic about going to the doctor! He tried to persuade Chris and me that it wasn't necessary. He'd be fine.

"I'm not even really sick! Besides, I want to stay here and play. It's Mama's birthday, anyway!"

Nonetheless we had made up our minds. I quickly ran a comb through his hair and then told him to put on a clean T-shirt and change his trousers.

"When we're finished at the doctor's office, we'll go to 'Snowcream' and get some ice cream, okay?" Chris promised.

That persuaded David. He couldn't resist an opportunity to spend time alone with his Papa. And he loved going to Snowcream, a local ice cream parlor. My two men got going.

If I had known what would happen over the next few hours, I might have decided to go along to the hospital instead. I went to the kitchen to start cooking before Tim woke up. I wanted to prepare something special for us when Chris and David returned. I had just started to make the Swabian noodle dough when the doorbell rang. It was probably somebody from the neighborhood. Locals would always ring the doorbell or pound wildly on the iron gate, until somebody opened up.

"Oh, no! I have so much to do. I haven't even started on the cake," I said under my breath.

I quickly dried my hands and hurried to the door, remembering, of course, to wrap a headscarf around my hair and tuck it in, as modesty dictated in these parts.

"*Miin maai?*"[31] I asked, before pushing back the lock and opening the door a crack.

A Bedouin family stood outside. I knew them from one of our project villages where we had built a school with the help of the locals. Mariam, the wife, had never seen a city apartment from the inside. She stood there, covered from head to toe, but through the eye slits in her face veil, she curiously looked all around the place. Her husband, Amer, and her 13-year-old son, Mahmud, were with her. Their clothing was dusty and soiled, not only from their journey but also from living in the desert. It was easy to tell that they came from a poor environment, but their glowing faces compensated for any sense of lack.

"What a surprise! Come in!" I said cheerfully while wondering what I was supposed to do now. I couldn't invite the man and the boy to come inside. That wouldn't be appropriate. Since my husband wasn't here, it would be best if they were kept separate from us in the men's mafraj at the front of the apartement.

I motioned with my right hand for the men to have a seat and attempted with my left hand to keep my headscarf in place. Mariam followed me at each turn through the apartment and marveled at everything she saw. Our house must have seemed like a palace to her in comparison to her humble home. She and her family lived in a straw hut on a dune. It was a simple construction that could quickly be taken down and set up somewhere else. They were nomads and didn't own much. Whenever their goats finished grazing the scant grass in one area, the family would move on to more fertile fields. After a few months, they would return to their original location and set up their hut once again.

---

31 Who is there?

I needed to start grating the dough into the pot of boiling water to make the noodles. My Bedouin friend joined me in the kitchen, and we chatted about this and that. I tried to keep the chicken fricassee from overcooking and to make sure the pasta didn't get too soft, all the while keeping an eye on my visitor. Martin had retreated to the playroom. I needed somebody right now to take care of the male guests. Then I had an idea: I could get Mariam to do it. I grabbed a tray and put some cold drinks on it, as well as a plate full of baked cookies, and asked her to take it out to her men on the *mafraj*. Then I returned to preparing the meal.

Mariam came back shortly after that. She was holding Tim in her arms. He had been sleeping peacefully in our bedroom. Mariam's robe was dusty and full of lice, and her headscarf was filthy. She babbled some baby words at Tim and gave him a big kiss. I swallowed hard when I thought of how the lice were going to have a heyday at our expense in our bedroom that evening.

Mariam asked where Chris was and when he would be back. She had come with her family by bus from Al Qariyah, a village about 40 miles away. For these Bedouins, who rarely leave their village, that was the equivalent of a trip around the world! Now it appeared that they planned to stay at our home the entire day and maybe even the night. Mariam went back and forth between the kitchen and the *mafraj* and relayed my messages to the men and their responses to me. She spoke a peculiar Arabic dialect, running her words together, which made me dizzy. The baby was crying impatiently. Normally, Tim didn't require much attention, but now he was hungry and wanted to be fed. And through Mariam, Amer asked me time and again to give Chris a call.

Even though I rather doubted that the Bedouins would appreciate my foreign cooking, I served them the chicken, noodles, and salad, anyway. I didn't have anything else to offer, so I hoped that their hunger would outweigh their reluctance. Unfortunately, they hardly touched the food. Apparently Bedouins are not very adventurous when it comes to trying out new food!

I was happy that the family had come for a visit, because in this culture it should be considered an honor. But it was the wrong moment for me because I had not gotten much sleep lately and was tired. The past few days had been incredibly busy. Impatiently I hoped that Chris and David would come back from the hospital soon. But it seemed like time had stood still—the minutes ticked away so slowly.

Finally, I heard the car pull up. I was anxious to know if they had found the cause of David's symptoms so I ran downstairs to the entrance, opened the door and looked at my husband and son with great anticipation and demanded: "Don't keep me in the dark! Tell me what the doctor said. You know how curious I am!"

Chris answered quietly, "They found signs for an infection in his blood. He's got malaria and something else. But the liver is all right. They gave me a prescription for the pharmacy. We'll have to return to the lab later to get the other test results." Chris handed me the prescription slip.

Before we entered our apartment, I whispered to Chris: "By the way, we have guests from Al Qariyah. Amer and his son are in the men's living area. Mariam is in the kitchen. I'm sure glad you're back. As you know, I couldn't enter the *mafraj* while you were away."

Chris went into the men's living room and began a friendly conversation with his friend. In Yemen, it would have been utterly impolite to let our guests know that their visit had come at an inconvenient time for us. Chris was not about to violate etiquette and hospitality conventions. So the two of them just sat there sipping their tea and eating cookies, but on the inside, Chris was like a cat on a hot tin roof. He was hungry, but he couldn't just leave his visitor alone and go enjoy the birthday party meal. Perhaps he ought to tell his friend that it was my birthday. But that wouldn't do any good. Most of the people here were illiterate. They couldn't grasp the concept of birthdays and never celebrated them. The oriental way is, "live for the moment." They had no need of calendars and appointment books.

After a while, Chris realized that our guests had no intention of leaving anytime soon. But today was his wife's special day! He just had to do something to get rid of them without offending them. This was, after all, the first time they had ever come to visit! Then a brilliant thought came to our rescue.

He told his friend, "Our son is sick and needs some medicine. We're going to drive over to Ibn Siina to the pharmacy there and see if they can fill his prescription. Do you want to come along?"

When Chris told me what his plans were, I realized how clever it was. I quickly draped my black coat around my dress and made sure my headscarf was in place. I picked up Tim and grabbed a hat for him on the way out, inconspicuously shoving Mariam in front of me the whole time. She was still completely robed, so it would be no problem for her to go outside as she was. David and Martin were almost ready to go, as well. They just needed to get their shoes on. We all went down the stairway, chatting the whole way. Chris locked up the apartment and followed.

Soon we were all on the way to Ibn Siina together. While talking with Amer, Chris had found out that Amer's brother, Bassam, was a patient in the hospital there. So when we arrived, Chris dropped our Bedouin friends off in front of the hospital and sent them on their way. Mariam and I kissed each other good-bye, twice on the left cheek, once on the right. As soon as the Bedouin family had disappeared behind the hospital doors, Chris went over to the pharmacy across the street. To our surprise, they were able to fill the prescription right away. I was relieved to see the bag in his hand as he returned to the car. He was beaming as he got in. He turned toward me and grinned.

We took an indirect way home, along the freshly-paved street that followed the shoreline. Chris was making sure we didn't bump into our Bedouin friends again by accident. The five of us were happy. We enjoyed the ride, admiring the beautiful shades of blue gleaming on the ocean. When we arrived home, we all shared a relieved smile and entered the house. We had used an oriental trick, and it had worked! We got rid of our guests without insulting them. I quickly discarded my *balto*, took off my headscarf, and headed for the *mafraj* to gather up the dirty dishes. I opened the door to the living area, started to hum, and was feeling very satisfied with myself when I stopped in my tracks and held my breath.

What is that strange smell? I thought and looked around.

And then I saw it: Behind the door lay a brown heap of a suspicious-looking substance.

"It looks like somebody had a problem here!"

My sense of humor got the best of me, and I laughed out loud. I held my nose with my left hand and used my right to clean up the mess with a rag.

Then I reasoned to myself: "How could the Bedouins have known that there was a toilet in the blue-paneled bathroom right next door? They have probably never seen a toilet seat, and certainly not a blue one! And there was no sand here for them to bury their little gift."

None of my friends back in Germany would ever believe what I had experienced today. I'm sure none of them ever had a birthday like this! At least I couldn't complain about being bored!

Before my black humor could turn into self-pity, the doorbell rang again. My next guests had arrived to celebrate with me.

I sighed: "I'm afraid we're going to have to make the *mafraj* off-limits for the rest of the day. The guests will just have to be entertained upstairs on the roof, I suppose. You have to be able to go with the flow!"

CHAPTER 19

Off to Jibla!

TIM WAS 25 days old by now and was a very easy-going baby. The whole family enjoyed playing with him and cuddling him. But David was still very ill. The medicine the doctor had prescribed a few days ago wasn't helping. He continued to lose weight and became weaker by the day.

It had been a long-standing custom of ours to enter the children's room to pray for them and bless them before we settled down for the night. It was wonderful to watch our three sons sound asleep and listen to them quietly breathing. Chris was away at a meeting on this particular evening, so I went into the kids' room by myself. I knelt by their beds and laid my hands on their heads to bless them. When I touched David's forehead, I noticed he had a high fever! Then I felt a cold sweat on his hot skin. That scared me! I listened carefully to his weak breathing. Usually, David was a light sleeper and would wake up as soon as somebody touched his bed. But now he wasn't moving at all. I tried to shake him awake, but he didn't respond. Then I realized to my horror, David was unconscious!

I checked his pulse. It was irregular and very weak. I trembled when I realized how sick my son was. I had to do something right away! I called Chris and told him to come home immediately. I paced back and forth, worried and scared, the whole time muttering a prayer or two and preparing cold compresses for my son's forehead. The fever occasionally caused him to hallucinate.

When Chris came home, he rushed in. I told him that David was not at all well. But when we entered the kids' room, Chris was shocked by what he saw.

"We need help right away! Let's take him to the Baptist Hospital in Jibla," I cried out.

"But that's 15 hours drive away!" he replied.

"I don't care! That's the only hospital around that is not run by locals. We are desperate! If the Hadhramaut Hospital can't figure out what's wrong with David, we'll just have to look elsewhere. The doctors in Jibla are more competent and trustworthy than those here. They'll be able to give us a more accurate diagnosis!"

Chris tried to calm me down. "Let's just pray and trust God to heal our boy!"

"Of course, we'll keep praying. But we have to go to Jibla. He needs medical help from the specialists there."

The alarms were going off in my head. Chris finally gave in:

"If he's not better by tomorrow, we'll leave first thing the following day."

David's condition didn't improve during the next 24 hours, in spite of all our prayers. His little body seemed to be collapsing more and more. We started preparing for the journey to Jibla. I was exhausted, but I managed to pack a few things we needed for the trip. I put some diapers into a suitcase and then tried to get the house ready for the time away from home, which could turn out to be quite awhile.

I breathed a sigh of relief when we were finally all in the car. It was very early, and the sun was just beginning to rise. It was still rather cool, so we wrapped David in soft blankets and got on our way. There were a lot of roadblocks and military checkpoints along the way which held us up. Many hours later, we finally arrived in Ibb. The fields around the city were beautiful and looked like colorful terraces. We had hardly stopped for a rest, and yet it was already dark outside.

The Christian hospital in Jibla was located on a wonderfully land-scaped estate with tall, shady trees. It emanated a sense of peace and refuge. The staff here had a reputation for being highly competent and experienced, and were acclaimed all around the country. We checked David into the hospital, and he immediately received infusions. An experienced doctor from America, Dr. Martha, examined him. She was a very conscientious and committed doctor who felt called to help the local population here in Yemen. David would have to stay several days in the hospital for observation and treatment. We were allowed to stay in the personnel barracks, located on the spacious hospital grounds. That way, we could be close to David.

For me, our stay here was a gift straight from heaven! God knew that I was at the end of my rope. This was like an oasis of green. Every-where we looked, there were park benches, tennis courts, playgrounds, and trees and bushes for playing hide-and-seek. They also had a library with a lot of English books. That was paradise for a bookworm like me. We all enjoyed the cooler climate and the fresh mountain air.

Here in this lovely environment, we could all relax. When David wasn't undergoing his various painful examinations, we enjoyed just lying around in the grass and playing with one another.

It turned out that our concern for David had been justified. Dr. Martha extracted quite a few tubes full of his blood, much to his chagrin.

When the results came back, she told us: "David is very ill, and the tests revealed several diseases. We found malaria and typhoid, as well as amebic dysentery. They could have been caused by impure water or unwashed lettuce and fruit. In these parts, the fields are often fertilized with human excrement. We also discovered a staph infection in David's blood. And since his immune system is under so much pressure, we think that he's been infected with mononucleosis."

That was quite an intense diagnosis. Five major diseases all at once! The doctor turned to speak with her patient:

"David, I'm going to give you some medicine. If you take it and drink a lot of water, you won't need the infusions anymore. After ten days or so, we'll check your blood again and see if you are doing any better."

David was upset and yelled: "You can't take any more of my blood! I don't have a single drop left!"

I felt for him, he had gone through quite a few treatments in the last few days. The doctor just laughed. She didn't take his comment personally.

"You just get better now, and then when I go to visit my patients up in the mountain villages, I'll take you with me, okay?"

David nodded and smiled. That sounded good to him. Unfortunately, it never worked out for him to accompany the doctor on her rounds through the mountain regions.

The side effects of the drug cocktail were dramatic, but during the next few days, we could see David's health slowly improving. Of course, we continued to pray for God to restore him completely.

On the weekends, David was spared any treatments and examinations. Since I was engrossed in a thrilling novel, Chris went with our two boys on a hike around the hospital grounds. There were so many things to discover! They skipped down the stone stairway which led to the hospital, and walked right up to the hospital director's house. Mr. Bill was sitting in the shade on his veranda. He didn't even look up, as they approached, while he was engrossed in whittling a wooden figure. The boys stopped in their tracks and watched him.

"Hi, Mr. Bill! What are you doing?" David asked curiously.

Mr. Bill wouldn't be disturbed. He just nodded and continued working. Chris tried to get the boys to leave him alone. But they were so fascinated by the masterpiece taking shape in the hands of this skilled craftsman.

"Look, it's a camel! It even has a hump. Papa, can we carve something, too?" Martin asked with admiration in his voice.

Although Martin had spoken German, Mr. Bill recognized Martin's appreciation of his workmanship and decided to look up after all. It turned out that he loved children and wasn't about to deprive himself of the wonder and awe this little boy offered.

"Come with me. I'll show you my shop!" Mr. Bill was usually very reserved, but now he laughed, stood up, and limped over to his workshop, which was adjacent to his house.

He didn't have to say that twice! David and Martin followed the elderly gentleman, skipping cheerfully while Chris brought up the rear. Upon entering the shop, the two boys were so intrigued by what they saw, that they just stood there in silence for a moment and took everything in.

The shop, although dark and cramped inside, had a wonderful smell of fresh wood. Wood shavings and sawdust covered the floor, and several unfinished figures sat on the planing bench. Pieces of lumber lay everywhere. All the tools were neatly hung on the wall. Shelves filled with lathed wooden figures reached all the way up to the ceiling. There were trains and all kinds of elaborate animals.

While Chris and the boys kept admiring the various carvings, Bill began to explain: "There are so many poor people in this area. They hardly have enough to eat. I've always loved to carve. Some time ago, I started selling my carved figures whenever we were in the States for a furlough. I'm just now working on filling a container that will be shipped over in a couple of weeks. The proceeds from the sales go to support the poor people here in Jibla and Ibb."

Chris didn't know what to say at first. Then he asked: "May we buy some of them from you?"

Mr. Bill nodded: "Of course. Whatever you take, I won't have to ship."

"Just let me get my wallet," Chris answered and ran light-footed up the steps to our accommodation.

He was out of breath when he finally reached the top. "Amiira, come quickly. Mr. Bill is showing us the wonderful collection of carvings he keeps in his shop. He said we could buy some of them. They're so beautiful, and with the profit, he helps poor people!"

He grabbed his wallet and was already on his way back down the stairway without waiting for a response from me. He didn't want to leave the boys alone in the shop any longer than necessary. Following on his heels, I greeted Mr. Bill upon entering the shop. I had always loved the smell of wood, and was amazed by the beauty of the carvings. I stroked the individual figures and just couldn't get enough! But Mr. Bill had more for us to see. He brought out an ark carved out of pine wood. When he took the roof off, we saw compartments containing various kinds of animals, all of them in pairs. Lions, elephants, giraffes, birds, snakes, cats, and every imaginable species—all very elaborate and made with much care.

He also had a key holder shaped like an ark. Then he showed us various bendable toys and some intricate key chains he had made. We were awestruck and bought several items as gifts for our friends and relatives back in Germany. We didn't know it at the time, but these pieces of art would later hold special memories.

The barracks we had been staying in were now needed for other purposes, so we had to move on. Chris suggested that we spend a few days in Aden, a city at the Indian Ocean, in the southeast of Yemen. We were planning to stop by there to meet some friends on the way home, anyway.

We shared the guest apartment of the Christ Church in Aden with an other Christian friend and his family. One evening, Chris and he laid hands on David and pleaded with heaven for his healing. And then the breakthrough finally came! We had often prayed quite fervently for our son. But now we saw real improvements. David was finally getting well!

CHAPTER 20

In Mortal Danger

GOD HAD TRULY stepped in and healed David. He was doing significantly better, and we were finally able to get on our way home. The journey through the "Wild East" in our Land Cruiser seemed to take forever. We drove as fast as we could and didn't even take any breaks, having prepared sandwiches and taken enough water along with us. Our kids loved the long trips through the desert. We listened to worship CDs and children's story tapes or played cards and read comic books.

I was holding Tim on my knees. He was fidgety and wouldn't take a nap. He had grown so much that he took up my entire lap and I couldn't move an inch. I read some stories out loud, turning my head to one side so the boys in the back could hear. I was getting very tired and my shoulders and back hurt. We'd already been on the road for nine hours and we still had at least six more hours ahead of us.

At the final military checkpoint, the soldiers had us stop at the roadblock. Chris got out and went over to a heavily-armed guard, speaking with him in perfect Arabic. We could feel tension in the air. Inside the car, the temperature was rising. Tim was still awake and crying miserably.

I hope we can get back on the road soon, I thought.

Chris returned to the car and explained: "We are about to enter Shabwa, a wild tribal region. It's a very dangerous area. Many kidnappings have taken place here. The guard recommends we take a military escort along with us. The police, who usually escort travelers, aren't available right now, and the guards don't know when they'll be back."

"Oh, no!" I exclaimed. I wasn't very keen on having a so-called escort of armed soldiers! Whenever they came along—hand grenades and all—I always felt like our car was a bomb just waiting to explode.

"We don't have any room in the car. The backseat is full of toys, books, and cassette tapes. Besides, we know these 'bodyguards' will run off as soon as they smell danger! Please talk to the officer on command again and ask him to let us go on our own," I begged Chris.

"I'll give it a try," he promised and disappeared into the guardroom, which provided the soldiers with a little shade from the scorching heat.

The boys and I prayed as we waited for the answer.

A few minutes later, Chris came back to the car. He got behind the wheel and drove off. His grin revealed that he had just attained a victory. I merely stared at him.

"Well, come on. Tell me what they said!" I blurted out.

"They said we should drive as fast as we could," he answered brusquely.

But I wanted to know all the details and pestered him impatiently with a load of questions.

Later, I found out that the officer in command had only reluctantly given his approval. There were not enough soldiers on duty that day and we had arrived just at the time they always took a break to chew their *khat*. But he warned Chris urgently: "Drive as fast as possible and don't stop for anything. If you see anything unusual on your way through Shabwa, just keep driving! Don't stop! Don't ever stop!"

Chris didn't want to worry us, so he didn't tell us exactly what the soldier had said. But we had often driven this route before, so Chris just told the guard: "We have an invisible guardian on board. God will take care of us!"

Chris pressed the accelerator to the floor. He was happy to comply with that order since he wanted to make up for lost time. The road was fairly straight and bordered by thick undergrowth on both sides, and there was nobody to be seen far and wide. The rhythmic vibrations of our car moving at such a high speed finally rocked Tim to sleep. I closed my eyes and could relax a bit.

Suddenly, two sheep jumped out of the bushes and ran directly in front of our car. Chris slammed on the brakes and I was rudely awakened, my eyes instantly open. But it was too late; we had run over the sheep. Martin and David screamed and Tim was awake again and started crying. David looked behind us and saw the sheep lying on the road, bleeding.

He cried, "Papa! Why did you do that? Those poor animals!"

Chris was pale from shock, but he instinctively stepped on the gas. He remembered what the officer had said: "Drive as fast as you can! And don't stop for anything!"

We had to get away as soon as possible to avoid getting into trouble with the local Bedouin tribes. I tried to calm the children down and comfort them. However, we had no idea that this was just the beginning of our problems.

Chris was worried and mumbled: "It's only a few miles to the winding gorge. We have to hurry. Who knows where tribesmen might be hiding!"

But suddenly gunshots cut through the silence like claps of thunder. A white Toyota Hilux was approaching at high speed from behind and quickly catching up with us. Chris looked in the rearview mirror and exclaimed: "The guy in the passenger seat is shooting with a Kalashnikow at us!"

"Duck! Get your heads down! Throw the luggage into the back for protection!" Chris demanded.

The boys could tell by the tone in their father's voice that he was serious. They obeyed his orders immediately and stuck their heads down between the front and back seats. Chris knew this was a very precarious situation. We were far from any settlement or community. I felt fear rising inside me, almost paralyzing me. Without thinking twice, I began to pray.

Our two-and-a-half ton Land Cruiser was losing speed. Chris stepped on the brakes and began to slow the car down. He knew we didn't have any chance of escaping our pursuers, so he decided to stop the car and face them. He wanted to make sure that the gunman wouldn't hit the car or maybe one of us.

I felt helpless, so I just cried out to God that he would protect our family and the car. We came to a halt, and our pursuers caught up with us. They jumped out of their vehicle and approached our car. The men were furious, but Chris remained very calm. He opened the door and got out, then crossed over to the other side of the road to put some distance between our car and the men, trying to protect us. He stared fearlessly at the two men who had chased us.

In the rearview mirror, I watched as the two men walked up to Chris and got right in his face. They held him at gunpoint and screamed:

"You damned *Ajnabee!* What have you done?"

Chris displayed an inexplicable authority as he calmly spoke to the men. "I am truly sorry. Of course, I'll pay you for the sheep! I wasn't try- ing to get away from you. The guards back at the checkpoint told us to drive as fast as possible without stopping through this region."

The man holding the rifle waved it about in Chris's face.

"Follow me!" he growled and pushed Chris toward our Land Cruiser.

He opened the door on the driver's side and pushed Chris into the seat behind the wheel. The boys and I had already locked all the other doors. The two troublemakers got back in their vehicle and spun it around 180 degrees on the narrow road. Then they pointed the rifle at Chris and told him to turn the car around. He was to lead the way, and they would follow close behind. Chris had no other choice but to obey. He knew that we probably wouldn't survive a second escape attempt.

After a few minutes, we reached the place where the two dead sheep lay. A crowd of men had gathered there. The atmosphere was extremely tense, almost explosive. Chris glanced over at me without saying a word. His eyes were loving and reassuring, as he got out of the car and slowly approached the hostile group of men awaiting him. At that moment, I thought I might never see my husband again.

When the children saw the dead sheep again, they were upset and began crying. The two men with dark beards led Chris in the direction of the nearby mountain village. I remained in the car with our three sons. We gradually lost sight of Chris, and I tried to calm the boys down. The situation was tense, but strangely enough, I felt a supernatural calm come over me. It felt like I was being wrapped in a nice warm blanket in the deep of winter. A sense of peace overwhelmed me in the middle of my storm. God was with us. He placed his peace within me, and I could think clearly again. I explained to Martin and David what was happening. They had been so shocked by the death of the sheep, that they hadn't even realized the danger their father was in right now.

"There wasn't anything Papa could've done to avoid the sheep. They just suddenly jumped out in front of the car. We should be glad we didn't have a bad accident. Everything is going to work out all right. We don't need to be scared. God sent his angels to watch over us. They'll watch out for Papa, too."

I was aware of the law of blood revenge that was prevalent in this region. Sheep were so valuable that sometimes a human would be killed as payback.

The minutes dragged on and on. It felt like hours had gone by. It was extremely hot and humid in the car, and we were all soaked in sweat. The kids were grumpy and began to whine.

"When is Papa coming back? We want to go home! We're hungry and thirsty!"

But there was still no sign of Chris or anybody else, just the dead sheep lying in the middle of the road.

I started to consider leaving the kids in the car and walking in the direction the men had taken Chris. But I hesitated, thinking, "What if they kidnap me, too? What would the kids do if both their parents were gone?"

But then I saw Chris in the distance and began to weep for joy. I loved my husband so much and was relieved to see his smiling face as he approached the car. Looking like he had achieved a victory of sorts, he got in, closed the door, and got the car going in the direction we had come from. He was in a hurry to get away from here and return home. After a while, he began talking about what had happened:

"I paid the owner sixteen thousand rials for the sheep, eight thousand rials apiece. The sheik was a fair man and didn't want more than that. The hostile man with the rifle tried to pit us against each other. He seemed to have it in for foreigners. But the old sheik was a well-respected man. And fortunately, he was considerate and peaceable toward me. He didn't want the situation to escalate. I'm just glad I had enough cash on me. I had withdrawn the salaries for the workers in Mukalla while I was in Sanaa. It was enough to pay the fee we agreed upon. We wouldn't have escaped if I hadn't had the money on me. There's no bank out here in the desert. Let's just thank the Lord and hurry home. It'll be dark soon, and we still have a long way to go."

We kept checking the rearview mirror to make sure nobody was following us. It began to dawn on Chris and me that we had just narrowly escaped a very dangerous situation. The shock ran deep!

"You need to drink some Coke, your face is so pale!" I suggested.

But he refused. He just wanted to drive. Dusk was setting in as we came near to the winding gorge. The surface of the road was bumpy and hazardous, so Chris had to slow down. The long journey and the traumatic experience had affected us more than we realized. The two of us just sat in silence, while the kids played in the back. Occasionally I glanced over at Chris, thankful that God had returned him to me safely.

When we finally arrived home from this adventurous journey, I hoped that things would get back to normal. During the last few days, I had felt like I was on a speeding freight train, unable to find the emergency brake!

CHAPTER 21

The Monsoon of the Century

A FEW DAYS later, black, dismal clouds filled the sky. It remained dark and eerie all morning. All of a sudden, the clouds broke and heavy rainfall put the sandy and arid countryside under water within minutes. The earth couldn't contain the amount of rain that fell. Gale-force winds began ripping away everything that wasn't fastened down, and everyone retreated to the protection of their homes. Suddenly, the mountains gave way, and torrents came flowing towards the city, dragging boulders and everything else with them. The poor slum dwellers who lived in makeshift sheet metal huts were at the mercy of the floods. The severe storm did extreme damage to the city.

The heavy monsoon rain continued for an unusually long time. There hadn't been a rainfall this intense for over 40 years. This was the first time we had seen any rain here at all!

The effects of this natural catastrophe shocked us. Chaos broke loose in the entire region around Mukalla. Homes, cars, shops, and even people were carried away by the storm. Electricity and telephone lines were damaged, as well as pipelines. That caused the precious water to sink into the ground, gone for good.

We had no idea that our neighborhood would be affected. The flood reached its peak the following day. The roads were flooded and full of rubble from the mountains. Nobody could get through. Our neighborhood was completely cut off from the rest of the world. But we didn't know this when my friend from next door, Chatija, went into labor.

It was very humid in spite of the storm, and I was cleaning the dishes after dinner and looking forward to a short nap. I was just going to lie down on the bed with Tim, who was now five weeks old, when there was a loud knock at our front gate. At first, we didn't hear the impatient hammering, since we had closed all the windows due to the storm, which was still roaring wildly. David was playing with Martin down in the playroom. After a while, he noticed that somebody was trying to get our attention.

"Mama, there's somebody outside!" he yelled up the stairwell.

I got up and ran down the stairs. On the way to the front door, I passed by David and told him, "You stay here. Otherwise you'll get soaked and catch a cold. I'll go see who's there!"

I grabbed a plastic bag as a substitute for an umbrella, hurried out to the gate, and pushed back the heavy latch. It was pouring, and within seconds, I was soaked to the skin. I looked like I had jumped into a swimming pool fully clothed.

Hussein, Chatija's eldest son, stood at the gate. His voice was hoarse, and I could see fear in his dark eyes.

"My mother is in labor. She has to get to the hospital. Can you take her? She's so afraid. Our phone isn't working, so we couldn't call our father. He's downtown, stuck in his restaurant."

Without a second thought, I nodded. "Tell your mom to get herself ready."

I turned and ran back into the house and shouted to Chris: "Chatija is having her baby. She needs to get to the hospital. I'm just going to change into some dry clothes."

Chris was home today, and to my relief, he said he would drive our pregnant neighbor to the hospital since it was still very turbulent outside. He quickly put on a fresh shirt and slipped into sandals. The moment he stepped out of the house, he was completely drenched! He quickly opened the heavy gate, got in the car, and backed out of the driveway.

Chatija's sister, Alia, had arrived a few days earlier to assist her pregnant sister with the housekeeping. She helped her sister Chatija out the door, and immediately they were both soaking wet, in spite of their *baltos* and headscarves. Alia shoved her sister into the back of the car, got in next to her, and slammed the door shut. Every minute counted. I watched through the window as Chris sped away with the two sisters. In my thoughts and prayers, I was with them all the way to the hospital. Then I hurried to the bathroom, where I peeled off the wet clothes, dried off, and put on a fresh dress. While I was still drying my hair, I heard Chris's voice from behind the front door.

I was surprised. *"He hasn't been gone that long. The drive downtown usually takes a lot longer!"*

Chris had returned without having accomplished what he went out to do. That wasn't typical for him.

Chris was out of breath. "The road to Mukalla is cut off. It's completely flooded. Our neighborhood is like an island. The valley at *Wadi* Fuwah is several feet under water, and the *wadi* has turned into a torrent. It was impossible to take Chatija to the Bashraheel Hospital in Mukalla. I turned around and tried the other route. But the road to Ibn Siina is also impassable. Cars are stuck in *Wadi* Khirbe and are under water. Traffic has come to a standstill. There's no way to get through. It's really bad!"

Chris continued, panting his words: "Chatija is home again and needs you. She's in great pain and is scared. I'll go out and try to find a midwife."

"Where in the world do you hope to find a midwife in this storm? Heidi is over six hundred miles away right now."

"Leave that up to me! Bawasiir, the mayor, told me that Wafa lives just a few blocks away from here. She's a midwife and could help. Pray that I'll be able to find her and bring her back. But right now, you need to get over to Chatija!"

He didn't need to say another word. I wanted to be there for my friend in her time of need. I just quickly checked in on the baby. Tim lay peacefully in his crib, so I didn't have to worry about him.

I told my two older sons: "I've got to go help Chatija. She's having her baby! Please let me know if the baby starts to cry. Just yell through the bedroom window. I'm right next door."

"OK, Mama. We'll check on him. We're all grown up now, and you can count on us. But first, we want to finish building this castle!"

I just smiled, put on my black *balto* and a headscarf, and then ran over to the house next door. Chatija lay on the bed moaning. Her three sons in the living room were edgy and getting at one another's throats. Their grandmother, who was almost bigger than her pregnant daughter, sat next to the bed.

I sat down next to my suffering friend and spoke calmly to her, trying to comfort her. I held her hand, rubbed her back, and wiped the sweat from her forehead with a damp washcloth. It was strange to see Chatija's mother sitting there next to her, so lifeless. It seemed to me that she should be the one taking care of her daughter and not me. Chatija yelled with each contraction, and we were relieved when Wafa, the midwife, finally arrived. She had dyed her gray hair carroty-red with henna, but the wrinkles on her face revealed that she was up in years. She quickly slipped out of her *balto* but left her large headscarf in place, which covered her entire body. Chatija and her mother also wore these long *nuqbas*. It was very humid in the room, and the ceiling fan only circulated the hot air. We were all covered in sweat and wished things would cool off a bit. The midwife greeted us quietly, and then went right to work. She examined Chatija's belly without saying another word, listening to the heartbeat of the child, using a strange wooden tube that looked like a trumpet without valves. She seemed to know what she was doing. I could tell she had a lot of experience.

It was only a few weeks ago that I had been in Chatija's position, but my delivery had been fairly quick and easy. I felt sorry for my friend. I prayed that everything would go well and that she would soon be able to have her healthy baby in her arms!

It seemed to take forever. But finally, the baby stuck his tiny head out and gave his first cry. I had tears in my eyes as I took little Sinan, wrapped him in a warm blanket, and placed him in his mother's loving arms. Only then did the grandmother finally seem to come alive.

She mumbled: "Another boy?! That's the fourth one! She needs a girl who can help her around the house!"

I tried to calm the old lady down. "But look! He's such a beautiful baby with brown, curly hair. His brothers will love him!"

As if on cue, the three older boys rushed into the room and marveled at their newborn baby brother.

It was still pouring outside, but we had completely forgotten the storm, even though the windows of the house were simple openings in the walls. But what was happening outside was not nearly as exciting as what was going on inside the house. Chatija was overjoyed and pressed the little bundle of life close to her breast. She thanked me time and again for staying with her.

* * *

It took several days after the flood subsided for us to determine how much damage had been done. The rockslide and the rolling rubble had been devastating and catastrophic. When I finally realized what had taken place, I cried. There were many people missing in Mukalla, and we suspected that some of them had drowned in the flood and were buried under the debris. Many of them would never be found.

The poor people were hit the hardest. They didn't have much to begin with, but now their homes and all their possessions were gone. Numerous sheet metal huts were blown away, and entire slum districts along the Mukalla waterway were destroyed. Debris filled the spaces where homes and shops had previously stood. The torrents from the mountains had brought boulders and lots of rubble with them.

It looked like an earthquake had shaken the city. It was a horrible sight and shocked us all to the core, foreigners and locals alike. The narrow side roads were filled with what used to be automobiles. All the colors of the city had turned pale and were covered by a sludgy brown coat. A great sadness and a feeling of helplessness dominated the atmosphere. And there were no insurance policies in place to help out!

We were thankful that our home remained undamaged from the storm, and that we were all safe. But we felt badly for our neighbors and friends. Once again, we became very aware of how close together lie life and death, joy and sorrow.

The heat from the sun did a thorough job of drying things out. Within a few short days, the entire disaster area was as parched as it usually was. But the sludgy brown color remained as a reminder of the flood of the century.

* * *

Shortly after the flood, our entire family visited one of the project villages for the first time since the birth of our baby.

The destruction around Burum wasn't quite as extensive as elsewhere since there weren't many settlements or villages in this uniquely beautiful coastal area. Our project area in Al Qariyah was spared from rainfall altogether. David and Martin were in the backseat playing "I see something you don't see," and Chris was at the wheel. He was whistling and obviously excited about visiting the village. Tim was sleeping quietly on my lap and had no idea he was to be introduced to the Bedouin society this very day. We all enjoyed the ride and sang children's songs or worship choruses together. The sun was shining, and it seemed that life was being good to us again. Then it happened: Right outside the fishing village of Halla, we were crossing the only bridge in the area, when suddenly there was no more connection and the road ended without any warnings or signs. Chris stepped on the brakes and was able to stop the car just in time, only inches away from a deep abyss.

The rest of the bridge had been washed out by the flood. Chris gasped and got out of the car:

"That was close! Thank God I had the brake disc replaced last week. Otherwise, we'd all be down there right now!"

He got back behind the wheel and put the car in reverse. Slowly and carefully, he maneuvered it backward along the narrow bridge. My heart was pounding wildly, and I held my breath. If he were to stray only a few inches to the left or the right, the car would most likely plunge over the side because there were no guardrails. After about 150 yards, we finally had solid road under us again. Chris stopped the car and got out. I could tell how shaken he was.

His shirt was dripping with sweat as if he had taken a shower with it on. With the scorching sun beating down on him, he let some air out of the tires of the SUV. Then he got back in and steered the car off the road. He drove it through the sand, put it in first gear, and headed down the embankment to the *wadi*. The car took a good shaking, and we all held our breath. The kids enjoyed the bumpy ride, but he and I knew how much trouble we'd be in if we got stuck in the sand.

The desert sun continued to bear down on us mercilessly. Our air conditioning had broken down a long time ago, so we were all sweating profusely *At least we have enough water and provisions with us, and even some Pepsi*, I thought.

I was proud of my husband. I glanced over at him and saw his sunburned face and the adventurous look in his eyes. I could tell he was having a great time. He drove us safely along the deep, washed-out riverbed, the car occasionally jostling through a puddle or two of mud. We were relieved when we finally made it to the other bank of the river.

After another hour, we arrived at Al Qariyah, the main village in our project area. We were tired but happy. Our Bedouin friends, who had been cut off from civilization for days, came out to meet us. No buses or trucks could have navigated the bumpy, damaged roads. Our friends were all curious to find out what had been going on in Mukalla. Nobody here in this impoverished area owned a car, so there was no way for them to visit the province's capital, except perhaps on the back of a camel, which would have been a day's journey. And even if buses were able to drive, the fares were too expensive for most people here.

Many of these southern Yemenis were very dark-skinned and had black, curly hair. Our white baby with his soft, light brown curls was a stunning contrast to these African-looking people. They just adored him.

Tim had survived the first adventurous ride of his life and was now fast asleep in my arms. Bedouin children quickly circled David and Martin. They wanted to show them a litter of brand new puppies. Our boys immediately fell in love with the little whelps.

"Mama, look! They're so cute. They haven't even opened their eyes yet, and their legs are still wobbly. Please, can we have one? Please, Mama, pretty please?"

"They're too small. They need their mother."

"Then let's take the mother with us, too!"

The last time we were here, the Bedouin sheik gave us a baby goat. On a different occasion, Chris and I intervened just in time, before the kids adopted a donkey into our family. If it went on like this, we'd soon own an entire zoo! Well, the goat remained with the Bedouins, and these puppies would stay here in Al Qariyah, too. But David and Martin still felt like they were the proper owners.

After lunch in the restaurant—there was only one item on the menu: rice and fish—we drove to the gas station to put air in the tires. Then Chris took David and Martin with him to visit some of the villagers and catch them up on the newest developments. I stayed behind with the baby and the Bedouin women. They relaxed in the shade of one of the huts and talked about everything—from their maize or wheat to which village women were expecting a baby. I was tired, so they brought me a mat to lie on. I just rested while the other women kept on chattering, drinking tea, or going about their chores. It was pleasant here in Al Qariyah, much more laid-back than in Western parts of the world. When visitors came by, the locals just took them in and made them feel at home.

David came running toward me from a distance: "Papa wants to visit Hayla before we go home. We have to leave right away. He wants to be home before sunset because of the bad roads."

I quickly said good-bye to my friends and left with David to join the rest of my family.

CHAPTER 22

Help! Sinan Is Dying!

WE HAD BEEN living with our three sons in Hadhramaut, the Valley of Death, for over two years now. So much had happened in that time! There was no chance of us getting bored! We had become a part of the community, although our light-colored skin still betrayed us as foreigners. Southern Yemen felt like home to us now, in spite of the heat, humidity, and difficult living conditions.

We all loved the friendly *Hadhramis*.[32] They were always very eager to help. Chris's skills and gifts made him particularly well-suited for this work, and he quickly adapted to new situations. That afforded him friendships with the governor and various other high-ranking authorities, as well as with the simple folk. To his advantage he looked like the Arabs, with his dark mustache and hair, which was always covered with a traditional Arab wrap extending down to the shoulders. He spoke Arabic with almost no foreign accent, and was also proficient in

---

32 natives of Hadhramaut

Fusha.[33] Whenever he arrived in the city, people greeted him from all sides with a friendly, "*Salaam aleikum,* Abu David!"

This was a title of honor and meant "Father of David," and had been given to him by the neighbors. Chris was constantly surprised how many people knew him! As foreigners here in Mukalla, we felt like fish in an aquarium. We were being watched closely every moment of the day and the bush telegraph worked very well in these parts of the desert. The locals were always grateful and treated us with respect, realizing that we were friendly and easy to get along with. They also recognized our fear of God and accepted it, even though their belief system was different than ours. The respect and affection they had for us were a direct result of our reaching out to them and trying to fit into their traditional Arab culture.

* * *

The phone rang. I picked up and heard Chatija's frantic voice: "Sinan is dying! He's dying!"

"Don't panic! We'll take him to the hospital," I answered, already on my way down the stairs. I grabbed my *balto* and a headscarf and was out the door.

Sinan had turned blue in the face. I realized he had suffered a pseudo croup seizure. One of our sons had been hit with two similar attacks while we were still living in Germany.

Chris drove Mohammed, his terrified wife, Chatija, and their little patient straight to the hospital while their other children stayed with me. Before I sent them off to play, my boys and I prayed for little Sinan's healing. The three neighbor boys just looked on with mouths wide open. They had never seen anyone pray to God without first performing ceremonial cleansings and other religious rituals. When Chris returned from the hospital, he shared what had happened.

"We made it just in time! Fortunately, a doctor came along right away and shoved a tube down Sinan's throat before it had swollen completely shut. Then he gave him some medicine and set him up with oxygen. Chatija was hysterical and couldn't stop crying. Her firstborn

---

33 the written Arabic language

son died of this very disease. She was not able to get him to the hospital in time."

David said, "Yeah, back then, nobody in the neighborhood owned a car or even a telephone!"

We were so relieved and thankful. Little one-year-old Sinan had survived, and his brothers had witnessed a miraculous answer to prayer. After that, Chatija often took me with her when she visited her relatives, where she proudly introduced me as her friend. It wasn't long before I had developed a good relationship with each of her sisters and many other relatives.

Chatija and I often talked about our belief systems and our different views of things concerning faith. We always listened carefully to each other and respected each other's opinions. I tried to avoid subjects that would lead to a quarrel, preferring to ask thought-provoking questions and being careful not to demean Islam.

"What do you think happens when you die?"

"Why does Allah desire for people to sacrifice themselves in suicide to promote his agenda? Couldn't he attain his goals without shedding blood? Why do these people have to die for him?"

Yes, we had our differences of opinion, but we didn't let our conversations affect our friendship. Chatija's sister Alia, though, had just finished her Islamic studies. She was a fundamentalist and tried to convert me to her "true religion" by quoting the Quran and arguing every point in detail. But after a while, both Chatija and Alia realized they were not going to convince me. I was a hopeless case and very resistant to their attempts to convert me. And so it became an unwritten rule that, whenever we were together, we would not talk about religion. We knew one another's point of view and left it at that.

I was occasionally able to slip in a reference to my faith, though. Once, when we were talking about child rearing, I told her how I depended on God to help me deal with difficult situations. But I was careful not to get onto religious topics.

CHAPTER 23

An Adventure with Grandma and a Khat-Chewing Angel

SHARIIFA HAD GIVEN birth to her second child. Rania was a happy, little girl and a ray of light in this hour of darkness. Unfortunately, Shariifa's husband, Sultan, was often away from home.

Our team leaders had left with their family for the capital to take part in a language study course. About the same time, our good friends, the Webers, were preparing to move far away to start a new project. They were often gone since they had to find a place to stay and wanted to get to know the people there.

Chris and I were left to head up all the projects in the villages close-by. That was a huge responsibility! Even though money was tight, we couldn't just abandon everything we had worked for. The people here were depending on us to fulfill the commitments our team had made.

A highlight of the summer was a visit from Grandma. She was especially excited to meet her youngest grandchild. Tim was five months old now, and the two of them bonded immediately. The older boys were glad to have their grandma around, too. She loved to play cards, or other games with them.

One day, we all went to one of "our" Bedouin villages for a visit. For Grandma, that was like jumping into the deep end. She knew nothing of the oriental culture and, of course, couldn't speak a word of Arabic. But we prepared her for the customs and taught her a few words on our way to the village. I had set her up with a traditional wardrobe, including the obligatory black coat (which covered her entire body down to the ankles), and a headscarf to hide her hair.

"Just smile and greet the people with a simple *Salaam aleikum!* When you meet women, kiss them on the left cheek first, then on the right, and then on the left again."

Grandma objected. "Is all that kissing really necessary?"

"Yes. That's the way they do things here. Then you smile again, and when they ask you *Kiif haalik?*,[34] you just answer *Alhamdulillah.*[35] Come on, try it. Just remember to smile. Your facial expression is very important. Most of these people are illiterate, but they can read people well and are very intelligent. They're masters at interpreting facial expressions!"

Upon arrival in the project area, our Bedouin friends Amer and Mariam welcomed us heartily. Memories returned of my recent birthday and their visit when David had become so ill. Today we just sat in the sand and chatted casually about everything and nothing. Grandma sipped her cup of tea and experienced Yemeni hospitality firsthand. After a while, she was ready to go home. If only she had known what Amer and Mariam were planning! They wanted to join us on our trip back to Mukalla. One of their relatives was in the hospital, and they wanted to save the bus fare and ride with us to visit him. And to pay the doctor for his care, they needed to take a goat along with them. They just grabbed the poor animal and stuck it into the back of our vehicle. Then they laid some hay at its feet and jumped into the front seat.

Grandma, the three kids, and I sat in the back. The goat kept sticking its head over the back of the seat and poking its snout directly in Grandma's face. It seemed to have taken a liking to our guest. It bleated

---

34 How are you?
35 Thank God!

loudly and drooled all over her headscarf, snapping and nipping at it as if starving. Grandma was horrified and freaked out:

"Help me! This beast stinks, and it's eating my scarf!"

Chris and I wanted to stop at a remote settlement before we went back home. But then we got stuck in the sand and couldn't drive any farther. *That's my chance*, thought the goat. It jumped over the back of the rear seat and landed on Grandma's lap, which served as a trampoline to hop into the front and out the open passenger window. It was such a funny situation! I glanced at Chris and we both burst into laughter.

While the men worked to free the car from the sand, Mariam and I, along with the kids, chased the goat trying to capture it. Grandma remained with Tim in the car, grateful that she had a chance to rest a bit. She didn't hide her feelings and hoped that we wouldn't capture the goat.

We had a hard time catching the goat, which was enjoying this moment of freedom. As soon as we thought we had it, away it would scamper. Apparently it wasn't keen on visiting Mukalla. It certainly wouldn't have been looking forward to the butcher's knife! Due to this unexpected turn of events, we lost a lot of time and the sun began to set. "Well, we can't go to that village now. It's almost dark, and it would be too dangerous to try to drive on the loose sand without being able to see properly," Chris said impatiently.

The goat was still on the loose. Chris put an abrupt end to our game of tag.

"We've got to move along. It's getting dark. Either we go on without the goat, or the two of you stay behind," he said to our Bedouin friends.

But just then, Mariam managed to grab the goat's horns and dragged it back to the car. She opened the hatch and shoved the stubborn animal inside. Grandma wasn't happy at all. Chris got back into the car and began to maneuver it out of the sandy ruts that he and Amer had dug.

"Well, at least it's only one goat!" he said and winked at Grandma. Then he turned around and concentrated on the road in front of him.

The rest of us managed to jump into the rolling car just in time. The remaining one-hour drive back to Mukalla was something Grandma would never forget.

When we finally arrived at the hospital, we dropped our passengers off, along with their bleating goat, and Grandma breathed a sigh of relief.

"Thank God that animal is gone!"

David tapped her on the shoulder. "Grandma, you know that poor goat is headed for the butcher! At least he could enjoy his last hour with us!"

That was too much for me. I couldn't control myself any longer and laughed out loud. Chris couldn't hold it back, either. He laughed so hard, that tears ran down his cheeks. Grandma just smiled.

* * *

A few days later, we took Grandma on a sightseeing tour of the country. Our first stop was the Baptist Hospital in Jibla. It was the only Christian hospital in Yemen. Our guest marveled at the difference between the luscious northern regions and the desert wastelands around Mukalla, in the Valley of Death, where we had been living for the past two-and-a-half years.

After leaving Jibla, we headed for Sanaa, the capital of Yemen. From there, Grandma was to catch a flight home. Our vehicle began to sound like it was sick. It started spitting and coughing even before we were on the road. We decided to make a short stop in Ibb to have a mechanic check it out. He found the problem and was able to fix it right away. And so we continued along the long winding road to Sanaa. While driving up the 9000-foot-high Sumara Pass, Chris tried to overtake a truck on a sharp, narrow right-hand curve. At that very moment, while we were on the wrong side of the road, our engine gave out. Chris tried to start it up again but in vain

Grandma and I started praying loudly. This was a precarious situation! If a car were to come from the other direction, there was no way we would be able to avoid an accident. The driver would never see us in time, and besides, his brakes could be faulty, like most cars in Yemen. Chris stepped on the clutch hoping to slowly roll backwards and try to get over to the correct side of the road.

But it was almost impossible since the gearshift was stuck. The children were scared. Chris was edgy. He knew that buses, cars, trucks and vans drove down this pass at high speeds. One only had to look below to know that in the chasm lay dozens of cars that hadn't made it.

"Pray everybody! Pray!" he said.

When Martin prayed: "Please, God, send us an angel!" it seemed like God answered immediately.

Chris was able to park the car on the right side of the road next to the guardrail. He got out, found a large rock and placed it under the rear tire. Then he grabbed the warning triangle and placed it a few meters farther up the pass.

We remained in the car to stay out of the blazing heat.

"Watch out! A truck is coming from behind!" Chris yelled. He waved his arms up and down, trying to warn the driver of the danger ahead. Grandma and I continued to pray for God's protection and help.

Amazingly, the driver stopped his truck just in time and got out. The friendly, gray-haired Yemeni truck driver had his mouth full of *khat*. It looked like he had a tennis ball in his cheek. He turned to Chris and asked, "You guys have a problem?"

Chris explained our situation, and without further ado, the driver pulled his truck around in front of us, took out a simple towrope, and connected it to our car. Then he hooked it up to his vehicle.

"Get in!" he ordered and put his truck into gear.

Chris got behind the wheel and put the car into neutral. He was rather skeptical and didn't truly believe this was going to work.

"There's no way he'll be able to pull the extra weight. And that thin rope won't hold going up this steep slope. The pass has a thirty-degree incline, and it's another twelve miles to the top."

But today, Chris would be wrong. The truck was apparently empty, and so the driver revved the engine and began to move forward. The towrope became taut and...didn't snap! A short jerk and we were on our way up the mountain, slowly but surely.

"Yippee! We're moving again!" The children were excited, and we adults were also very happy, as well as amazed. It was a miracle!

We were moving in slow-motion speed and could have walked faster than we were driving. We were so happy that we began to sing "Thank you, Father!"

It seemed like it took hours, but eventually, we reached the top of the pass.

I told Chris: "Why don't you offer him some money for his efforts? He lost a lot of time helping us out."

Chris replied: "No, that would offend his sense of honor. The Yemenis are all very eager to help and would never want to be paid for their services."

David called from the backseat: "Why don't you give him an *Injil?*"[36]

Martin joined in: "That's a great idea! And we have some Coke we could offer him!"

"Where is he, anyway? He was just here. And now he's nowhere to be seen. His truck has vanished into thin air!"

We asked around at the gas station, but nobody had seen a truck. There was no trace of him.

Martin laughed out loud. "It must have been an angel! A *khat*-chewing angel!"

Our sons never doubted again that angels exist!

---

36 New Testament in Arabic

CHAPTER 24

Run-in with the Police

DAVID, MARTIN AND the Webers' children were at school with their teacher, Peter. I decided to take Tim with me and drive to Mukalla. I wanted to pick up some photos at the Kodak store and get the mail from the main post office. We were expecting important papers from Germany: David's corrected tests from the correspondence school in Hamburg. The school had sent them off several weeks ago, and they should have arrived by now. Today was the last opportunity to pick up the mail since the post office would be closed the next few days during *Eid al-Adha Sacrifice Feast*. This was my only chance to get these errands done. I had another hour before school was out when my kids would need something to eat. I was glad that Chris had taken the Land Cruiser to the project area that day and had left me the SUV Normally, I wouldn't have driven the 12 miles to the city in the hot, midday sun. The car's air conditioning was still on the blink.

Tim sat directly behind me in his safety seat and babbled away. He was an uncomplicated little boy and always happy. The heat never seemed to bother him. I guess that's because he was born in Yemen. I let my thoughts wander and hummed a catchy tune.

Party atmosphere was in the air, and many people were out making last-minute purchases in preparation for the big feast. It was obligatory to bring sweets with you when visiting relatives. Every daughter got a new dress and the sons a new pair of trousers and a shirt. This was a must, even if it meant there was no money left for food. After all, nothing is more important than image and tradition. Even for the poorest of the poor, this was a matter of honor. Sometimes they would save for months for these purchases.

The city was very crowded and bustling. I should have considered that before coming to town.

Suddenly, there was a loud bang. It sounded like a rifle being shot. The car shook fiercely. Tim was scared and started to cry. My heart began to race. Then I saw it: A blue police car was wedged into my car's left rear fender. I was shaking in my shoes and knew I was in trouble. Women were often blamed for any problems and if a woman drove a car, that was really suspicious. The only women who ever drove a car in all of Hadhramaut, were the foreign ladies from our team.

I was baffled. "What had happened?"

I took a quick look at Tim to make sure he wasn't hurt. I handed him his teddy bear and spoke to him softly, and he began to laugh. His optimism cheered me up, and I was able to smile again. I slowly got out of the car. Had I been distracted by the vast amount of traffic? A bus had tried to pass me, and a donkey cart had been parked in the curve up ahead. Several people on foot had been trying to cross the street. Then there was the man in the pedestrian area, standing next to his festively adorned horse and offering people a once-in-a-lifetime opportunity to take their photo with the beautiful pony.

I still had no idea what had happened. The road I was on was a one-way street. The lane coming toward me was also one way but turned away at this juncture. There no thoroughfare on my left, so I hadn't even glanced in that direction.

It surprised me to see a crowd of people surrounding me. I was the center of attention. I thought for a moment that this must be what movie stars felt like.

Usually I'm not afraid of people, but this situation was a bit embarrassing. Most of the time, the Yemeni people were very friendly and generous to us foreigners. But today it seemed they had banded against me. "A woman at the wheel! That was bound to end badly! What was she thinking?" Many of the men here couldn't afford a driver's license, and the poor people just couldn't comprehend that I had one. It was hard for them to grasp that a woman—who in their eyes belonged in the kitchen—would be out driving a car!

I smiled as I remembered our beginnings here in Yemen. Shortly after arriving, I had a strange encounter during one of my first drives. I was just about to turn right out of our driveway onto the main street when a local man returning from his noon prayer at the mosque, started to cross the street. He then noticed something very strange about the car in front of him: A woman was behind the wheel! A woman! He was taken aback and just stood there on the road with his mouth wide open.

When he finally composed himself again, he shouted: *"Hurma bit-suuq, hurma bitsuuq sayaara!"*[37]

I just gave him a friendly nod and made a big detour around him. I thought it was funny, but I tried to keep from laughing. I didn't want to make matters worse or perhaps even give him a heart attack!

In these parts, it was very unusual to see a woman driving a car. And come to think of it, if the local women were to get behind the wheel with their faces completely veiled, that could be very dangerous indeed!

Over time, though, the people here had become used to the women in our team driving.

The driver of the police car got out. He was heavyset and bald and was sweating profusely. He left the car running, and the putrid smell of gas filled the air. The policeman did his best to rile up the crowd and convince them—and me—that the accident was my fault. He stopped the next car that came by and had the three other policemen who were with him leave the scene. He also tried to get rid of any other potential witnesses, yelling at them and telling them to leave. After a few minutes, a second patrol car arrived, and the police officer helped his colleague disperse the crowd. He ignored me altogether. I was merely

37 A woman driving a car!

a light-skinned foreign woman, after all. He didn't even answer my question:

"Aish ilmushkila?"[38]

He hid behind an Islamic law that forbids a decent man from talking to a woman he doesn't personally know. I was starting to become desperate. Then I remembered that my husband couldn't be reached since he was out in the project area where there were no phones. I nearly panicked when I realized I couldn't expect any support from him. I forced myself to remain calm and remember that I wasn't alone, after all. Immediately, a supernatural peace came over me. The fear and confusion left, and I was calm again.

Finally, the overweight officer, who could hardly keep the buttons on his uniform from popping open, spoke to me and ordered:

"Give me your license. And follow us to the police station!" he demanded in Arabic, because he did not know any English.

Holding Tim close in my arms, I pleaded with him. "First, I have to go to the post office! After all it's only 200 feet away!" The police station was in the other direction, three miles outside the city. But the officer insisted.

"You follow us!" he snapped and looked right past me.

Then he got in his patrol car, crammed his fat belly behind the wheel, released the parking brake, and put the car in reverse. He tried to move it away from my car, but it wasn't as easy as he had thought it would be. The car creaked and banged terribly as he tried to get it untangled.

I had to drive a few yards in the other direction toward the roundabout since I couldn't turn around on a one-way street. I was so close to the post office and the Kodak, shop that I thought about slipping in to take care of business. I could always tell the officer that I hadn't understood him. But then I remembered that there was usually a long line in these places. I wouldn't be able to find a parking space, either, so I dropped that idea and turned around in the direction I had come from. My adversary was waiting for me at the accident site. He turned on his siren and flashing light and drove off. It was hard not to feel a little amused by his obvious need for attention. I followed him

---

38 What is the problem?

inconspicuously. When I arrived at the police station, the fat officer had disappeared with my license, so I waited in the car for further instructions. For the policemen there, I was a welcome diversion. They rarely had to deal with women here, especially not "exotic" ones like me. I had my hair covered and was wearing a modest black *balto,* but they were still able to see my face and light-skinned hands and ankles.

It was hot in the car, and unfortunately, I had not thought to bring any water along. Time passed, and nothing happened. Maybe they were out to lunch? Or was it prayer time? Tim started to cry. I was a bit tense because I needed to nurse him, but I didn't want to do that with curious eyes looking on.

I bargained with the officers standing around: "I need to go home now. My children are hungry. They are probably wondering where I am. Do you want them to go hungry? They need their mother."

The policemen were empathetic. They knew a mother should be there for her children and that a woman's place was in the kitchen. Besides, I couldn't do any more damage than I already had!

"You may go, but you have to leave your driver's license and car here!"

"I can leave the license here, but I need the car. How else will I be able to get home? It's over fifteen miles from here. Besides, my husband would be furious if I came home without the car!"

I had figured out by now that women should mention their husbands in difficult situations like this. That would always be respected since only men's opinions really counted. So I wasn't surprised when the officer allowed me to take the car, after all. But before I could drive off, the chief of police came down the stairs and had one more stipulation:

"Send your husband around tomorrow. We are having a police celebration and need a special guest for the press. When he comes, we'll discuss your accident with him."

Before the officers could reconsider their offer, I got in the car and drove away. It had scarcely been damaged. I kept checking the rearview mirror to make sure nobody was following me. I was quite relieved when I finally got home, exhausted and famished.

While I was preparing dinner, I told David and Martin what had happened.

They pouted: "Oh, Mama! Why didn't you take us with you? You have all the fun, and we have to go to our boring school!"

Neither of them believed that I would have loved to exchange places with them.

As a consolation, Chris took them with him the next day when he went to the police station. Who would have suspected that my husband would be the guest of honor at the celebration and sit on the stage next to the chief of police, drinking tea and Cola and being photographed by the press?!

Over tea, he took it upon himself to convince the chief that I couldn't have caused the accident the day before. The place where it happened proved that it was the stout, low-ranking policeman who had violated the law. He had turned illegally onto a one-way street. Chris gained a few new "best friends" at the police station that day. It would prove later to be a great asset. Without further ado, they gave him my Yemeni driver's license back, and Chris was proud of himself for how he had managed the situation. It had been so simple. But being a man had given him an advantage over me. In this culture, men were privileged. I had to accept the fact that Chris would probably never understand what it felt like to be a woman in this male-dominated society!

When he returned home, he triumphantly gave me my license and grinned. The boys were happy, too. They had been allowed to drink as much Coke as they wanted to.

* * *

Some time later, I had a pleasant experience involving another police officer. I was in a hurry, as usual. I needed to pick up a dress from the tailor's shop. There was a lot of traffic, and I couldn't find a parking space. So I parked our car—which everybody in the entire community recognized as ours by now—in a wide curve and got out. I checked to make sure I had everything I needed and was about to move on when I looked around and saw a tall, short-sleeved officer standing directly in front of me. He grinned at me and pointed to the no-parking sign. Apparently, he thought that I couldn't understand Arabic since I was a foreigner. He was quite taken aback when I answered him fluently in his own language.

"Yes, I know. But there isn't a parking space anywhere to be found! I just need to step into that shop over there. It'll only take five minutes." The officer was inspecting the car and saw that the window on the driver's side was open. I seized the opportunity and said: "Officer, my electric window opener is broken, and I can't shut the windows. Would you mind waiting here until I get back, so nobody tries to steal the car?"

He just smiled, so I hurried off. Unfortunately, I got lost and couldn't find the tailor's shop right away. There were just too many narrow roads and alleyways! Worse still, when I got there, the customer in front of me was ordering her wedding dress, and the discussion about the form and the accessories seemed to go on forever. I was just about to leave without picking up my dress when the customer finally left. It was my turn.

"I'm sorry. Your dress isn't finished yet. But it will only take another two minutes!"

I figured that two more minutes wouldn't be such a big deal. I had waited so long already, and the policeman was certainly gone by now.

The two minutes turned into thirty. I should have known! I returned to my car almost an hour later, and to my chagrin, the officer was still there watching and protecting it. He had sprawled out on the hood and laid his head on the windshield. I apologized to my "gentleman protector," but he just smiled at me, flashing his white teeth, then hopped off the hood and said:

"*Misch Muschkila!*[39] Everything takes longer around here!"

I gratefully returned his smile.

"The police: your friend and helper!" I muttered in German, half laughing. I got in, closed the door, and started up the engine.

I waved at the officer as I drove away, eager to get home. I had made a new friend. From that day on, every time that officer saw me somewhere, he smiled and waved!

---

39 No problem!

CHAPTER 25

Shariifa's Dreams

ONE MORNING, SHARIIFA came much later to work than usual. She was quite upset.

"I had a terrible dream. I was dressed in white. That means somebody in my family is about to die!" she said. (In Islam, white is the color of death and sorrow.) "I'm really scared! Will it be my son? Or my father who is far away in Africa? I haven't seen him in years!"

I tried to calm her down. "Come here and sit for a moment. Drink some tea. Just relax a bit, and then we'll pray to see if God has something to say to us."

As we prayed, a deep peace came over us both.

"You have no reason to be afraid, my dear! In our book about God, it says that we will receive white clothes when our sins are washed away by his blood. Wearing these white robes will be a sign of our redemption. You belong to the family of God."

Shariifa's face began to glow, and she laughed and jumped for joy. She was relieved beyond words when I read this Bible verse to her.

A few months later, a house was built directly next to ours. Through the kitchen window, we could hear all the noises the family made. Like many Yemeni houses, this one didn't have glass windows, only blinds with little openings in them that didn't allow much air to get in. But they also did keep the curious glances of the neighbors out.

One night, Shariifa had another dream. The following day she shared it with me:

"It was summer, and I was a 'guardian' of your home. A wedding was imminent in the neighbor's house next door. Through the openings in the blinds, I could see all the delicacies in the house. They made my mouth water. A beautiful white light shone out from inside. All the women wore gorgeous white dresses and were marvelously adorned. I desperately wanted to join them, but I didn't have a gown that fit. I decided to ask Chatija if she could loan me a dress. Chatija said she was sorry, but she didn't have anything my size. But she offered me a black robe and all the gold she possessed. I turned her down. Another friend offered me a freshly-washed red gown. But I refused that, as well. Then I went to the next neighbor, and she had a white dress for me. Unfortunately, it hadn't been washed recently. Normally, I wouldn't have worn an unwashed dress to a wedding ceremony, but I took the dress and put it on. I don't know why."

After a while, I said: "Perhaps these neighbors will become children of the King one day. Our book says that they will all be dressed in white robes. These neighbors reject us foreigners for now. They don't want anything to do with us. But perhaps the dream should be understood differently. Maybe the neighbors see the light shining from within our house and all the delicacies. That might get their attention and draw them closer to God."

I paused, and then continued:

"Your role in this matter is very important, Shariifa. You feel drawn to the celebration. You want to join in. But Islam wants to prevent that and is tempting you with gold. You feel drawn back and forth. In any event, you have been invited and will be allowed to attend. God knows that you are still undecided. The colors of the dresses have a special meaning in our holy book, as well. Red symbolizes the blood of Jesus. White is for purity. And black represents sin."

CHAPTER 26

An Oil Tanker Explodes

October 6, 2002

WE WERE CONCERNED about the future of the project. Chris wanted to do more sustainable work which reflected our faith, even if that meant more effort and less free time. Long-term projects would be effective only if the quality of the work was first-rate. The government's stipulations had to be fulfilled, as well. Otherwise, we would lose all credibility.

Chris had to fly to the capital again for several days to sign new contracts with the government. That would guarantee the future of the development projects.

The kids and I stayed home alone as Shariifa had skipped work that day without giving us any notice. Maybe she was sick? Martin had been attending the Arab school in the mornings for a couple of weeks now, and David was down in our homeschool classroom with the other children. Sabine, the new tutor, and the Weber family tutor were with them. My youngest son sat on the kitchen floor and was having fun emptying all the cabinet drawers, while I was kneading bread dough. My thoughts wandered to the attack that happened on September 11, 2001, just over a year ago.

The phone rang, and I hesitated, glancing back and forth between the phone and the bowl of dough.

"I can't right now! My hands are all sticky!"

But then curiosity got the best of me. With these old telephones, there was no display to tell you who was calling. I quickly washed the dough off my hands, grabbed Tim, and picked up the receiver.

"Hello, *miin maai?*"

It was Tobias, my youngest brother-in-law. He rarely called, and he got right to the point. "Don't you guys think it's about time to get on a plane and come home?"

"Hello, Tobias! Is that really you? How are you doing? This is a nice surprise. Do you have good news? Or did somebody die?" I was surprised to hear his voice.

"Haven't you heard?" Tobias asked, obviously upset.

He waited a few seconds and then continued: "There was a terrorist attack right near where you live. An oil tanker exploded. Poisonous gases are escaping. Haven't you noticed? The news reports show a thick, black cloud of smoke directly over Mukalla. Haven't you heard anything about it?"

I just shook my head in bewilderment.

"It's weird that you guys already know about it, and we're still completely in the dark. But we keep our ceiling fans on all the time, and they're really loud. Maybe that's why we didn't hear the explosion."

Tobias repeated his concern for our safety. "Seriously! You should think about coming back to Germany! I'm beginning to worry about my nephews, especially when I see what's going on over there!" Then he said good-bye and hung up.

Meanwhile, the bread dough was flowing out over the brim of the bowl. I had completely forgotten it. I ran up to the roof with Tim in my arms and looked toward the city. Sure enough, I saw the dark cloud of smoke rising high into the atmosphere. Fortunately, it was still quite a distance away.

The phone rang again! I ran down the stairs carrying the baby, taking two steps at a time. This time it was Sultan, Shariifa's husband. He worked at the oil harbor. Without even saying hello, he yelled his urgent orders into the phone:

"Close all your windows and doors! There was a terrorist attack at the oil harbor in Mukalla. A huge French oil tanker exploded and is in flames. Be careful! The terrorists apparently come from your immediate neighborhood. Don't leave the house! I can't say anything more on the phone right now."

Before I could even ask about Shariifa, he had hung up. I was confused and concerned. The fear in Sultan's voice was alarming. He was usually so calm. Suddenly, I realized the gravity of the situation. Fear gripped me, and I immediately followed the instructions Sultan had given me. As if in a trance, I went from room to room and shut all the windows and doors, even in the school classroom.

"You boys stay in the house today, even during recess!" I told the children, trying to sound casual.

"But Mama, we wanted to continue building the bird cage today. Please let us go outside!" David begged.

"Don't argue! It's just for today. We don't know exactly what's going on, but down at the oil harbor something terrible happened."

"But that's so far away!" David answered. "What does that have to do with us?"

"Good question. One that I can't answer at the moment. But we have to be careful. The poisonous vapors could reach all the way to our place. And they are very dangerous, even though you can't smell them."

The tense situation and uncertainty about the extent of the danger made the kids restless. They had a hard time concentrating on their "boring" lessons and wanted to know just why they couldn't go outside. But I had no time to argue with them. My mind was spinning. Suddenly, I remembered the bread dough and darted up to the kitchen.

"What a mess!" I said with a loud groan.

I put Tim down on the floor and took a closer look. The sticky dough had risen due to the heat in the room and had swelled over the edge of the bowl and onto the counter. But it hadn't stopped there. It had dripped down the counter all the way to the floor.

"Oh, no!" I sighed.

About the same time, Chris's cell phone was filling up with missed calls and messages from news services, security agencies, and various Western embassies in Sanaa.

"You're the expert on things like this. Please tell us what you think. Who's behind this attack? What did the terrorists hope to achieve?"

Suddenly, Chris was a sought-after man. Everybody wanted to interview him.

On his return flight to Mukalla the following day, the plane was full of journalists, as well as French and American security experts. In his conversations with them, he found out that most of them would be staying at the Holiday Inn. He had to smile at the irony! That hotel belonged to the Bin Laden family. And Bin Laden's terrorist organization Al-Qaeda was being suspected of the current terrorist attack!

It quickly became clear that this was a well-planned attack. Everybody knew it, but the government kept the public in the dark and tried to convince everyone that it was just a tragic accident. The administration didn't want to validate the bad reputation Yemen had as a "country of terrorists" by conceding that this had been an attack. But after a while, they couldn't deny the evidence any longer. The situation could have been much worse, though. The French oil tanker *Limburg* that had exploded was constructed in compliance with the latest international security conventions to prevent an oil catastrophe. It had been built after the infamous *Exxon-Valdez* oil spill in the nineties and had an improved double hull and compartmentalized tanks to help limit the damage that could be caused by a leak or an explosion.

During the week of the explosion, international newspapers reported that the cause was still unclear. One sailor was killed, and 25 of the crew were injured that Sunday morning. The captain of the *Limburg* asserted that the explosion was not the result of a technical problem. He said that at least the first of several detonations had occurred outside the tanker. One of the sailors had seen a small boat speeding toward the ship just before the explosion occurred.

Yemen was considered to be a sanctuary for terrorists, and many suspects were detained at first, only to be released soon after.

An Arab newspaper reported some time later that the explosion had been planned and executed by the Islamic Army of Aden and the Al-Qaeda terror network. These organizations confessed to the attack but stated that they had mistaken the tanker for a US battleship.

* * *

A few days later, Chris, who had finally returned from Sanaa, took us all to the beach. The kids built sand castles and looked for seashells. Suddenly, we realized that our feet were all black and sticky. We hadn't noticed the dark streaks in the sand at first. As we got closer to Mukalla, we discovered a couple of dead birds amid the regular flotsam in the sand. Their wings were covered in oil. We also saw a few dead fish floating belly-up toward the shore. It was a terrible sight! When we looked more closely, we saw a mile-long oil spill stretching all the way from here to Mukalla.

It shocked us at first when we realized this was the oil which had spilled from the tanker that had been attacked. Even though it was a fairly secure ship, the explosion had ripped a 25-foot hole in one of the tank walls. We stopped at the Diving Center and were told that the new Dutch owners were already packing their bags and closing shop.

"We're leaving. The oil is killing all the fish, and the coral is dying, too. It will be years, if not decades, before the fish stock is replenished. There's no future for us here. We were crazy to set up shop in this remote area!"

Later while sitting on the cliff looking out at the ocean, I was filled with sadness. The oil spill glistened from the oil harbor on my left and was being carried by the tide toward Mukalla.

I protested to nobody in particular: "Why should we just sit here and do nothing about the destruction that is going on? We're on good terms with the Creator of the universe, aren't we?!"

"Chris, let's get the team together this evening up on the roof. We need to start battling this oil contamination in prayer. We ought to believe the song we sing 'Possess the good land the Lord is giving you,' don't you agree?" Chris did.

That evening, he and I and two other members of the team went up to the roof of our house and prayed under the starry sky:

"Lord, you are in control of everything. It's no problem for you to push this oil back. Please protect this beautiful part of your creation and keep the fish from dying, so the fishermen can survive. Turn this curse into a blessing. Take the chaos and create something wonderful from it, even as you did in the very beginning of creation."

After talking to God, we were able to sleep well. The very next day we discovered that God had, in fact, miraculously intervened. The oil spill could still be seen at the place we had been the day before. It remained there for many weeks, but it never moved on to Mukalla and the suburb where we lived. Burum and Al Qariyah remained untouched, as well. And most of the fish and coral survived!

"Apparently, no prayer is foolish in God's eyes! Everything is possible with him!" I felt victorious and danced around joyfully.

The owners of the Diving Center had taken a huge loss when they sold it. They had left this pristine paradise because they didn't know there was a Father in heaven they could talk to.

CHAPTER 27

Radical Changes

SHORTLY AFTER OUR team leader, Sebastian, decided to take over the projects, his wife, Larissa, announced she would be returning to Germany. She packed her bags and grabbed the kids and was gone before David and Martin were even able to say goodbye to her and the two girls, Mia and Lea.

Just a few days later, the Weber family packed up the car with their belongings and prepared to move to their new project area. The moving van would follow. Only a small team was left: Sabine, the children's tutor; the midwife, Heidi; and Sebastian, Larissa's husband. He would be joining his family in Germany just as soon as he could tie up loose ends on this side, and the remaining project money had been spent.

With all the others leaving, Heidi decided to join them. It was a sad time. Chris and I lost most of our friends and colleagues within a matter of a few days. David and Martin lost all seven of their German playmates, and that hurt!

We promised we would visit often, but we all knew that with the Webers' departure, a fresh chapter in our lives was beginning. It was a day's journey to their new village, deep in the province of Hadhramaut. The dirt roads would make traveling tedious. Our team had completely dissolved.

This was a difficult time for us. We felt abandoned, disappointed, and fully exhausted. Now the responsibility and the workload were entirely on our shoulders.

"If I had known from the beginning that the other families would be here for such a short time, only to leave us behind in the diaspora all alone, I'm not sure I would have come in the first place," I sighed.

Was our project over? Would we be the only *ajnabees* left here in this huge southeast Arab province, far away from any English-speaking, like-minded people? And how were we supposed to deal with the other challenges we were confronted with, for instance, the increasingly difficult financial situation hanging over our heads like a Damocles' sword?

We were encouraged that many of the local people and government officials approached Chris, begging him to keep the projects going, no matter what it took. After talking intensively with some friends, Chris and I decided to continue our work, in spite of the lack of financial security. We would trust God to provide the funds and new workers if he wanted us to stay on.

"I promised the locals we would finish these projects! What kind of testimony would it be if we were to break our promises? These people need to know that Christians are reliable and do sustainable work," Chris said resolutely. He peered over at me with that mischievous grin of his that had given me new courage many times in the past.

I truly admired my brave husband. He wasn't about to give up!

"God's going to have to speak clearly if he wants us to leave. He was the one who sent us here, and he has confirmed it time and time again. We're not going to be chased away by a few problems. Our family will not be defeated!"

CHAPTER 28

Pray for Healing!

ONE OF OUR sons needed medical treatment, so we made the journey once again to the Baptist Hospital in Jibla up north, in the western highlands of the country. All around the hospital grounds, armed soldiers had been posted at the tall, barbed-wire fence. They were there to protect the foreigners, the Christian workers, as well as the patients of the hospital. Anybody who wanted to ascend the grassy hill to the hospital was checked for weapons. In spite of everything, the international personnel here were fully committed to their work, and it was obvious that they did it out of love.

Our stay in Jibla was refreshing. There was a relaxing and friendly atmosphere there. The Jibla Baptist Hospital was an oasis where we could renew our strength and be encouraged.

During our visit, I got to know Helen, who had a very strong and contagious faith. She was a pretty nurse from India, who had lost her husband years ago. As a widow and a guest worker in this country, she had to work very hard to earn enough money to support her family. Her two teenage daughters lived in India with her mother. Indian workers here in Yemen labored long hours and were often discriminated against. They had very little free time. Every two years, they were allowed to visit their families in India for three months. Indian women were treated especially unfairly and sometimes exploited by men.

In spite of all this, Helen had a big heart for the Yemenis. Her desire was to draw as many of them to God as possible. She did this by living out her faith. She regretted not being able to speak Arabic very well. She was only familiar with a few medical phrases, such as: "Where are you hurting?" or "Here's your medicine," or "You have to stay in bed!"

But what she lost out on for not being fluent in Arabic, she made up for in prayer for the lost souls in her care. Her loving service to these people was vivid proof of the compassion she was unable to express through words. I greatly admired this woman. She had suffered so much. I could learn a lot from her example.

Meanwhile, our son had improved, and we would soon be saying good-bye to Jibla and the friendly hospital staff.

Helen knew we would be leaving the next day. "Before you go back to Mukalla, would you please help me with something? You speak Arabic so well. Please come over this evening during my shift. One of our young patients is on her deathbed. She had an abdominal operation, but the incision didn't heal. We've tried everything. We think some resistant hospital bacteria entered her bloodstream during the procedure. This evening, I would like to pray for her and need you to translate. We'll have to wait until the Muslim workers have left since they are always suspicious. So don't tell anybody you're coming!"

Even though this was officially a Christian hospital, the staff was subjected to constant regulation and control.

I arrived at the hospital at the time we had agreed upon and waited until Helen finished her rounds. It was interesting to observe all the commotion in the hospital ward. The smell of blood and disease, medicine, and disinfectants filled the air. I had no idea that I was about to learn an important lesson that evening, one that would be very significant and groundbreaking for my future.

Helen briskly led me into the darkened hospital ward, where 20 critically sick patients lay in beds. On the bare floor next to them or underneath their beds lay the mothers or sisters of the ill. Many of them sat up and looked at us when we entered the room. They were curious to see what was going on. Helen spoke with the mother of the sick girl in English, but the mother couldn't understand her. She tried to communicate using gestures and facial expressions. The sick girl's eyes were open, but she was staring into nothing. She was apathetic, and her skin was discolored. The sight of her reeking, pus-filled wound shocked me and made me sick to my stomach.

I was unable to get a word out. I prayed quietly for God's help to find the right Arabic words.

I translated what my friend had said. "Your daughter is very ill. We've tried everything, but it seems that humans cannot help her. But I know somebody who loves your Fatima. Would you like me to pray for your child?"

"But we are Muslims! Would my daughter or I have to change our religion?"

Helen affectionately shook her head.

"No, it's not important which religion you belong to. God loves all people. And I know he can do a miracle."

The mother hesitated and considered the offer carefully. Then she said, "Yes, please! Please pray for my daughter, Fatima!"

The other women in the ward, sick and healthy alike, came over and stood around Fatima's bed. They were curious to see what would happen. I hardly noticed them. I was so focused on Fatima, her mother, and Helen. The smell of death filled the air. That bothered me. Doubts began to fill my heart. I wasn't so sure God would answer Helen's bold prayer and heal this girl. However, I translated every word she said. Then we both laid our hands on the young woman, and I prayed a short prayer in Arabic. Although we couldn't see any physical change immediately, something wonderful happened at that moment—an indescribable peace overwhelmed us. Not only did Helen and I feel it, but we could see it in the faces of the dying teenager and her mother.

The following day, Chris and I wanted to get on the road early. It was a 16-hour drive home, and we wanted to be in Mukalla before dark. If we arrived at the last checkpoint too late, they would hold us back, and we'd have to remain in the desert until dawn.

I was disappointed, of course, that I wasn't able to visit Fatima again before we left. I was curious to see if our prayer had been effective.

When we arrived back in Mukalla, we were appalled to discover that the incision from our son's operation had become infected due to the extreme humidity. He was in a lot of pain. I felt sorry for him. We did all we knew. We tried various medicines and prayed for him frequently. In the end, however, we had to admit him to the local hospital in Mukalla to have a follow-up operation. After that, his wound healed quickly.

The first few days at home kept me busy. But finally, I couldn't take it any longer. I called Helen to find out about Fatima. I was prepared for the worst:

"Is Fatima still alive?"

She answered: "Yes! She is alive and was released from the hospital two days ago. She is completely healed, soul and body!"

I could hardly believe it! Completely healed only after a few days? I was so happy, that I laughed out loud.

"Oh, that's just wonderful! I wish I could be there with you. Please give me more details!"

Hearing about Fatima's healing was one of the most encouraging and inspiring moments of my entire life. I had so many questions, and I just blurted them out:

"How did you know that Jesus would heal her? Have you ever prayed for somebody who wasn't healed? How do you know if Jesus is going to heal the person? If you don't know beforehand, how can you pray for healing?"

Helen answered quietly: "Don't forget: When we pray for God to do a miracle, it's not important how big or small our faith is. The important thing is that we turn it over to God. All we have to do is give him praise and leave the results up to him. It's not your faith that is almighty. God is almighty! He can do it, even when human knowledge and medicine can't. And it's entirely up to him to decide how he will respond to our prayers. Don't look at the circumstances. Just be bold and listen to his voice. Pray for healing and leave the rest up to God. The blessing will come when you are obedient. Just trust him!"

CHAPTER 29

Comfort in Sorrow

December 2002

TOWARD THE END of December, my friend Rachel called. She was hysterical, which was alarming since she was normally very reserved. I had known her for some time, ever since our language studies in Jordan. She lived with her husband, Bob, and their three boys in the capital city of Sanaa.

Rachel was weeping uncontrollably over the phone. I felt my muscles tighten and my heart began to pound. I held my breath and feared the worst. Rachel was crying so hard that I couldn't understand a word she was saying.

"What's going on? Calm down, Rachel. Tell me what happened!" I begged.

But she just couldn't stop crying. It was quite a while before she blew her nose and tried to speak. Her words were still shaky:

"It's horrible! An attack in Jibla. Dr. Martha…" Rachel started to sob again and was unable to continue.

I started to cry, as well, although I still didn't know what had happened.

"What about Dr. Martha? Is she…?"

I started to stammer and couldn't get that terrible irrevocable word out. I shook, and my teeth were chattering. It was over 100 degrees outside, but I was freezing. I waited in silence until my friend was able to speak again.

"Dr. Martha, Mr. Bill, and Kathryn were shot to death. A pharmacist is severely injured. It's just terrible! I still can't believe it! We are all affected by this. Some of our friends here in Sanaa are packing their bags and getting ready to leave."

How could this be possible? Everything in me refused to believe it!

"How could something like this happen, Rachel? The grounds are shut off and under strict security. Besides, wasn't the administration of the hospital supposed to be handed over to the locals in a couple of days?"

"Yes, you're right. My husband said that a local man came into the hospital a day before the transfer was to take place. He had a gun wrapped in a blanket and carried it like he was holding a baby in his arms. When he entered the consulting room, he just opened fire, shouting 'Allahu akbar'. If somebody hadn't stopped him, he would have killed more of the American staff."

Rachel began sobbing again. I groaned. Could this really have happened? It wasn't long ago that Dr. Martha had treated our eldest son. After this phone call, I couldn't get anything done. I was just too upset. Fond memories of Mr. Bill and his wood shop and Dr. Martha treating our son filled my thoughts. In the evening, after I put the kids to bed, I sat down and closed my eyes to collect myself. At that moment, I remembered a conversation Dr. Martha and I had engaged in once over dinner.

She had smiled and said: "If I had my way, I'd just stay here and work until the day I die!"

It was as if I could see Dr. Martha sitting there in front of me, smiling. I started to cry again and then reached for the phone.

"Rachel, you know that Dr. Martha loved her job. Just a couple of months ago, she told me she wished she could stay in Jibla and work there until the day she died. But she was afraid she wouldn't be allowed to stay after the administration of the hospital was turned over to the locals. You know what? Dr. Martha's heart's desire was fulfilled. She didn't have to leave Jibla, after all. She completed her race and reached the finish line. She is with Jesus and is happy! But we will miss her very much!"

A few of the staff left Sanaa after this attack that killed three people. The mourning for these martyrs lingered on, but eventually, the situation returned to a kind of normalcy. The remains of Dr. Martha Myers and Mr. Bill Kohen were laid to rest on the Jibla Hospital grounds. They had an honorable burial. We were reminded of our friends every time we took out the carved wooden toys that Mr. Bill had made. Even after many years, our boys still played with them.

The situation in the Middle East was very tense and constantly in danger of escalating. The father of our children's tutor, Sabine, was concerned for his daughter's safety and insisted that she returned home in January. Her contract was through the end of June, and Sabine wanted to stay. She felt safe and comfortable here. But I knew what I had to do. Even though it would be difficult for us as a family, I told Sabine that she should listen to her parents.

"We'll really miss you. You've been such a blessing to us. But it's true: We can't guarantee your safety. If something were to happen to you, we'd never forgive ourselves."

We had taken this helpful, cheery girl into our hearts, and it was extremely hard to say good-bye to her.

We wouldn't be able to get a substitute for Sabine, so I stepped in to teach our two sons for the rest of the school year. In addition to teaching them all the required subjects, I still had my other responsibilities and little Tim to take care of. After three months of these extra duties without even an assistant teacher, Chris suggested that I take the boys back to Germany for our furlough earlier than planned. He would join us nine weeks later around the end of June.

While we were on furlough, David and Martin attended the little German elementary school I had gone to as a child.

* * *

We were relieved to return to Mukalla in September. We were tired and sweaty, but glad to be home.

Shortly after we got back, Shariifa told me she was worried about her friend: "Samiira is very ill. She had a miscarriage and was stitched up afterward, but now she is in great pain."

I knew what Shariifa was referring to. Female genital mutilation is officially illegal. In spite of that, this maltreatment of woman is quite widespread, especially in rural areas since people still think and act very much according to tradition. Genital mutilation is a barbaric ritual practiced for the sole purpose of protecting the virginity of young women, to maximize their sale price as brides.

"There was a complication during Samiira's delivery. The baby died because the opening was too narrow. They cut her open, but during the operation, a fistula formed and became infected. It's festered, but Samiira was ashamed and didn't go to the doctor. The whole issue is very taboo, you know. Now the infection has spread throughout her entire body. Her husband, who loves her very much, has taken her to a hot springs resort. That could be her last chance. I'm so worried about her. She's not eating and is quite apathetic."

"Maybe she has given up hope and no longer wants to live," I said. Then I made a suggestion: "Perhaps you ought to pray with her!"

Shariifa sighed: "Right. I thought about that. Can't you come along and pray for her? You could lay your hands on her like you always do with me when I'm sick. God listens to you."

I tried to encourage her. "Shariifa, God knows your voice and listens to you, too. But I'd be happy to come with you as soon as she returns home. Just let me know."

Samiira came home earlier than planned, but her husband drove her straight to the hospital because she had taken a turn for the worse. Unfortunately, it was too late. Within an hour, she had passed away.

When I heard of her death, I was shocked. I just couldn't believe it. "How can that be?"

Shariifa grieved deeply for her friend. She didn't leave her home for several days. When she finally came over, she said:

"I dreamed that a corpse was brought to me. Nobody wanted to perform the last washing ritual, so I did it. After I washed the body and put beautiful robes on it, the corpse sat up! It was alive again and threw off all the ceremonial robes. And when I looked more closely, I recognized Samiira! She was laughing, and the wounds were healed. Even the scars had disappeared."

I swallowed hard, trying to understand what that could mean.

"Your dream seems to imply that Samiira was born again. But she was a Muslim. She hadn't known anything about our faith, had she?"

"Yes, she knew, Amiira, and she loved everything about Jesus. During the time we guarded your home, she often stayed overnight. She never got tired of watching the *Jesus* movie. Sometimes she stayed up all night watching it! She was so touched by the man in the film and all the miracles he performed. She knew a lot about Jesus and truly loved him."

"In that case, we don't have to worry about her. I believe she is with God now, and he has taken all her pain away. She has a new body and is perfectly healthy."

We both missed this young woman. She had been like a sister to Shariifa. But the dream gave us great consolation. I recognized that God can touch people's lives without any help from us! That was comforting, and I realized that he is more merciful than people are. It amazed me how he would speak to my friend, who had absolutely no formal education. Perhaps that was why she received deeper insights, much like a blind person, whose hearing ability is sharper than people who see.

CHAPTER 30

Typhoid and Encounters with Angels

LISA, OUR NEW teacher's assistant, arrived shortly after we returned in September 2003. She lived in the large room on the ground floor of our house. She taught David fourth grade and Martin second grade. The classrooms were on the same floor as her room. I prepared the curriculum in accordance with the school system requirements in Germany and taught English and German myself.

During the last few weeks, I had stayed very busy and began to feel drained. We set up a new office, and Chris had given the project a new name. It felt to me like the project was his "baby." He felt a sort of fatherly responsibility and invested a lot of time in it.

Chris had to travel to the capital for a few days to renegotiate some contracts and apply for visa extensions. I hoped that things would calm down a bit and that we could get back to some routine. But that didn't happen. Shariifa didn't show up for days to help around the house. Lisa was often faint and weak, so I had to take over her teaching responsibilities.

When she got even weaker, I reluctantly decided to take her to the hospital in Mukalla. In Yemen, it's inconceivable that a woman would enter a public facility without being accompanied by a man—either a brother, husband, father, uncle, or grandfather. So the two of us foreign-looking *ajnabiyas*[40] raised quite a few eyebrows when we entered the hospital. The patients and the Yemeni hospital staff all stared at us with a curious look on their faces. It was quite a sight for Yemeni eyes: A petite adult woman trying to prop up a heavy-set young lady, all the while completely ignoring the suspicious glances of those around them.

The waiting room was filled, as always. There was no place to sit. Poor Lisa would have just plopped down on the dirty floor, but I leaned her up against the wall instead and tried to encourage her.

It seemed like hours went by before we were finally called into the examination room. A dark-skinned, middle-aged, female doctor from Pakistan examined Lisa.

"She has typhoid," she said. Her diagnosis confirmed what I had feared all along.

She gave us a prescription for an antibiotic and something for the fever, as well as advice on how to treat the illness. The whole procedure, from the waiting period to the examination, had taken up half a day, and I was eager to get back to my kids.

When we arrived home, the kids were all alone. They had wanted to do me a favor and had poured soapy water all over the living room floor. It was one big Slip'n Slide!

When the boys saw my startled face, they innocently defended themselves: "Mama, we washed the floor so you wouldn't have so much work to do. Now we're skating."

The whole room was under water, and the rest of the apartment was also a catastrophe. I suppressed my anger, as well as a bit of a smirk—those little scalawags! I helped Lisa to bed, since she was too weak, and brought her something to eat and drink. I also left a bell for her to ring if she needed anything.

The next few days were extremely stressful for me. I was concerned about Lisa. She seemed to be getting more confused and apathetic by the day, in spite of my care. Shariifa still hadn't shown up. I had to wash

---

40 foreign women

Lisa's dishes with disinfectant due to the risk of contamination. It was beginning to take its toll on me.

Then Martin, our 7-year-old, contracted a high fever. He had been complaining of dizziness and fatigue for several days, and now he had stomach cramps as well. These symptoms looked a lot like those Lisa had. I knew that typhoid could be fatal, so I took a deep breath, grabbed my next patient, and drove him to the hospital. Martin was so weak that he couldn't walk into the hospital on his own. So I carried him in my arms through the large hospital entrance. I prayed. The examination and laboratory results indicated, to my relief, that Martin didn't have typhoid. It was a severe intestinal infection that displayed similar symptoms.

I was relieved as I drove home and put Martin to bed. When I saw him there, all pale and in pain, it was just too much for me. I felt alone and helpless and broke into tears. How was I going to deal with everything—handle two patients, homeschool David, do the laundry, wash the dishes, care for the baby—without a husband around to lend me a hand?

I sighed, frustrated: "Where am I going to get help?"

I would have loved to lie down next to my son. But I forced myself into the kitchen to get started on the dishes. Oh, how I missed my German dishwasher!

All of a sudden, my knees became weak. I held on to the kitchen sink as I sagged towards the floor. I tried to continue working in this posture since my patients were waiting for their tea. In the playroom, it was suspiciously quiet. I wondered what my two healthy boys were up to. But I just had to lie down for a minute. For the last two nights, I had mostly been up and around, cleaning up vomit and taking care of Lisa and Martin. I was dizzy and weak, and I began shivering, even though it was over 100 degrees outside. I got a blanket from the cabinet and lay down on the bed. Normally, we sleep with only a thin sheet over us, but I was freezing. I even put on a sweatshirt and then covered up with the blanket.

I told myself, I would just rest for a couple of minutes, and then…

Before I could even complete my thought, my eyes had closed, and I was fast asleep.

I don't know how long I slept. I just remember feeling someone stroking my cheek.

Am I dreaming, or did my husband return from the capital earlier than he planned?

I slowly opened my eyes. I couldn't see anybody! And yet I heard a voice saying: "Don't be afraid. I am with you. You are not alone. I give you my peace!"

I heard the voice loud and clear. But nobody was there. Was it all a dream, maybe caused by the fever? No, that couldn't be. I sensed a powerful, profound peace, and my cheek felt warm from someone's touch. Strange! I had never experienced anything like this. I was no longer concerned that Lisa and Martin were sick, or that Chris and Shariifa had not yet returned. I felt God's supernatural peace. I knew for certain that Jesus had visited me, or had at least sent an angel. That was a great comfort, and my strength was replenished. I rose up and went to check on the children and my patients.

After a few days, they seemed to be getting better. Martin wanted me to read him a story, and Lisa began writing letters.

I felt like I was finally approaching the light at the end of a long, dark tunnel. The following day, Chris came home. By then, everything had returned to normal. He had no idea how turbulent the last few days had been for me. But he did notice that his wife was a little pale in the face and had lost some weight. I was merely happy to have my husband back. He decided he would cheer me up, however, and during the following days, he occasionally took the kids off my hands until I regained my strength.

CHAPTER 31

Chipped Teeth

Summer 2004

SUMMER VACATION ARRIVED! We loved Mukalla, the beautiful white city on the vast blue ocean. We loved the neighborhood, our friends, and our work in the project areas. And yet, when summer vacation time came around, we all got excited. It was our habit to drive to the cooler parts up north to escape the sweltering heat and intense humidity. Lately, there had been several blackout power outages in Mukalla. Usually we kept our air conditioning on at night to help combat the 95-percent humidity and lower the room temperature. Our bodies needed a good night's rest for the following day's work. Without our air conditioning, ceiling fans, and refrigerator, we had a hard time coping with the sultry weather. Occasionally we woke up in the middle of the night, fully drenched with sweat. The power had gone out, again! Whenever that happened, I would get up and turn off all the electrical appliances, so they wouldn't be damaged by a power surge once the utility company got the electricity back up and running. Our first air conditioning unit, as well as various electrical devises had been destroyed by these voltage swings.

We planned to spend this summer in the capital city. Chris had to take care of some administrative business there and didn't know how much time that would take. The kids and I were excited about spending time with some friends, who had invited us to stay with them during our vacation.

The first day was our travel day. We loaded the car to the brim and made our way through the desert. It was usually a 16-hour drive, but because of the many delays at the various checkpoints, we arrived in Sanaa late that night. We were all exhausted.

Martin begged his father: "May we go to the amusement park tomorrow? You promised you'd take us!"

Chris was worn out, but he agreed.

The climate here was different from where we lived, and I always got headaches when we were in Sanaa. The capital city had an elevation of about 7,000 feet. Hadhramaut was at sea level. The difference in altitude always took its toll on me. I told the boys and Chris to go to the park without me. I would stay behind with Tim and rest a bit.

The two boys were up very early the next morning. They stood at the side of our bed, ready to go.

"Can we go, Papa? I can't wait to drive a bumper car!" Martin said.

Right after breakfast, Chris and the boys were on their way.

My friend Mirjam and I took care of the most urgent chores around the house and got caught up on each other's news. Then I sat down to relax with a good book. I hadn't read in ages! Hours later, I looked at the clock and was surprised to see that it was already afternoon. I began to worry. Where were Chris and the boys? Had they lost track of time? Or had something happened to them?

Finally, I heard their voices. They were still outside, so I ran to meet them. When I saw David, I was startled. His lips were all swollen, and his face twisted with pain. He was smiling, but his mouth was a little lopsided.

He tried to explain with a mumble I could barely understand: "Bumper cars. Crash!" His lips were still bleeding.

"My mouth hit the steering wheel..."

Chris translated: "David had an accident while driving the bumper car. You can't tell right now because of the swelling, but his two front teeth are chipped, and the nerves are exposed. I'm sure he's in much pain. But David's a brave boy. You know that!"

I swallowed hard. "Oh, no!"

My son's handsome smile was ruined! It was only a while ago that the permanent teeth had come in.

I took my brave boy and hugged him. He whispered in my ear: "Mama, it hurts so bad!"

He had kept himself together in front of his father and brother, not wanting them to think he wasn't cool and brave. But he didn't have to pretend in front of his mother. We knew each other so well that we could pretty much read each other's mind. My heart ached for him. But I knew he was strong.

None of us enjoyed supper that evening. David couldn't chew at all.

I was concerned. What if his teeth turned black because of the damaged nerves? Where would we find a good dentist? How long could we wait without risking permanent damage? The next day was Friday, the Muslim equivalent to our Sunday. There wouldn't be any doctors on duty.

The night was restless for us all. We could hear David tossing and turning in bed, moaning in his sleep. He was obviously in pain and having nightmares. I sought refuge in prayer, as I often do when problems arise. I knew my God always had a solution, even if we were at the end of our rope.

We had a worship service at our friends' house the following day. Dr. Payo, a friend of the family, was attending. He told us: "Go visit Dr. L. in Dubai. He's an excellent dentist, and I know him well."

He exuded a deep sense of confidence and explained that there are good dental implants available these days.

"Don't worry. Everything will work out fine!"

The entire group prayed for David.

Dubai was far away, but our son was worth the trip. Chris was able to book an inexpensive flight for the following day. Somebody told us we could stay in a nice apartment in the Emirates free of charge. The people who lived there were in America for a visit. God is indeed awesome! The owners had five children, so their place had several children's rooms fully stocked with toys, books, and audio cassette tapes. It was in an apartment complex in the center of Dubai with a nice pool, which we often took advantage of. We had the swimming pool to ourselves most of the time. What a haven God had provided! When we arrived in Dubai, Dr. L. told us to bring David in that very first evening. It amazed us how much time Dr. L. took with his patient. After a lengthy and tedious procedure, the two upper front teeth were like new! Soon after that, there was no trace of the damage. Since our international health insurance didn't cover dental procedures of this kind, we would have to pay for it ourselves. We knew it would be very expensive. But Dr. L. was a Christian, and when he found out that we lived and worked in Yemen, he didn't charge us a penny. He told us to return after 10 days for a follow-up examination. So we spent the next few days discovering Dubai. It was a special vacation, and we enjoyed various excursions and shopping sprees. The kids needed new clothes and, of course, a few new toys. We could get anything here, things we could only dream of getting in Mukalla. And so the tooth catastrophe was a blessing in disguise! We were amazed how God turned things around and allowed us so many beautiful days together.

* * *

After we returned to Sanaa, we had one more tooth adventure. David was building paper boats with his friend. He used his teeth to tear off some Scotch tape, and part of his tooth stuck to it and broke off! He screamed out in pain and stomped his feet, mad at himself!

"Why did that have to happen to me again, Mama? And it's the same front tooth!"

I wasn't very good at consoling him. I had a hard time controlling my own tears. "Come on, David. Let's pray. Our heavenly Father knows that we can't go back to Dubai. Now he's just going to have to step in and repair your tooth without a dentist. He promised he would take care of us if we would only cast all our care on him!" Even though it sounded a bit crazy, we prayed, and soon we felt better.

A few days later, the broken piece of the tooth had grown back entirely. There was no sign that it had ever been broken! This miracle filled David's heart with joy. And ours, too.

CHAPTER 32

Layla and Afrah's Dream Wedding

NEW NEIGHBORS MOVED into the house two doors down from us. It was the detached house we had looked at when we first moved here, the one with the Quran verses written on the walls and all the rubble lying around. The day after they moved in, four children stood at our front door and asked if they could use our telephone. I let them in, and when they had come upstairs, the doorbell rang again. Two more children wanted to come in. After several journeys up and down the stairway, all nine of the new neighbor's children were in our apartment, and I was completely out of breath. It rang once more. This time it was their mother, Layla, and their sister. They curled up on my *mafrajj* and relaxed while the gang of little rascals ran around the house. Layla paid no attention to them. I tried to follow protocol and start up a conversation with the two women. I served them the obligatory tea and cookies, all the while trying to limit the damage the kids were doing to the house. Layla told me that her second-eldest daughter was taking care of her household so that she could recuperate from the delivery of her latest child. She had given birth to ten girls before finally having a boy. He was very frail and cried a lot. The baby was not gaining weight. She also told me that her eldest daughter was married and had children of her own.

I wanted to spend some time with our new neighbors, so I asked my sons to play with the children. They weren't excited about that! I could understand why. The neighbor's kids threw things and fought over the toys. One of Martin's favorite cars was broken in the process. He was devastated. David shoved the ill-mannered children out of the room and locked the door from the inside. That didn't stop these uninvited guests. They just took over the rest of the house and created chaos everywhere they went. All this commotion was stressing me, and I hoped the *muezzin* would call to prayer soon. When he finally did, Layla wasn't fazed a bit. She just remained lying on the *mafraj* and told me she wasn't a very religious person.

Layla was an attractive woman about my age. You couldn't tell by looking at her that she was the mother of so many children. Her oldest daughter had a three-month-old child—the same age as Layla's youngest. Sometimes she would call her children *shaitaan*,[41] but I told her not to use that name in my house. She was a very feisty lady who loved to visit her neighbors but hated taking care of her own home.

One day, Layla came by again and plopped down on our *mafraj*.

"I'm pregnant again! I don't want any more children! I'm tired, I have heartburn, and I'm vomiting a lot."

She also suffered from an iron deficiency. I was suffering from her bad mood!

Layla appealed to me as her friend: "You have to get your husband to check up on mine. He comes home late every night. I think he's seeing another woman. He's probably having an affair."

I just sighed and explained to her that my husband wasn't a private detective and that he wouldn't have the time, anyway.

I tried to calm her down. "You have to trust your husband."

Layla let out a loud curse. She was upset because we wouldn't dance to her tune.

---

41 devil or satan

It seems that Ahmed had noticed that his wife had been complaining on the phone about him to the neighbors. He cut off the telephone line on the spot or it might have been that he hadn't paid his telephone bill. In any event, Layla couldn't make calls from her home anymore. So she would come over to our house regularly and scream obscenities into our phone. While she was on the phone, I'd be busy letting her children in and out and making sure they didn't tear our place apart or shove a toy or two into their pockets.

I had to find a solution that wouldn't be impolite but would save my few remaining nerves.

I explained to Layla: "If you want to use the phone, you need your peace and quiet, so come alone. If you want to visit me, bring no more than three children with you."

That was a little impolite, but even the Arab neighbors wouldn't allow Layla's children into their homes anymore. Layla wasn't welcome.

One day, Layla suddenly disappeared. Her husband had sent her away. She was allowed to take only her two youngest children with her and would have to stay with her mother. There was much gossip about her in the neighborhood. I felt sorry for the children. Now they would be neglected even more. Occasionally, I invited them over for dinner or brought them something to eat. But I soon realized that this was a bottomless pit. Besides, there was rarely an opportunity to have a conversation with the children.

* * *

Layla's second daughter, Afrah, was a lovely 15-year-old girl with beautiful almond-shaped eyes. She was soon to be married, and Layla returned to help with the wedding preparations. Afrah's bridegroom was a very wealthy 56-year-old man from Saudi Arabia. He was willing to pay a high price for Afrah and offered to buy his teenage bride gold jewelry and glamorous clothing in every imaginable color. Perfume and makeup were also part of the deal. The financial benefits were supposed to make up for the fact that he was quite old and already had several children from his first wife. One of his sons was even older than Afrah.

She was to be his second wife and live with his children in their home, which she was to keep clean.

My friend Shariifa told me all about Arab weddings.

"A traditional Arab wedding goes on for several days and is like a dream from *The Arabian Nights*. The day before the wedding, the bride has to go through a painful procedure to remove all her body hair. The hair on her head is all that remains. Her entire body is covered in a sugar-lemon mixture, which makes her skin is soft and hairless, like a baby. Then her arms and legs are painted with *sabra*.[42] For this event, only women are allowed in the room. Music and dancing fill the room, while decorative designs are drawn on her skin. Afterward, henna powder is mixed with a little water and lemon. It has to have the proper consistency, not too fluid or too solid. Then a brush is used to apply this sludge-looking, reddish mixture to fill in the details of the drawings."

It was amazing to me that an artist could make such elaborate flower-tattoos on fingers, feet, and even toes with just henna and *sabra*-paste. All that trouble for only a few days of pleasure! But beautification wasn't the only reason for using henna. This plant also had traditional significance. People here believed that henna healed evil. The bride's hair was set in hair curlers which were later covered with a light green towel. The bride herself was also draped in light green until the henna powder dried, which could take several hours. The female guests at these proceedings celebrated the bride with dance and tambourines. When evening arrived, and the henna paint began flaking, they washed it all off with water. The result was a beautiful, black-red pattern.

On the following day—the day of the wedding—the bride was made ready and her hair styled. An enormous hairdo was created with dozens of hair curlers and spray. Then it was time for the cosmetics. To us Europeans, the bride's makeup would look as elaborate as a clown's. A dense layer of white was painted on the face, neck, and décolleté. In these areas, light skin is considered attractive. Kohl was used to darken her eyes, eyeliner and fake lashes to intensify them. Bright lipstick accentuated the sensuality of her mouth.

Then the bride put on her colorful wedding gown, covered with glitter and lace. Gold jewelry was placed on the dress to symbolize

---

42 black paint used to create temporary flower tattoos, lasts 10 days

the value of the bride. She had at least one ring on each finger, many bracelets around her wrists, and around her neck hung several necklaces—some with pendants, others without. She had earrings in all the piercings in both earlobes, and an elegant gold belt graced her slender waist.

Afrah looked like a princess—exotic and beautiful, delicate and frail. Like a model from a wedding magazine. But her eyes looked sad. You could tell she was fighting back the tears. After the ceremony, she would have to say good-bye to all her loved ones and leave with this bald, fat-bellied stranger to go to a foreign country. It made me cry to think about that. Layla, the mother of the bride, scolded me.

"You shouldn't cry at a wedding. That brings bad luck. You have to laugh and be happy at weddings. And Afrah is a lucky girl. This man is very rich!"

I was shocked and wondered whether this woman had any heart at all. It was almost as if she had just sold her child.

I asked Layla: "Who is going to help you around the house now and take care of your children? Won't you miss her?"

"Of course, I will. But her fourteen-year-old sister will have to step in and take over. We have to marry these girls off. For every one that leaves, there is one less mouth to feed! And it's better for them, too. It's the best thing that could happen to them."

During the next few years, Afrah would have one baby after the other and never see her family again, in spite of her husband's promise otherwise. She wasn't even allowed to go home for her deliveries, as is normal in these parts.

Shortly after Afrah's wedding, the entire family moved to the downtown section of Mukalla. The house two doors down was empty again and stayed that way for some time.

CHAPTER 33

Blessing or Curse?

TIM HAD TURNED 2, David was 9, and Martin 7. When David was younger, he had always been a relatively large child. Now he was quite small in comparison to other boys his age. I hadn't noticed it, but now I realized that he hadn't grown an inch since he had become ill two years ago. Was it by chance that I just now came across a medical data sheet in German from the same typhoid medicine David had taken back then?

Two years ago, we couldn't read the data sheet. It had been in Arabic. Now I read, to my dismay, that this medicine was not to be administered to children since it could stunt their growth! I was shocked.

"We didn't know. And if we had, what else could we have done? We had to give this medicine to our sick child for him to recover."

I was worried and felt guilty. But then I made a decision. I was reading a book by Derek Prince entitled *Blessing or Curse*. He wrote that words have power and that we can decide to be blessed. After all, what good would it do to blame myself or to worry about what happened back then? What happened, happened! And yet, I didn't have to give up and watch my child suffer from a mistake we made two years ago. There was a solution: prayer. I decided to pray that the "curse" caused by the side effects of this typhoid medicine would be broken. And I was going to pray that my son would grow again and reach a certain height by his birthday.

I went straight to my husband, who was in his office writing a report on the computer.

"Chris, we have to pray that God intervenes and helps our son grow again. Let's stand together in prayer that he'll regain the height he was robbed of."

Chris put his work aside. It was already late in the evening, and the children were sleeping peacefully. We went over to David's bed, and Chris laid his hands on his head. We began to storm heaven's gates with prayer. We asked our heavenly physician to break the curse the side effects of the medicine had caused and to help our child start growing again.

We went to bed that night full of confidence and worryfree. In the middle of the night, I woke up. Somebody had touched me softly on my shoulder and shaken me. I was still drowsy, but I recognized our eldest son.

"Mama, my arms and legs hurt really bad!" he said.

"Come lie down in our bed next to Papa and me. I'll give you a nice back rub, and then you'll feel better. Maybe these are growing pains!"

The following morning, I was baffled when I saw what had happened. David had actually grown almost a hand's width during the night!

Once again, we could only stand in awe at how clearly and quickly God had answered our prayer. Our wonderful God, who loves to take care of us, did this miracle. There would be no need for growth hormones or other medical treatments.

* * *

After living here for over five years, I was sometimes amazed how well I was feeling physically. About a year before we came to Yemen, a medical specialist had told me her devastating diagnosis, without batting an eye.

"The findings are clear. You have third-stage Lyme disease. The bacteria that cause this disease are everywhere in your entire body, not only in your bloodstream, but also in your nervous system, your cerebrospinal fluid, and your bones. In this stage, there is nothing you can do. The only treatment is long-term inpatient therapy, in which you would receive antibiotics intravenously. But the drugs are so strong that they will ruin your veins. You should stop nursing your baby immediately since breast milk transfers the medicine to your child and cause irreversible damage. Furthermore, we can't guarantee that the therapy would help. We are still experimenting with it. The chances of it succeeding in an advanced stage like yours are about fifteen percent. This much is certain: an oral therapy with antibiotics is effective only in the first and second stages of this disease. Unfortunately, we discovered your illness too late."

At first, I was shocked. I couldn't believe it! After consulting various doctors, I realized that traditional medicine would not be able to help me. Every time I went in for a consultation, I received only brutally honest and discouraging opinions thrown at me. It was all very depressing. And sobering. And frightening.

So I sat down and read everything I could find about this disease and its symptoms. Then my husband and I made a decision: we would not let this disease get the better of me.

To leave Germany, we had to obtain a health certificate. The doctor told Chris bluntly: "Your wife is very sick. How can you even think about taking her to a country in which medical care is so poor?"

The doctor ignored the fact that there wasn't an effective treatment for this bacterial tick-bite disease even in medically advanced Europe.

After several disappointments with various doctors, we had become disillusioned and skeptical. We had lost faith in the "all-knowing" medical science. But we hadn't lost faith in our all-powerful God! We decided to put all our trust in the best physician, Jesus, and not begin therapy. Shortly after that, I began to show some signs of improvement. A one-sided facial palsy I had been suffering from completely disappeared. It had distorted my face, but now I was able to smile again.

However, I continued to suffer from circulation problems and general weakness. One day, I cut my finger while opening a tin can. The wound was not very deep, but I could not stop the bleeding. Apparently, the Lyme disease had caused a blood clotting disorder. After two-and-a-half hours, I was still changing the bandage every few minutes.

My husband was very concerned for me, but then finally something miraculous happened and the bleeding stopped.

Two years later, after we had moved to Yemen, I was attending a conference, when Hamish, a colleague of ours from Scotland, came over to me and asked sheepishly: "Amiira, could I pray for you? I believe God wants to heal you completely. Please tell me about your medical conditions. I'll ask your husband to come and lay hands on the diseased areas while I pray. Would that be okay?"

At first, I was skeptical and didn't want to agree to it. Previously, I had hardly been able to take a step without passing out. I'd get terrible headaches, and my joints were extremely painful. Now I was fairly well and was content with the way things were.

But Hamish was persistent! He was convinced that he had a mandate from heaven he had to fulfill.

"I believe that God wants to restore your health entirely! Don't be content with just a little healing. God is capable of complete healing, and he wants you to have more than just a little."

That sounded convincing. And even though it was strange to me at first, I agreed to let him pray. I didn't actually believe anything would happen, but I didn't want to offend my friend and his sincere faith. So I decided to "give him a chance." Hamish prayed for my knees, my elbows, my ankles, my wrists, and my entire nervous system, while Chris laid his hands on those areas. The earth didn't shake; I wasn't slain in the Spirit; the man of God didn't scream—he just prayed to God in simple words. And yet afterward, I felt that "something had changed" and that surprised me!

I sensed a deep peace. At that time, this was a new experience for me, and it was very encouraging. I felt God's healing touch in my own body. This time of prayer had left me very weak, although I hadn't done anything. Two days later, I realized that something had changed: I didn't get tired as quickly, and even the constant little aches and pains were gone. I didn't even notice that at first since I had become so used to them. I was ecstatic and in awe!

Back then, I did not doubt God's ability and willingness to heal others. But for God to heal me was a new and wonderful experience. It was a miracle!

CHAPTER 34

Tragedy at the Beach

September 17, 2004

OUR NEW MIDWIFE, Helena, had arrived only a few days before from the language school in Taiz. Until her apartment in our neighborhood was ready, she was staying in our office. Her new house was the one in which Layla and her family had lived. We had been alone without a team for sixteen months. Now we were finally getting some co-workers in Mukalla. I admired Helena's courage. Life in this remote area and foreign culture wasn't easy for single women. In addition to Helena, our children's new tutor, Pia, had arrived two days ago.

We had only recently returned from our summer vacation in Sanaa. I wanted to spend some quality time with our newcomers so we could get to know each other. The boys wanted to stay home and play with their toys. Chris offered to stay at home and watch them. So I took the car and we drove to the beach.

There were no clouds in the beautiful azure sky. I looked down at the ocean and admired the sparkling reflection of the sun on the waves.

The beauty of the sea and the deserted shore once again took my breath away. I glanced over at my two companions and saw that they, too, were awestruck by the magnificent setting. The beauty of God's marvelous creation overwhelmed us all. I smiled. The ocean roared, and as we got out of the car, a light breeze blew through the black, floor-length *baltos,* which covered our colorful dresses. The wind cooled us off a bit. The air had a salty taste to it, and hungry seagulls circled above the ocean.

The hot, golden sand crunched under our flip-flops. I led my two new friends to a solitary, sheltered location—my favorite spot on this beach. A low wall separated us from the road. Usually there was very little traffic around here. The panorama view of the bay was awesome. It was about 650 feet wide and surrounded by coral reefs, which extended into the ocean from both sides of the spacious shore.

When we reached the beach, we spread out our picnic blanket, and peeled off our cloaks and veils. The ocean looked inviting. Only a few tiny waves rippled across the shore, and the surface of the water was smooth and calm. The heat from the noonday sun had subsided, and I was looking forward to a peaceful afternoon with our new team members. We just wanted to enjoy the ocean, take a swim or two, and get acquainted with each other.

I suggested, "Hey, let's take a dip! We'll have to leave our dresses on, though."

For Helena and Pia, it was a strange thought to swim fully clothed in their long, loose dresses. Tradition didn't allow women to show themselves in only a swimsuit in public. In this conservative region, it was even objectionable for a man to glance at a woman without her veil. There was no one around right now, but somebody could show up at any moment.

The sparkling ocean was bidding us to come in for a refreshing swim. A breath of wind gently caressed our skin as we entered the water up to our ankles. Our feet sank into the sand, and our wet dresses stuck to our legs.

Just then, other people arrived at the beach. Helena noticed them first. Six women, clothed entirely in black, got out of their truck, which their driver had parked directly behind the wall. About 20 children between the ages of 5 and 16 were with them. They approached the place where we had spread out our blanket, and I sighed when I realized that the three of us wouldn't be able to have a nice private visit, after all. I was disappointed.

"Well, we can forget swimming now. The Bedouins will probably sit down right next to our spot, although the entire beach is empty. We need to cover our heads since there's a man with them. It's indecent for a woman to wear her hair uncovered when others are around. If we were to swim, our dresses would stick to our bodies and reveal too much. We don't want to act indecently."

The elderly driver of the truck remained at a respectable distance, but the women and children kept coming closer. They were chatting away and laughing. As I suspected, they sat down right next to our picnic area and stared at us—the exotic, light-skinned European women. I tried to fight back my disappointment. We would have to share our afternoon with this group of Bedouins. I was the only one of our trio who knew the ways and the culture of these parts. The other two couldn't speak the Arabic dialect, either. So it was up to me to have small talk with our intruders. The Yemeni children sat quietly around us and looked at us curiously with their big, dark eyes. When they smiled, their teeth sparkled in bright contrast to their mocha-shaded faces. They probably thought we were Hollywood stars since they had only seen such pale creatures in the movies!

The Bedouin women were very hospitable and offered us cookies and sweetened *chai*[43] from their Thermos. Then they began their small-talk interrogation.

"How are you? How is your family? Do you have children? What's your name? Are you married? What did you cook today? Do you own any goats? What kind of soap do you use to make your skin so light?"

I chuckled under my breath while answering their questions. Pia and Helena had been involuntarily thrown into the Bedouin way of life, but they seemed to relish the generous hospitality shown to them. I drank some tea and began to enjoy my conversation with these local women. Then I noticed that Pia—our quiet high-school graduate, who had been in this country for only two days—was having a lively conversation with the women, although she didn't speak a word of Arabic!

---

43 tea

I was amazed! There was a gleam in her eyes, and I was sure she was going to like living here in Yemen!

The boys and girls ran barefoot across the golden beach, dressed in their best clothes. They scrambled back and forth, laughing and splashing water on each other. Then they boldly jumped into the water, still fully clothed. The boys competed in a speed-wading contest to one of the dark, towering cliffs on the side of the beach. The water was shallow and barely covered their knees. Like most Yemenis, they couldn't swim and had a healthy respect for the infinite ocean. Soon they had reached the cliff and skillfully climbed the sharp-edged rocks. The children laughed and screamed as the spray from the gentle waves got them all wet. Suddenly, a jet of water gushed onto the rocks.

A young Bedouin wearing a knee-long, checkered *futa* appeared in the parking area and frantically waved his arms at us. I watched him quickly approaching us and saw that the truck driver was also quite agitated.

"Move your car!" the young man yelled as soon as he was close enough for us to hear him.

Helena glanced over at me. "The car is in his way. I'll go and find another place to park it!" She jumped up to follow the young man's order. I stayed behind on the beach with Pia. Helena put her shoes on, took the keys from my purse, and trudged through the sand to the car. We watched her disappear behind the wall that separated the beach from the parking area.

When I looked back at the ocean, I was shocked, and my heart skipped a beat. What happened next took my breath away. The rest of the children had joined the boys on the cliff. They were all waving and screaming.

"Something's wrong! Something's happened!"

Intuitively, I sensed that a catastrophe was imminent. Far out in the deeper parts of the ocean, I saw a dark head bobbing up and down. Or was it more than one?

All the Bedouin women began howling a bloodcurdling dirge. I recognized that sound. The Arab women were all screaming the "lament for the dead." Our peaceful outing had turned into chaos. The women ran down toward the beach to the shrieking children, who were looking out into the ocean.

I shouted to Pia: "We have to do something. Most Yemenis can't swim, and it looks like somebody is drowning out there!"

With the crescendo of the women's lament, dark clouds appeared above the horizon. It was as if the dreadful clamor had cleared the path for evil spirits to close in on the ocean—gloomy, powerful, terrifying spirits. The dark facade stretched across the entire horizon and rose higher and higher. The clouds were coming closer by the minute. My blood ran cold, and I was terrified. The women's screaming grew louder and louder and sounded like the howling of a pack of wolves.

I felt like it was freezing outside, and a tingle went up and down my spine. The atmosphere was spooky and horrifying.

I started to pray softly. "Jesus!"

That was all I could say at that moment. I knew one thing for sure, though: I had to save that drowning child! Without a thought of the consequences that might follow, I ran down to the shoreline. The water seemed calm enough, so I jumped in, headscarf and all. Out of the corner of my eye, I saw Pia to my left jump in as well. She quickly passed me and swam over to a spot just below the cliff, where the frightened children were still standing and screaming. A tremendous, invisible pull from below drew me abruptly downward in a powerful whirlpool. It caught me by surprise. I swallowed large mouthfuls of salt water and had to cough, all the while trying to grab onto something to keep from drowning. What was happening? The surface of the water was deceptively still, but then I was pulled down under again. Was I experiencing the infamous and dangerous riptide that usually occurs during monsoon season? The locals had warned us about them time and time again.

We had just shrugged our shoulders, never expecting to need those warnings. Suddenly, I felt something hit my temple. Apparently, the current had hurled me into the coral reef. Then I felt nothing. It was dark all around me. My limbs were heavy, and my lungs were on fire. It seemed to last forever, but it was actually only a fraction of a second. I opened my eyes. My head was pounding as I broke through the surface of the water. I choked and tried desperately to catch my breath. At first, I couldn't tell how far I had drifted. I couldn't hear or see a thing. I could only feel the sand and the water surrounding me. My head was barely above water. Slowly but surely the pressure lessened, and the water became shallower. Carefully, I tried to stand up without losing balance. The current had become weaker, and I swayed back and forth.

I was relieved to see Pia on my left. She was swimming in an area where apparently the current wasn't quite as strong. With great effort, I managed to get back to shore, and then desperately yelled:

"Pia, come back! Please come back! It's too dangerous. Turn around! Don't swim out so far!"

But Pia couldn't hear me. She kept swimming calmly and steadily farther into the ocean. I screamed louder and tried to get Pia to come back. I prayed fervently that nothing bad would happen to this young girl. A crippling fear for her overwhelmed me. I felt responsible for the safety of our two new co-workers.

The Bedouin women were desperate, and their piercing "dirge of death" seemed to be reaching its climax. To this day, I cannot remember how I got back safely to the shore. I was groggy and lightheaded and just let my body flop onto the sandy ground, where I threw up. I felt exhausted and empty, like a balloon that had been popped. Helena returned from moving the car and made a beeline for the beach. She immediately noticed that something was wrong.

"Don't go into the water! It's too dangerous!" I shouted.

Meanwhile, Pia had returned as well. She collapsed at the edge of the water, dizzy, her drenched clothing clinging to her, and the waves rippling through her toes. Her dress was torn, and strands of hair plastered her face. She stared at the ocean and seemed oblivious to everything around her. As if in a trance she let sand sift through her fingers.

I finally regained control of my limbs, retrieved the car keys, and headed for the parking area. I grabbed one of the older Bedouin girls by the hand. She was screaming frantically, but I told her:

"Come with me. We have to get the fishermen to help us. There's nothing we can do here on the beach."

The girl just froze and cried even louder: "My brother, my cousin, my niece! They're all going to drown!"

"God is going to help them! He is here! They can't fall deeper than into God's hand!" I tried my best to calm the desperate girl.

I believed with all my heart that God would intervene in this situation.

"But first, we have to get help. Come on now!"

Wafa—I found out later that was her name—finally unstiffened and stumbled along beside me to the car, which was parked at quite a distance. She was still crying and screaming uncontrollably. As fast as the car would take us, we drove over the sandy slope to Halla, the nearest fishing village. The fishermen were dozing in the shade of their beached boats, relaxing and chewing their *khat.*

I yelled at them: *"Yella, bi suraa!*[44] Children are drowning!"

But the men seemed dazed by the sight of a foreign woman seated behind the wheel of a car, screaming and gesticulating at them, her clothes fully drenched and tattered, and her hair uncovered. They didn't move. Were they dreaming? Or had they already consumed too much *khat?* Maybe they thought they were hallucinating.

Suddenly, I became aware that I had lost my scarf in the ocean. These simple Arabs had probably never seen an unveiled foreign woman with her hair uncovered before, unless perhaps on television. I was certainly an unusual sight for their eyes, maybe even indecent!

I was ashamed and frustrated and angry, as well. I turned the car around without confronting the fishermen. Wafa cried and screamed incessantly. Her wailing sent a shiver down my spine, and I knew only one way to counteract it: pray loud in Jesus' name! I sped the SUV along the rocky, bumpy dunes toward the beach. I was determined to get back as quickly as I could and didn't care about the car possibly blowing a tire or breaking down altogether.

When we got back to the scene of the disaster, a few motorboats were speeding toward the beach. Apparently, the men in the fishing village had realized that something was wrong. Many curious onlookers had stopped their cars and were standing around, doing nothing. Just then I noticed that I had lost my shoes. My bruised and bleeding feet were full of thorns. But at that moment, I couldn't feel the pain. I was horrified to see the corpse of a child lying on the shore. Helena had retrieved the young boy, but too late! Apparently, there were other children still in the water. I saw a head bobbing up and down and swam out to rescue the child. It was a pretty young girl with long black hair. I dragged the pale-faced child from the ocean. She coughed and spat up water.

"Hurry! She's alive, but we need to get her to a hospital!"

---

44 Hurry! Move it!

I tried to pick the girl up and carry her to the car, but she was soaked and too heavy for me.

I screamed at the people standing around. "Please help!"

I looked around. Pia was a few feet away, but she was unresponsive. I couldn't expect any help from her.

I shouted to her: "Pia, I can't take care of you right now. Just rest a little. I've got to get this girl to the hospital. I'll be right back!" Then I headed for the car.

An elderly woman stood in my way, screaming hysterically. I spoke to her in a soft voice and asked her to help. But she was frightened and apparently in shock. She just looked right past me and continued screaming. It was only a few days later that I found out her name was Umm Mustafa. The men standing around just shook their heads and looked at me with a blank expression on their faces. Although I had lived among these people for almost five years now, I still had a lot to learn. Didn't I know that a man should never touch a girl he isn't acquainted with? I was aware that as a woman, I was not supposed to take a stranger to the hospital all by myself. I had to be accompanied by a male relative.'

Our car was boxed in by other vehicles, so there was no way I could take it. I didn't want to get stuck in the deep *wadi* while trying to maneuver it out of the parking area.

With my last ounce of strength, I placed the girl on a white pickup truck parked in the front and went to look for its owner. Which of these gawking bystanders had the keys?

Abu Mustafa, the man who had driven the original group of Bedouins to the beach, seemed to wake up from his stupor. When he realized that his granddaughter was fighting for her life, he went over to the owner of the pickup and asked him to take the girl to the hospital, since his car was also blocked by other cars. Their owners had just stopped and left the vehicles this way and that all across the parking area.

I was completely exhausted and trembling all over when I returned to the scene of the accident. The traumatized Bedouin women had stopped screaming, but they were still reeling from the shock of what had happened. Meanwhile, two other corpses lay on the shore—both boys, one about 7 and the other about 8 years old.

It was a tragic scene, as those remaining of the Bedouin group began to return to their vehicles. They were still very upset, but Islamic law dictated that they be home in time for dusk prayer.

They all slowly climbed into their SUVs, their minds still baffled by what had happened. A bewildered young boy named Hamza stood next to the truck and just stared out into the ocean. He wanted to wait for his twin brother, who had been swallowed up by the tide. *They couldn't just leave him here! He could not imagine that life just went on without his identical brother: They had always done everything together.*

My heart broke when I saw him staring at the water in agony. These children were about the same age as my boys!

I gently stroked Hamza's hair and put my arm around his shoulders. He looked up, surprised. He hadn't been touched like that since he was 3. In this culture, only small children receive affection. Although he knew that it was *haraam*[45] for strangers to touch each other, a slight smile appeared on his face. He understood! A curious, indescribable bond had formed between me, a light-skinned mama, and the traumatized Bedouin boy. We nodded at each other, and then he slowly got into the overfilled vehicle and rode off with the rest of his relatives.

Now it was mysteriously quiet. Dead quiet. The screaming women and the haggard children had left. A couple of fishing boats were still looking for children in the water. Pia, Helena, and I were stunned and sorrow-stricken. Four children lost! Just a short while ago, they were sitting here next to us. Now they were gone! We were too distraught even to move. We needed a few minutes to process what had just happened. The sun had set, and it would be getting dark soon. So we suppressed our grief just long enough to pack up our things and leave.

Just as we were heading for the car, we saw fishermen coming ashore. They had found another victim. The young girl was about 14 years old and had beautiful porcelain-colored skin. With her long black hair, she lay there peacefully, as if she were asleep. A car stopped, and the driver helped us load the lifeless body into the vehicle to take to the hospital where a death certificate would be issued.

We couldn't stay a minute longer in this horrible place! We hurried to the car and drove off. Helena seemed calm and collected. Pia remained silent, except for an occasional murmur:

---

45 forbidden

"I'm so sorry. I ripped your dress!"

She was obviously in a state of shock.

I asked Helena how she was doing.

That was when she broke down and wept. Tears filled my eyes, as well, and I felt faint, so I pulled over on the side of the road. We all sobbed. The tears just wouldn't stop flowing, but nobody spoke a word. There were no words to be spoken.

We couldn't understand why we had been at this place at precisely the moment such a tragedy had happened. We felt like extras in a dreadful movie that just wouldn't end.

* * *

It was quite late and fully dark outside when we finally arrived at home. Tim was chattering away, totally oblivious to the tension in the air. Chris, David, and Martin, however, noticed right away that something was not wrong.

"What's wrong? Why are you so quiet? Why aren't you saying anything?"

During supper, my new friends and I just poked at our food. We had lost our appetite. Afterward, we went up to the roof and just sat there in silence. It was good to have each other. I was thankful I was not alone. This tragic incident had bonded the three of us together, and there was no need for us to say anything. We had been changed in an instant. Everything was different now and would probably never be quite the same again. And yet, life must go on. After a while, Chris joined us on the roof and cautiously asked what had happened. Our report of the events came slowly and in fragments. It was difficult to talk about. Chris only vaguely grasped what had happened that afternoon at the beach. He was shocked and didn't say a word.

The following day, Chris was on his way to the project area, when he drove past the place where the catastrophe had occurred. The coast guards were out searching for the rest of the missing children. Our red SUV was well-known around here, and people had recognized it parked at the beach the day before. Everyone was talking about the three courageous European women, who had tried to save the children from drowning. The newspaper listed the names and ages of the children who had died. Helena, Pia, and I didn't feel like heroes, but rather like failures, especially when we read that a total of eight children from two different families had drowned. It was terrible!

We were struck by guilt and remorse. We just couldn't understand why we had survived, but eight children between the ages of 6 and 16 had lost their lives in the ocean.

The news also mentioned two local men who had died at the same time in a tsunami. They had been swimming in the ocean a couple of miles closer to Mukalla.

Pia was not doing well. She would only rarely speak. Later, she told us that she had reached one of the drowning girls and grabbed her hand. But the girl held her so tightly that both of them were about to drown. Suddenly, the current got stronger, and Pia had to make a difficult decision. She knew what she had to do since she had attended a lifesaving class in Germany. She had to let the girl go. She knew she could not save the girl's life and her own, too.

During the next few days, Pia needed a lot of encouragement.

I felt responsible for our two newcomers, and I was sorry that their start here was such a horrible experience. Only later did I realize how much I myself had been affected by this tragedy. I was having problems sleeping. As soon as I closed my eyes, the whole scenario replayed itself over and over in my mind. And when in the wee hours of the night I finally did fall asleep, I had nightmares. I envisioned the drowning children, but imagined my sons' faces instead!

This crisis situation was a challenge for my family. The children had never seen their mama so sad and discouraged. I fell into a deep emotional abyss and couldn't eat or sleep. I was tormented by unanswerable questions:

"Why did these children have to die? Why weren't we able to help them? Why did we survive? Why were we even there that day? Why didn't God intervene? He could have helped."

For the first time in my life, I doubted God. I didn't doubt that he existed, but I was beginning to question my longstanding faith in his goodness.

The tragic death of these Bedouin children changed me. My life was turned upside down. After everything we had been through, I wondered how I would manage to survive this agonizing experience. It was just too much for me!

How could I keep my heart from breaking over and over again? I often thought about the pretty girl I had carried to the car. Had she survived? I asked myself that question many times. And if she had survived, had she perhaps suffered brain damage due to a lack of oxygen? Every time I remembered the desperate look on the children's faces, I started to weep. Their ages were so close to my own boys. And yet, I didn't want to become hardened because of the misery and suffering I was experiencing. I was determined to continue caring, yet I had to steel myself up in the process. That proved to be quite a challenge!

When I was alone with Chris, I asked him: "Please tell me if you notice me getting cold-hearted or uncaring. I need to protect myself, so I can cope with it all and not go under. Chris, please tell me why nobody asks how I am doing?"

Chris looked me in the eyes and said, full of appreciation: "You are a strong woman. You're known for your courage and calm manner."

"I don't want to become hard inside. I don't want to become heartless. I want to keep my heart tender, but I'm afraid I might crack under the memories of all that happened. Please tell me if you notice that I'm being cold and indifferent towards others."

I tried to keep myself busy with work. That distracted me and helped me momentarily to push aside my feelings of despair.

But when nighttime arrived and I had nothing to divert my attention, the visions and nightmares of the tragic event reappeared. Every time I closed my eyes, I saw the traumatic accident unfolding. I tossed and turned all night, reliving those terrible hours on the beach over and over again. I remembered the awful frustration, the agonizing helplessness, and the painful desperation I felt. I saw the horror-filled eyes of the children and heard the bloodcurdling screams of the Bedouin women. I tried in vain to forget it all and put the images out of my mind. But suppressing my feelings didn't turn out to be a good strategy for me.

When my restlessness became unbearable, I got out of bed, so I wouldn't wake my husband. Trying desperately to keep my mind on other things, I would read a book or listen to a worship CD. Sometimes I would go up on the roof. The clear and starry sky stretched over our house like a black, silk blanket speckled with hundreds of dots of golden lights. I would pace back and forth and argue with my Father in heaven until I was so tired I would finally go back to bed. I tried to relax and make myself lie still. My body needed that. I didn't dare look at the alarm clock! That would just remind me that I wasn't asleep and upset me even more.

Emotional reactions to suffering and calamity are hard to predict. Each person reacts differently. Outwardly, I remained relatively calm and detached. But I knew that my emotional dam would break sometime soon, probably without warning. The trigger could be something trivial. I knew that from my training in counseling. I also knew myself well and could tell how things were affecting me. And yet, I didn't know how to escape this minefield of explosive feelings.

I knew I couldn't expect other people to understand. That's why I withdrew more and more and shut myself off from others. In the end, I would have to go through this dark valley alone, as I usually did. I was aware that a crisis could either make or break a person. I decided I wasn't going to let this break me. I was going to hold on tight to my heavenly Papa! At times, all I could do was stammer a psalm or two and ask God for help.

Eleven days had passed. Since the day after the tragedy, Pia, Helena, and I had planned to visit the families that had lost children. We wanted to express our sorrow that we weren't able to save them. But we still hadn't managed to go. Now that we had regained a little strength, we mustered up all our courage and went to visit them. We got their address from the newspaper. The Ataas family and their neighbors, the Baad Bayaans, lived in a part of the city near Fuwah. Sitting behind the wheel, I was all uptight and feeling sick to my stomach. What would the families think? Of course, we had tried to save their children, but we had failed! Lying awake in bed at night, I had thought a lot about what I would say. I even memorized an Arabic elegy and taught it to my two colleagues.

I parked next to their house, and we slowly got out of the car. We were all very nervous.

Helena said: "You go first, Amiira. You've lived here for five years and know what to do and say." I wasn't so sure about that!

The door opened, and suddenly we were encircled by a throng of women and children. They stared at us in silence. The words I had memorized got stuck in my throat. Tears of compassion rolled down my cheeks. And before we realized what was happening, the three of us were all hugging and embracing the Bedouin women. They led us into the women's living area, and we sat down and just wept with them. It was an unusual feeling. We were of one heart and one soul with these women, although we had only known of them since that day at the beach. The shared trauma had created a strong bond between us.

Officially, the time of bereavement was now over. After 10 days of weeping, the mourners were to say *Alhamdulillah,* and were not allowed to question the sovereignty of Allah by continuing to shed tears of sorrow.

After a while, the master of the house, Abu Mustafa, entered the room carrying a freshly washed and ironed veil with silver stitching on it. Ceremoniously, he handed it to me, and I recognized it as the one I had lost in the ocean while trying to save his children. Mustafa was the elderly driver of the van, whom we had met that day at the beach. He was extremely grateful for our "help."

"You are now part of my family!"

We were quite moved and speechless. That had never happened before. A man had entered the women's living area and spoken directly to me, a woman. He had even touched my hand. That was certainly not considered acceptable in Islamic society. But since he had "adopted" us into his family, the rigid rules regulating the interaction between men and women no longer applied. Abu Mustafa felt obliged to apologize that his wife, his daughter, and his daughter-in-law were still weeping. He was embarrassed about it, but we could tell that he was having a hard time holding back his own feelings. I was moved by the respect and hospitality this family showed us. But now I felt an urge to tell the master of the house what he needed to hear:

"God gave women tears to channel their feelings. When they weep, their souls are cleansed. If they are not allowed to weep, they become ill."

Surprisingly, Abu Mustafa welcomed my words—the words of a foreigner. He even made concessions and allowed the women to weep, as long as the neighbors weren't watching. But that was a luxury he could not afford himself. Some time later he became depressed and experienced serious heart problems.

As we were leaving, the Bedouins asked us to visit them again soon. As we were driving away, the entire neighborhood gathered around and waved good-bye. Some of them ran alongside our car. It almost felt like we were in a parade!

Our healing process began that day. We became close friends with these Bedouins. We visited one another regularly and enjoyed our fellowship together. My two colleagues were especially touched by their "adoption" into the Bedouin family. We were overwhelmed by the love, gratitude, and respect the entire family showed us.

But still I couldn't sleep at night. So I began to compose a psalm:

Lord, where were you?

Why did you allow this to happen?

Why did we happen to be there on the day of the tragedy?

You see me and know me. Even if nobody understands me, you do. I can't even understand myself anymore. I am confused. I feel lonely and miserable. People try to explain things to me, to analyze me, to offer me solutions. They say everything will be all right. But nothing is all right, and nothing will ever be the same.

I can't cry anymore. I'm out of tears, and yet deep down within my soul, I weep day and night.

Nobody understands me. My children ask: "Why are you sad? We're still alive!"

My husband asks: "Why are you still mourning? You're a nurse and know that death often comes unexpectedly. Besides, you didn't even know these children."

Maybe you have chosen me to share in your grief for these lost children. Could it be that you are looking for somebody who will just sit there and silently grieve with you? Who will simply listen to your voice and not try to explain or analyze it all away? Could it be that you long for a deep, solid friendship?

I am honored! But I cannot yet fully grasp it. Words do no justice to my feelings. Have you chosen me to share in your deepest feelings? Wow! I am beginning to understand. You have chosen me to be your friend, to relate to you in a unique way at this very hour. That is exhilarating and, in an odd way, brings me comfort.

You call to the lost: "Please, please, turn around! Be careful! Your destruction is a vacuum that will suck you in and ruin you!" But in spite of your warnings and your calling and wooing, they are all headed for destruction. It hurts so badly to watch them get swallowed up!

How often have I been indifferent or distracted by less important things? I allow opportunities to pass by without sharing your good news. And these children are among those who will never hear about you.

* * *

During our first visit to the Bedouin family's home, I noticed a beautiful young girl with captivating almond-shaped eyes. She stared incessantly at me, and I stared back. It was as if I had been hypnotized by this charming girl. She had golden-brown skin, which was lighter than that of the other girls. Her high cheekbones accentuated her pretty face, and gorgeous black pigtails peeped out from under her headscarf.

I asked her: *"Aysch ismik?"*[46]

The girl, who was probably 12 or 13 years old, smiled shyly but didn't say a word. Somehow, I felt a connection to this oriental beauty, and so I tried again to find out her name. I just couldn't escape her charm. After a while, her mother realized I had been talking to her daughter, but not receiving an answer in return.

She said: "Her name is Jawaahir. That means 'gemstones.' You saved her life that day at the beach and carried her to the car."

At first, I was speechless. I had assumed the girl had not survived the accident. And now she was sitting directly across from me, staring into my eyes. She was traumatized and needed help, but she was alive! I was so happy and grateful! And yet I still felt responsible for what had happened to her.

During the next few months, Jawaahir and I got to know each other better. But it was only quite a while later that she finally opened up.

"My soul drowned in the ocean that day. That's why I can't go to school anymore."

Her mother, Jamiila, wasn't too concerned about that.

---

46 What is your name?

"That's just the way it is. She was the best in her class and really enjoyed going to school. She had big plans for her life. But since her brother died, she's become a different person. Education is not all that important to us. Jawaahir helps me out around the house and takes care of her brothers and sisters. She's going to make a good wife and mother. She doesn't need school for that. And since she has such light skin, we're going to get a good price for her as a bride."

I swallowed hard and kept my mouth shut. I knew I shouldn't respond right now. It was difficult for me at times to understand and accept the way Arabs thought about things like this. I had grown very fond of Jawaahir and prayed for her often. Slowly but surely, a friendship formed between us. I remember how happy I was when she smiled for the first time. And later on, I told her about the hope and the future God had in store for her.

CHAPTER 35

Scars

MY FRIEND JOY worked for a company in Saudi Arabia. She had a flight voucher that had to be used by the end of the year. The cab that took her to the airport was involved in a severe accident on the way. Her friend traveling with her was killed.

It took a while for Joy to get over the trauma of that tragedy, but now she was doing better. She wanted to get away from her strenuous job for a few days and spend some time relaxing and shopping in Dubai with a good friend.

Joy and I were very close. We had been friends since our school days. She had helped me with Tim's birth. After the tragic incident at the beach, she called me several times to see if I was all right. Her compassion and levelheadedness helped me deal with the anguish of that awful experience.

Joy was determined to get me to join her in Dubai for a shopping spree. At first, I couldn't imagine leaving my family alone and going on an outing like that. But Chris encouraged me to go. "It might be good for you to get away from the daily routine for a while."

So I finally agreed.

When we arrived in Dubai, we checked into a nice hotel in Sharja. There were many restaurants and shopping malls within walking distance. I had met some people here on an earlier visit, and they invited Joy and me to an Indian church service.

The Indian brothers and sisters greeted us with open arms and incredible love. That was a welcome we wouldn't easily forget. Sashi, one of my friends there, introduced us to the other believers, and they were amazed when they heard that we worked in Yemen.

I was especially impressed by Pastor Keith. He spoke that day on the subject of pain. As I listened, I couldn't stop staring at him. He was speaking out of personal experience. A supernatural peace surrounded him. Dark-red scars on his hands and arms were visible, even though he wore a long-sleeved shirt. His right cheek was also disfigured. When I first saw these bulging marks, which appeared to be burns, I felt sick at my stomach. But when I listened to him speak, my attitude toward him changed completely. I realized that this man was wearing these terrible scars with dignity. Suddenly, he didn't look unsightly anymore. These burns made him unique and very special. Now he even looked beautiful to me.

A still small voice whispered to me from within.

"This man has gone through hard times. His scars will be visible for the rest of his life. He can't hide them. They are a reminder of the devastating things he has had to endure. But he survived, and the scars are a sign of how precious he is because of the experience. My child, you have gone through hard times, too, and the inner scars remain as a sign of those difficulties you have endured. They are a part of who you are now. At first glance, they are repulsive. But they actually make you beautiful and very special. You can't remove the stigma of the scars, and you can't explain them away. Scars are inevitable after an injury. Sometimes they can be covered up and made less intimidating. But you don't need to cover these up, and with time, your wounds will become less painful."

This revelation moved me deeply, and I sensed that my emotional wounds would soon begin to heal.

Joy and I cherished our time together. I missed my family dearly during these five days away. But I savored the conversations I had with my good friend.

CHAPTER 36

The Sheik's Daughter

MY CO-WORKER, HELENA, and I were being bounced around in our car. We were on our way to the project areas, and our chauffeur, Rashid, was driving us to one of the villages. We were excited! We had medical and bandaging supplies in the car, even though I knew God had called me to "pray for healing and leave the rest up to me!" But I took my medical supplies, anyway. Just in case.

Chris had stayed behind with the kids. He wanted to take care of some office work and give me a day off. The kids always managed to preoccupy me when I tried to get any work done. I assumed it wouldn't be any different for Chris. He probably wouldn't get any work done, either.

My husband loved visiting the villages and talking to his Bedouin friends, always coming home so fulfilled and excited. He enjoyed listening to their stories and telling some of his own. He was usually very calm and laid-back, but when he got started with his friends, there was no stopping him. His friendly and receptive manner caused the locals to drop their reservations about us foreigners, and many friendships grew from that.

The women in these villages were very shy at first. They watched us suspiciously from a distance. We were the exotic light-skinned foreigners. It was seldom they got to see somebody who wasn't as chocolaty-brown as themselves, and they stared at us curiously. Centuries ago, their ancestors had been brought here as slaves from Africa. Now they lived as the poorest among the poor and were despised by the rest of society. Yet they accepted their circumstances and were somehow able to make ends meet in this desolate wasteland.

The women had to fetch water from a river several times a day, transporting it in clay jars on their heads. In the blistering heat, they walked a few miles each time, and never complained. Life for the women here was difficult and strenuous. It grieved me to find out that most of them had lost at least one child. The child mortality rate in this region was very high.

Rashid drove us safely along the desert roads from village to village. He drove without saying a word, all the while secretly watching us in his rearview mirror. Helena and I sat in the back chattering and noticed him glancing at us. We were careful not to make eye contact with him because that would have been absolutely *haraam.*[47]

In the early part of the afternoon, we arrived in the last village, which was probably the dustiest of all of them. Sherj consisted of a few clay structures with tin roofs and a couple of dirt alleyways covered with debris and goat dung. In the center of the village, an impressive white mosque with a green minaret rose high above the other drab sand-colored buildings. But it also was beginning to show wear and tear. The façade of the mosque seemed to be adapting to its surroundings and fading to a light sandy color. In the streets children played with tree branches or discarded car tires. They were barefoot and half-naked, their bodies covered by only a few tattered rags.

Many of them had matted reddish-brown hair, hunger-bloated bellies, and skinny arms and legs. They proudly showed us a car they had built from old tin cans. I was constantly amazed at how creative and content these children seemed to be.

---

47 forbidden

Soon we were surrounded by the village women, who were usually very timid and cautious. They were waving their arms wildly and pleading with us to help them.

"*Daktoora*,[48] come quickly. Safia, the sheik's daughter, is sick!"

The crowd of women accompanied us to the sick girl. They all tried to cram into the dark, windowless room where the pale little girl was lying on the floor on a thin mattress. Safia was unresponsive and had closed her eyes. She was wasting away and had lost a lot of weight. I hardly recognized the beautiful teenager I knew. She was usually very cheerful and full of life. Now she looked like she was on the brink of death. The smell of incense filled the stuffy room, and I held my breath. Several women sat around the sickbed and recited verses from the Quran. Others just nervously talked back and forth with one another.

"Please, help her!" Safia's mother pleaded.

The mother began to tell Safia's heartbreaking story. The teenage girl had undergone several operations during the last two weeks. She sighed, "We didn't have the money, but when Safia wouldn't stop throwing up and her skin turned yellow, we took her to the hospital in Ibn Sina. They operated on her there, but after that, she just got worse. She was very weak. So the doctors operated again. We ran out of money and had to pay for the second operation with our last goat. Now there is no more hope for her."

Tears flowed down the mother's haggard cheeks as she spoke. She was broken-hearted.

"Can't you do anything to help my child? Please!" she pleaded.

Then she looked down at Safia and realized that she was asking for something impossible. Overcome with hopelessness, she fell silent. She had already lost eight children—three of them in the womb, the other five before they turned a year old. Safia was her eldest daughter. She had always been a big help with the household chores, especially during her mother's pregnancies. These had taken their toll on the mother, and weakened her. She and Safia had been a good team, and the teenager had stepped up to the task, despite the hard work, sparse food, and the helplessness they felt.

---

48 a title of esteem for female medical persons

Helena and I looked at each other apprehensively as the mother told us what had happened to Safia. We spoke English so that those around us wouldn't understand. These dark-skinned women were all illiterate and couldn't speak any foreign language. Still, we had to be careful, because they could read our gestures and facial expressions better than anyone I knew from my homeland.

It sounded to me like Safia had developed hepatitis. In that case, an operation wouldn't have helped her at all. Had the hospital team not discovered the infectious disease? Is that the reason they performed the operation? Or had the doctor deliberately made an erroneous diagnosis? Perhaps they planned to remove some of her organs and sell them on the black market. Unfortunately, reports of such criminal practices were quite frequent in this corrupt, destitute country.

"There's nothing we can do about it," Helena whispered. Even though we spoke English, she was being very cautious.

The unnecessary operation had left the girl extremely weak and emaciated. She was suffering greatly.

Yet she refused our help. She didn't want any foreigners, even "medicine women," to touch her. She especially didn't want anyone to inspect her wounds, which were covered with soiled bandages. Safia just wanted to be left alone to die. She had refused to eat food for several days now. It didn't look good at all. Helena frowned and said: "There's nothing we can do here. Let's leave right away." We felt powerless.

If the girl were to die after we treated her, we could easily lose our good reputation or even be accused of murder! But I shook my head in defiance. I wasn't about to give up, not after the miracles I had experienced in recent weeks. One thing I knew for sure: My assignment was to pray.

I told the mother the truth in a very undiplomatic and direct manner. Arabs consider such bluntness to be rude.

"I'm sorry to say that we can't help your sick daughter. Nobody could help in this situation. But I know somebody who loves your daughter. Would you like for me to pray for your child?" My boldness actually surprised me. Here in this part of the world, people normally wouldn't speak so bluntly. They would prefer to tell a lie than to be the messenger of bad news. Lying is legal in Islam, especially if you are trying to go easy on somebody.

The room reeked of death and disease. It was packed with family and friends, all concerned and full of empathy. It was unusually quiet. Nobody dared to speak.

A light breeze occasionally crept in through the open door. All the women looked at us with expectation. Without anyone else noticing, Helena slightly shook her head. The child's mother didn't wait another second. She looked straight at me and pleaded:

"Yes! Please pray, *Daktoora!* Just do it, please!" To be honest, I didn't expect the 15-year-old girl to live much longer. I felt my courage fading.

Yet I was determined to fulfill my assignment! After all, I had experienced the power of God in situations like this time after time.

I closed my eyes and prayed quietly. I prayed that God would clearly intervene and touch the girl. I prayed that the family would experience his supernatural peace.

At first, I was a bit reluctant to pray for the girl's healing. I realized that I didn't really believe that Safia's condition could improve. In my heart, I confessed my doubts to my heavenly Father: "If she doesn't get well, the whole village could lose their trust in us—trust that took a long time to gain. Only you can intervene here. I don't know what you'll do or how you'll do it, but I leave it entirely in your hands."

Before we left, we were offered a sweet beverage, which we thankfully accepted and drank. Refusing would have insulted our host. We stepped out into the inner court and could finally breathe again. The courtyard was a roofless area surrounded by the kitchen, the goats' area, and two small, windowless rooms. Just as we stepped out, Sheik Faisal, Safia's father, returned from the mosque. He saw us and greeted us warmly, but cautiously, staying out of the curious neighbors' sight.

"How's my friend Chris doing?" he asked.

I could tell how much he respected my husband.

"And how is my daughter?"

I didn't want to lie to Sheik Faisal, so I answered honestly, and quite undiplomatically: "Safia is critically ill and will probably die soon. Only one person can help her. You have to pray!"

My bluntness caught the leader of the village by surprise. "I am praying! Look here!" he said and showed me a well-worn piece of paper full of Quran verses.

I hesitated for a moment before replying: "Only in the name of Isa Al-Masih can she be healed. Pray to him. He will help your daughter!" I nodded and turned to leave. The sheik just stood there with his mouth wide open, and I could feel him staring at me as I left.

I was emotionally drained, very tired and worn out and wanted to go home. But I couldn't leave just yet.

Several other women led us to their simple huts, where many other sick women were lying. They were all very pleased that the *daktooras* had come to their village since there were no infirmaries or pharmacies for miles.

It would have been impolite to reject their invitations. In these parts, it was an honor to be invited to somebody's home. So we suppressed our weariness and followed the colorfully dressed, dark-skinned Bedouin women to their simple abodes, although we would have preferred to be outside breathing the fresh air. We sat down on the bare clay floor, talked with the sick people, and treated their diseases.

* * *

"You did what?!" That evening, my husband scolded me when I told him about my day. "Faisal is not only the village leader and mayor. He's also the Imam of the mosque and a good friend. You shouldn't have spoken so directly to him! If he decides to turn his back on us, we won't be able to complete our projects in that village!"

I swallowed hard. I knew Chris was right. But I also knew I had not said anything for which I needed to be ashamed. I prayed that God would allow things to turn out for the best, despite my mistake.

"Don't worry so much, Chris!" I said. "You know that a woman's opinion isn't worth much around here, anyway. The sheik wasn't mad at me. He values your friendship and would see it as a great loss if you stopped visiting his village. Besides, what would become of the school, the water project, and the cement factory?"

Chris began to calm down. He came over, gave me a big hug, and whispered in my ear: "Oh, sweetheart, he appreciates you, too! Let's not worry. We'll just trust our heavenly Daddy to take care of everything!"

A couple of weeks later, I was back in Sherj, walking around and talking with a few other women. I looked over and saw a young girl standing in the doorway of one of the houses. She was smiling and waving at me. I nodded and smiled back.

Latifa, one of the village women I was with looked over at me in amazement.

"Don't you recognize her? That's Safia, the daughter of Sheik Faisal!" Actually, I hadn't recognized her. She looked totally different from when I saw her last. She was healthy and had gained weight. And she was all smiles. As Safia came closer, I realized that she had been standing at the door of the sheik's home. I hadn't recognized the house at first since we had approached it from a different direction than usual. I was surprised and laughed out loud.

I was so happy that I felt like dancing! I greeted the girl with a few conventional Arabic phrases and then asked her: "Do you know who made you well?" The girl responded with a timid and reverent nod.

"Yes. Jesus, the Messiah. The man from the pictures!" I smiled and nodded. Safia had remembered the flannel cutouts that we took with us to tell Bible stories to the women and children. It was sort of like a "portable cinema" we used to explain our faith in an entertaining manner. We usually had a crowd of mothers, grandmothers, teenagers, and children at our presentations.

Nobody wanted to miss these free open-air events. They all loved the flannel figures and often asked if they could take one of them home with them. The village had no electricity, so obviously nobody owned a television. Most of the people here only left the village to go to the hospital. The men of the village stood a few yards away and watched the presentation. They were interested and would have loved to join the group. But out of respect for the rules of etiquette, they watched from a distance. In these parts, men were only allowed to speak with other men, and then only if there were no women present.

I was relieved to hear that there had been no negative repercussions from the supernatural healing that had taken place. On the contrary, it had opened doors for us in this remote village.

* * *

Helena and I were on our way back to the car, where our chauffeur was waiting for us in the shade of one of the buildings. An elderly woman with a kind, wrinkly face, grabbed my hand and led me silently back to the village square in the center of the settlement.

Salmiin, an aged man with snow-white hair, was waiting there for me. He was just as wrinkled as the old woman leading me to him. Without hesitation, he showed me his finger and asked: "Please, can you heal my finger?" He was desperate. I looked at his lifeless finger. The skin was parched and had turned black because of an infection that had not been treated properly. Carefully and somewhat timidly, I touched the elderly man's hand and hoped I hadn't violated some Islamic law I was unaware of. Apparently, *daktooras* were allowed to touch a man, even a venerable old patriarch.

On the other hand, it might be that Bedouins just didn't adhere as closely to the strict fundamentalist rules as did their counterparts in the cities. All the women around me looked at me, their faces revealing hope and trust.

"I'm not a doctor and can't operate on you. The best thing would be to go to the hospital and have the dead skin removed. Unfortunately, I can't do that for you here." It was frustrating that I was not able to help him.

But the old man didn't give up that quickly.

"I am old and can no longer work. I don't have money for the hospital. Besides, it's too far away. I'm not strong enough to make it, and I can't afford a bus ticket, anyway. But you could pray to your God and ask him to heal me!" His childlike faith overwhelmed me, so I closed my eyes and prayed in simple Arabic words for his healing. Once again, I began to doubt. What if nothing happened? What if Salmiin boycotted our work here? After all, he was a respected Bedouin patriarch. Would we be allowed to return to the village? It had taken a long time for us to gain the people's trust. I decided it wasn't any of my business to know these things. It was up to God to reach out to the poor and needy. My business was to pray for the sick.

It moved me deeply that these people would put their trust in us. They had become very dear to me. I smiled and nodded as Helena and I returned to the car. We were silent during the entire trip home.

* * *

A couple of weeks later, a physician friend of ours, Dr. Payo, and his wife, Elischa, came to visit. They brought their two daughters, Grace and Joy, as well as their son, Samuel, with them. They lived in Taiz, a city north of Mukalla, and had set up a children's infirmary in the hospital there. Today, Dr. Payo and Chris were heading out to visit the remote project villages. They wanted to examine and treat the most extreme cases.

Before the two of them got on their way, I said: "Please check up on Salmiin. Maybe Dr. Payo can help him."

That evening, I stood at the door eagerly waiting for Chris and the doctor to return from their trip to the project area.

During supper, I asked Dr. Payo: "Did you see Salmiin? How is his finger?"

I was astounded by his report. "After treating several other sick people, we drove to Salmiin's village. I examined him and saw that the skin on his right middle finger was a little thinner and lighter than the others. But otherwise, he was fine. God had completely and miraculously healed the old man, entirely without an operation."

CHAPTER 37

Ramadan and the Missing Child

DURING RAMADAN, THE mornings were unusually quiet. It was very hot outside. Trying to get the laundry done, I wiped the sweat from my brow and shooed a couple of flies away. Most of the neighbors were still asleep, at least the men were. The women were tired, too, but rarely had the luxury of sleeping in after a night of excessive celebration. They had to take care of the children and prepare the elaborate meals for the next night's festivity. During this month of fasting, Muslims would turn the night into day. According to Islamic law, not even a crumb of bread or a drop of liquid was to be consumed during the day. That's why everybody took it easy and preserved their energy until the evening arrived. But by then they were completely exhausted, just the same.

As soon as the sun set and twilight broke, the muezzin shouted through the crackling loudspeakers: *"Allahu akbar!* Come to prayer!" The fast was over for the day. It was time to eat again!

For starters, the Muslims would eat five dates to break the fast. A tasty *shurba*[49] followed, then the heartier main courses of greasy meat and rice. Everybody filled his belly and tried to regain his strength. The feast ended with pudding and other sugary desserts, as well as baked goods rich in calories. Cake and mocha coffee topped it all off. Then, just before dawn, everybody stuffed themselves with *ftur*[50] so their stomach would be full when they lay down for their morning nap. This nightly gorge took its toll during the day. Most of the men slept until noon and didn't go to work. During the month of fasting, it wasn't unusual to find public officials sleeping on or under their desks.

Ramadan was especially difficult for the elderly and feeble. We noticed that quite a few more people died during the fasting season. The weak and elderly often didn't survive the fast.

But for pious Muslims, it was blasphemous to criticize this increase in mortalities that Ramadan caused. They even believed it was a special blessing from Allah himself to be allowed to die during Ramadan. Oh, how we longed to let the people here know how big our God's heart is—so much bigger than they could ever imagine!

One Monday morning around 9:30 a.m., the boys were downstairs in their classroom. The final days of Ramadan had arrived. It was very quiet. Even the birds seemed to be singing more quietly and less than usual, and apparently, the wind was being considerate of the slumberers. Or was this the treacherous calm before a storm?

I was just filling up the washing machine with water from a hose when suddenly there was an unrelenting knock at the front door. I didn't want the children to have to interrupt their lessons, so I turned off the water and rushed down the stairs, two steps at a time. I opened the gate and peered outside, wondering whom I would find. Was it another beggar? They often came around during Ramadan. Or was it one of my neighbors wanting to borrow a cup of something or visit for a while?

It was Ferouz, the cute 5-year-old girl from the yellow house across the street.

---

49 oatmeal soup
50 breakfast

"Is my brother Hamoudi here?" she asked. "We haven't seen him in hours. He just disappeared. Mama is crying; she's so worried."

Ferouz's family had only recently moved to our neighborhood. I had often wondered whether Fatima, the lady of the house, was the children's mother, or perhaps their aunt or grandmother. She was a very haggard and scrawny woman and probably looked older than she actually was. Yet when she smiled, her face lit up, and she appeared quite lovely and youthful. We had seen her with only her headscarf covering her hair. Whenever she came outside, she was completely veiled, and like most women here, even her eyes were covered. I smiled at the little girl and shook my head:

"I'm sorry. I haven't seen your brother today. He couldn't be with our children. They're in school right now."

Ferouz looked so desperate and scared that I felt sorry for her. Then I remembered a disturbing rumor I had heard the day before. During Ramadan, certain men had been driving around in a van, picking up children from the streets. They would kidnap them, and then remove their organs to sell on the black market. Immediately, I offered to drive around to help search for Hamoudi. Maybe he had just wandered down to the ocean like all the other rascals often did. The sea was very alluring, and it was almost as if the boys could hear the sirens calling to them. As a mother, I could certainly identify with my neighbor's fears. I slipped on my black *abaya* and a headscarf, and then stopped by the classroom to tell the teacher and the boys that I would be gone for a while. David and Martin begged me to let them go along:

"Please, Mama! Take us with you. We can help you find Hamoudi! The more people looking for him, the faster we can find him. And that way you can keep your eyes on the road while driving. We'll look to the right and the left. Please, Mama! Please!"

I didn't have the time to argue with them. Perhaps it wasn't a bad idea to take them along. I was really beginning to worry about the missing child.

So I said they could join me, and within seconds, they were in the car, along with their teacher and a few other eager neighborhood children. I opened the gate and drove out of the driveway onto the street. Which way should I go first? Fortunately, I was used to driving our SUV on sandy roads. It was almost like driving on ice. You just had to place the vehicle in a low gear and then be careful not to accelerate or brake too abruptly. I rarely got stuck in the sand.

I decided to head down to the ocean, which seemed very ominous today. My helpers looked to the left and the right, closely inspecting the ponds that had been formed by the recent rainfall. They were full of foul, brackish water and were surrounded by dense thickets and undergrowth. I was already nervous, and the children's bickering and nagging made matters even worse. I prayed for wisdom. Where was Hamoudi? Where should we search for him? It was like looking for a needle in a haystack. The odds were against us. The streets were empty, and there was nobody around for us to ask if they had seen a small lost boy.

The children in the backseat were chattering away, yelling back and forth each time they thought they saw something. I slowly drove down one road, then turned around and followed the next one back. Then I wondered whether I should have started at the neighbor's house and worked my way systematically through the side roads. Perhaps Hamoudi had already returned home and was safe and sound. We should return and ask my colleague, Helena, to help with the search. She could help me treat any wounds, if necessary.

"These kids are distracting me; I have to get them to calm down," I murmured.

When I rounded the next corner, the mosque came into sight. On the stone steps leading up to it lay a dark bundle of something. The children pointed it out and yelled:

"Look, Mama! There is something at the mosque!"

As we drove closer, the "bundle" moved and lifted its head. It was Fatima. She had gone out on her own to look for her son. She was frightened and fully distraught. The heat and her fasting had caused her to collapse on the steps of the mosque. She just lay there, a picture of misery, with tears running down her soiled face. David and I jumped out of the car and helped her get in. When we arrived back at her home, I sent Martin over to get Helena, who lived on the opposite corner.

"Martin, tell Helena to come quickly and bring her bag with her," I said. Martin hurried off to get my friend.

Fatima was screaming hysterically and shaking all over. I checked her pulse and noticed that it was irregular. It was difficult to calm her down. She was so distraught that she wouldn't even take a sip of the drink I was trying to give her. Helena came, bringing her blood pressure equipment with her. She did a quick examination of Fatima and said she thought that a heart attack was imminent. We decided that Fatima needed to go to the hospital, but it wasn't easy to calm her down enough to get her to agree.

Just then, Samir came through the door. He was holding his little brother by the collar. It was Hamoudi, who was trying to wrench himself free from Samir's grip. He finally managed to escape his older brother's grip and just stood there, looking at the floor. He felt uncomfortable with so many women staring at him. Samir said that he had found his missing brother in a kiosk, where he had laid down under the counter for shade and had fallen asleep. We were all greatly relieved.

However, Fatima was still not doing any better. This new twist of events was too much for her. Her emotions swayed between relief and anger, and her blood pressure was still unstable. So I urged her to let us take her to the hospital. I placed her *abaya* in front of her, tightened my headscarf, and straightened up my *balto*—a gesture that meant: "Whether you want to or not, we're going to the hospital!" She continued to resist until we were able to persuade Samir that she needed medical attention. When he ordered her to follow our advice, she finally gave in. Her lips were blue by now, and she was hyperventilating. Samir took her downstairs and forcefully placed her into our car, promising he would take care of the children. Then I told my boys to return to their classroom to finish their lessons.

"I don't want you going with me to the hospital. We might have to wait quite a while before it's our turn."

David and Martin didn't like hospitals, anyway, so I didn't have to do much persuading. They had unpleasant memories of their time in the clinic and were happy that they weren't the patient this time around.

"We've been to the hospital often enough. We'd rather go back to our classroom. Otherwise, we'll have so much homework to catch up on." The boys were reasonable, after all.

We arrived at the hospital, but when we came to the front gate, soldiers stopped and searched us. This was the Bashraheel Hospital, which was government owned and operated. It offered treatments for minimal fees but required rigorous controls at the entrances.

We as foreigners usually got special treatment. It was no different now, and I gladly accepted the offer to take Fatima into a treatment room without having to endure the usual hour-long wait. The smell of disinfectant filled the air of the large room. Bloodstained stretchers were separated from one another by thin curtains on either side. Meanwhile, Fatima was very weak and mostly unresponsive. The poor hygienic conditions here didn't seem to bother her at all. Helena took a handkerchief and wiped the worst of the grime off the stretcher before we helped Fatima lie down. She desperately needed oxygen.

I started to close the curtain on the right, so she could have a little privacy, when I stopped in my tracks. I gasped at what I saw on the stretcher next to Fatima. A young pregnant woman lay there in an oddly bent posture. She wasn't breathing. Her face was ashen and stiff.

An older man stood next to her with an infant in his arms and a 3-year-old at his side. He was crying relentlessly. When I recognized this family's misery, I felt like somebody had punched me in the ribs. I wished I could have eased their pain. But there was no more hope for the mother. Help had come too late. I hoped that it wouldn't come too late for Fatima.

The nurse finally showed up with an oxygen cylinder. She gave Fatima an infusion, as well, and I calmed down a little. I stayed at Fatima's side, but with one ear, I listened to the sounds from the next compartment. I was glad I didn't have to watch as they took the young mother's body away. Fatima needed to remain calm, so I decided not to tell her what had happened to this poor family.

I'm a highly sensitive person, and sometimes that can be quite a burden. How much easier would it be if I could just ignore situations like this? But I couldn't. I would hide them deep in my heart, and this particular painful memory was bound to remain with me forever.

I prayed quietly: "Lord, help me to be able to look past things like this. The sorrow is just too much for me to handle. I feel helpless."

Soon, the color began to return to Fatima's face. She was responsive again. However, Helena and I decided it was best for her to stay in the hospital a little while longer.

"They'll take good care of you here. You just rest now. We'll go home and fix some dinner for the children. A little later, we'll come back and bring you something to eat. And maybe we'll be able to take you home then."

Then we left her and went back. Our patient recovered and was soon able to leave the hospital.

CHAPTER 38

One Husband
with Two Wives

ONE EVENING, HELENA, our midwife, called while I was brushing my teeth and getting ready for bed.

"Our neighbor, Jamila, is having contractions. Her husband just called. Would you come along with me? It's only a few hundred feet to her home, but I really don't want to go out alone. It's so dark in our neighborhood without any streetlamps."

"Sure! I wouldn't leave you alone! I'll meet you at your place in two minutes!" I put my dress back on and then grabbed my headscarf and *abaya*.

While putting on my shoes, I told Chris: "Don't wait up for me. I'm going with Helena. Jamila's baby is on its way." I was just about to run out the door when Chris stopped me.

"Wait a minute. I'll take the two of you over." Within a few seconds, he was at my side. He escorted Helena and me to Jamila's house, which was located on a dark street not far from ours. Before he left, Chris said: "Call me when you're finished. I'll come and pick you up."

The apartment had only two rooms. In the living room, left of the stairwell, Jamila's husband, Abdallah, was watching television with a few other men and chewing away on his *khat*. To the right was a sparsely furnished room that served as a kitchen, as well as living quarters and bedroom for his two wives and his children. It was a big room with a simple concrete floor. In two aluminum boxes on the left wall, the women kept their belongings, such as clothing, jewelry, and makeup.

Opposite the door on the other wall was a small gas cooker with a few pots and dishes, as well as a refrigerator and a few cooking utensils. Even though they had no cabinets, everything was neat and tidy.

To the right of the door was a stack of thin foam mattresses, which the women and children slept on at night. An antiquated ceiling fan squeaked loudly and circulated the hot, sticky air throughout the room. The four children of the older wife, Hudda, sat on the floor playing marbles.

Both of Abdallah's wives were pregnant. Jamila would probably deliver her child before the night was over. It was her first baby. Hudda's fifth child would likely wait a few more days. The two women sat on the bare floor of the scanty room, the harsh fluorescent light mercilessly shining down on them. They were wearing long, flowing robes, and were sweating profusely. Their hair was tucked behind colorful *nuqbas*. They knew Helena well from her previous visits, and they greeted us warmly and with respect.

Although we immediately removed our *baltos* and headscarves, we were soaked with sweat in less than a minute. The ceiling fan was no help since it just circulated the muggy air.

The two women insisted upon keeping their heads covered since the birth of a child was considered a holy event.

When we asked them if they wouldn't be more comfortable without their warm scarves, they answered in unison: *"Aadi!"*[51]

For the next few hours, I watched as Hudda affectionately took care of her co-wife Jamila, who was several years younger, tall, slender, and very pretty. Hudda seemed to suffer with Jamila at each contraction. She stayed at her side and comforted her like a mother would. Her empathy amazed me. Hudda had to share her husband's affection with

---

51 That is normal! We're used to that!

this woman, perhaps even watching as they made love. I had a hard time comprehending this with my Western mind. These two women had become close friends and were almost like sisters. It was touching to see how tenderly these women treated each other. During the next few hours, the children fell asleep one after the other, and we laid them down on the mattresses. After a long and difficult delivery, Hudda took the newborn baby girl and placed her at Jamila's breast.

A few days later, we were called back to the house. Hudda was having her fifth baby! This time, Jamila was the one helping and comforting Hudda, who was Abdallah's main wife. But something seemed to be troubling Jamila, and her baby looked like it had lost weight.

When Helena and I returned a week later to check on the women and their babies, we were shocked to find out that Jamila was no longer there. At first, Hudda wouldn't answer our questions and refused to give us any details. Finally, she sadly and soberly told us that Abdallah had sent his second wife away. He didn't like her anymore. She had developed pimples, probably due to the change in her hormone levels. Since she had only borne him a daughter, he had sent her away to move in with her parents, who lived over 600 miles away. Abdallah kept the baby, and Hudda took care of it, along with her own five children and an unloving husband.

When I heard this, my heart bled for Jamila, and I was determined to tell Abdallah what I thought about his decision. I went over to his room and knocked at the door. He wasn't there, but I caught a glimpse of his living quarters. There were beautiful carpets and pillows everywhere. The room even had air conditioning! During the next few days, I tried several times to talk to him. But I was not allowed to come in. Unfortunately, I never got the chance to give him a piece of my mind. I would have asked him why he hadn't allowed his wives to deliver their babies in his air-conditioned room. Then I would have told him he shouldn't be surprised if the heat rash caused pimples.

I said to Helena: "Thank God not all Yemeni men are like him!"

CHAPTER 39

Fire (continued)

September 17, 2005

"CHRIS! WHERE ARE you?" My desperate cry echoed across the rooftops of the city. I was afraid he was unconscious with his head on the horn of our burning vehicle. I felt like I was trapped in a nightmare.

I finally heard him screaming at the neighbors, who were pounding at our gate:

"Intabihu-Dirubalkum![52] Move! The car will crash right into you, if you don't get out of the way!"

The impact of a three-ton car would blast the gate wide open and overrun our neighbors, who were just trying to help. I was still on the roof looking down at this frightening scene.

My heart was pounding, but when I heard Chris' voice, I breathed a sigh of relief. At least now, I knew he wasn't trapped in that burning car! Just then, I saw a trail of flames leading from the gate to the car.

---

52 Be careful! Watch out!

"What's that? I hope it's not..."

I suppressed the haunting suspicion for now. I had more important things to take care of. I'd follow through on that thought later.

The car was burning fiercely and still rolling backward, when it suddenly came to a halt in the middle of the courtyard. It had miraculously stopped at a safe distance between the group of trees and the house, at a spot where not much damage would be done if it were to explode.

It all happened within seconds. Chris finally got the gate open and let the neighbors in. They had witnessed the whole spectacle and shouted:

"Allah! Allah! It's a miracle. Allah is with you!"

It was comforting for us to know we were not alone. The neighbors stood by us and helped us while we waited in vain for the fire department to show up.

Finally, after almost two hours, we had extinguished the fire. The neighbors helped us push the charred remains of the car onto the road. We made sure to park it far away from the house and the trees, just in case the flames ignited again.

Chris thanked the neighbors and sent them home.

We were fully exhausted but grateful that nothing worse had happened. We flopped into our beds to try to get a few hours of well-deserved rest before the sun rose at around 5:00 a.m. and the *muezzin* called out the *fajr*.

* * *

The following morning, Chris was getting ready to go to his office at the university, when his plans were thwarted once again.

The neighbors were all standing around the remains of the burnt car. Even those who had not seen the inferno firsthand were there, talking loudly and gesticulating wildly.

"What happened? How was this possible?"

While Chris was talking to the neighbors and trying to calm them down, David found a folder in front of our house. There was a note in it with an unusual message.

"Mama, look! Somebody threw this folder over the wall. It looks like a school binder," David shouted up to me on the veranda.

I hurried down and took the white folder from him, opened it, and froze. David looked at me with a puzzled expression. I knew immediately that this wasn't just some kid's prank I held in my hand. The note was handwritten in Arabic, and I felt like my heart was going to explode. I read the foreboding message and told David to take it to his father right away.

"Hurry, David! Go! Tell Papa I need to talk to him before he leaves for the office."

David grabbed the anonymous letter from my hand and then ran out the door to try to catch Chris before he left.

"Papa, look here. I found something!" he shouted and gave the note to his father.

Chris turned white when he looked at the piece of paper. He immediately recognized it as a handwritten, anonymous death threat. He read the message out loud, but in a low voice:

> In the name of Allah and Mohammed, his prophet: Praise be to his name.
>
> Chris, don't think that you and your family are safe. Ever since you started Christianizing Muslims, you have walked a dangerous path!
>
> Today we burned your car and a part of your house. Tomorrow we will surely burn you and your family if you don't immediately stop trying to convert people. Just leave! We'll give you until Ramadan to shut down your organization and leave this country of Islam. You had better get a move on, otherwise we'll butcher you and your family.
>
> A Zealot of Islam
>
> P.S. Don't depend on government security forces for protection!

Basaam, a neighbor who lived three houses down the street, approached Chris. When he saw the document, he turned pale and became very agitated. Basaam worked for the government in the Department of Education. He was apparently very concerned by what he saw as he appreciated and respected Chris a lot. Since we lived in the same neighborhood, the two of them had become close friends and often visited each other. Instinctively and with much foresight, Chris took a picture of the document before giving it to Basaam, who would turn it over to the police. Chris suspected that the threatening letter might get lost in the piles of records and documents at the police station.

Somewhat impatiently, Basaam shoved Chris into his car.

"Come on, Chris! We need to go straight to the police station and file a charge against the unknown perpetrator."

"Don't touch anything! Be careful not to disturb any evidence! Let the forensic team do their work, then you can clean up," Chris ordered me, before he was pulled into the car.

That was going to take a lot of willpower on my part since I really wanted things to return to normal as soon as possible.

That day, Chris would have no time for breakfast or lunch. He had some important people to talk to, including the chief of police and the head of the East-Yemen secret service. He would also be talking to the prime minister personally. The kids and I were left behind to deal with the trauma of the previous night.

Everybody knew this attack was to be taken seriously. The police feared that the government might be in danger, as well. Nobody took the situation lightly. They even called it an international crisis since we foreigners were well respected here. At each of the meetings, Chris had to relate the whole ordeal over and over again.

After Chris returned home, police officers swarmed our grounds, inspecting the crime scene.

I was annoyed. "Why are there so many policemen here?" I asked him when we were alone for a moment.

"There are various agencies here investigating. Apparently, they don't work well together. First the secret service, then the political security police (Al'amn assiyaasii). When the criminal police officers came by, followed by the security officials, I had to answer the same questions over and over."

Then the inspecting officers discovered something very unusual: The car had rolled backward, even though it was in first gear!

Nothing was normal that day. I couldn't even let the boys play barefoot outside because of the broken glass. They were disappointed that they had slept through the agonizing situation.

"Why didn't you wake us up? We could have helped! It's not fair! Just when something interesting happens, we're sound asleep! We're never going to bed again!"

I had my hands full trying to calm my children down and keep them busy, all the while providing the officers in our living room with cold drinks and sweets.

* * *

Two days later, I asked Chris, "What do we do now? Are we going to take their threat seriously? And if we do, what does that mean for us?"

For Chris, the answer was crystal clear: "This is serious! We have to leave Mukalla before Ramadan begins next week!"

And yet we didn't want to run away in fear.

Chris talked to Saiidi Ahmed, the governor of Hadhramaut. "What do you recommend? We don't want to decide on our own. We respect your authority, so please tell us what you want us to do."

He answered: "You're in grave danger. We can no longer guarantee your safety. These men are al-Qaeda extremists. We can't do anything about them. They want to kill you. There's nothing we can do. You and your family have to leave."

Chris responded: "Okay, but please think for a moment: If we leave now, who will have achieved their goal? Your security force or the terrorists? The decision is up to you. Whatever decision you make, we will respect it. It's important, though, that the government keeps the upper hand. Otherwise, chaos will break out."

"You're right, of course. But I want to get you and your family out of the line of fire for a while. Please visit your other project area over in Taiz during Ramadan. We'll conduct the appropriate investigations while you're away."

Somewhat later, Chris told me what the officials had said. He asked me to start packing our bags immediately.

That was just too much for me, and I wept. So many things had happened. Besides the assault against us, it had now been exactly one year since the children had drowned in the ocean.

I had barely seen Chris since the attack on our car. The trauma of all of it was beginning to take its toll on me. During the summer, termites had invaded our home. They had nested in the mattresses, the furniture, the carpets, and even the books. I had spent days taking the books and the shelving units up to the roof to be "fumigated" by the sun. After that, we had to coat the wood with a special salt and oil compound to kill the eggs that remained. The locals usually used kerosene, but that was unhealthy and smelled terrible. Only after treating the furniture could we return it to the house. Otherwise, all our clothes, books, and other belongings would soon be eaten up by the termites, too!

"I haven't even gotten everything off the roof yet. And those termites are pesky little beasts. Just look at you. Your whole body is covered with bites, and Tim has red blisters all over. And they're getting itchier by the day!

"Chris, didn't you notice that all the bookshelves are gone?"

My "professor" was preoccupied and nodded absentmindedly: "Well, no, I mean yes."

I continued arguing: "And besides, the schoolbooks haven't arrived yet from Germany!"

But all my arguments didn't change a thing. He was determined for us to leave. There was a lot to organize and take care of, and many decisions to be made. I often felt overwhelmed by the workload. I wished that Chris would just put his arms around me to comfort me. He was learning that he didn't always have to have an answer to my questions. It was often more helpful if he just gave me a hug instead. Whenever he took the time to let me talk and cry, I always felt better afterward. If he listened patiently, running his fingers through my hair or rubbing my back, I knew that he loved me, and soon I was able to enjoy working and helping him again.

Although I knew that my poor husband had no time to slow down, I still felt the need for a little special attention. I was his wife, after all, and in my heart I longed for some time alone with him. Yet he needed to function like a smooth-running engine to get everything done on time.

He had to use every spare minute replacing locks and lamps in the house so that intruders wouldn't break in during our absence. And he had many other things to take care of before we left—for instance, repairing the calcified water pipes that had become clogged during the summer.

Rick, soccer player and teacher-to-be, helped as best he could with the repairs. He had returned with us from Germany to teach our children during the coming school year. But we couldn't even begin to think about school right now. There were more urgent things to take care of first. I felt sorry for Rick. His start here in Yemen had been turbulent and intense.

I finally gave in and called various friends in other cities to find a place for us to go.

"Do you know where our family could stay for a few weeks? Perhaps outside the country? Or maybe we could live with you for a while?"

But the bush telegraph had been quite active, and some of our friends thought it was even too dangerous to talk to us on the phone. We had been accused of proselytizing Muslims and turning them into apostates, and our phone was probably being tapped. We still had no place to go, and our future remained uncertain.

Colleagues from the capital city recommended: "Go back to Germany!"

I just sighed, "That's not an option unless our Boss in heaven says the word. We have a traumatic experience to deal with here, and who knows if we could ever return to Yemen if we were to leave now? Besides, where would we go? We don't have a home in Germany anymore. And we don't want to burden our friends again with more extended visits."

Months of living as vagabonds during our summer furlough had been enough!

After several restless nights and much prayer—and after quite a few disappointing conversations with friends in other parts of the country and abroad—a solution seemed to be on the horizon at last.

Chris said, "Tomorrow we're going to Taiz. A family who lives there is on furlough in Canada and has offered to rent us their house in the mountains while they are gone."

With a heavy heart, we said good-bye to our neighbors, our cat, and our house.

The children asked: "How long will we be gone? When can we come back?"

Chris tried to comfort them: "It won't be too long." I tried to be strong and keep from crying, but I was skeptical about ever seeing our beloved home again.

The Land Cruiser was packed to the brim, and we were on our way into an uncertain future. The children were atypically quiet. Normally, we couldn't keep them from gabbing throughout the entire drive. Only Tim chattered away. He was always happy when we went out together for a drive!

CHAPTER 40

Living in Exile

September 25, 2005

IT HAD BEEN eight turbulent days since the attack on our car. In a few days, the month of Ramadan would begin. Late in the evening, Chris and I and our three boys, along with the boys' new tutor Rick, arrived in the beautiful city of Taiz, which lay in the southwest part of Yemen's central highlands, close to Mount Saber with an altitude of about 10,000 feet.

David told his two brothers: "We're here! I get the biggest room since I'm the oldest."

I grinned. "Life just goes on!"

We were grateful and relieved to have finally found a place to stay after several stressful days of searching. The apartment had been empty for some time and was covered in dust, but at least we felt safe here. It was located directly in the city, so we went out and got some food before the stores closed. It had been a long 16-hour drive through the desert and the mountains, and we were all hungry.

The water pipes were clogged, the electricity was off, and there were absolutely no dishes or linens in the cabinets, but we were so tired, we didn't really care. We just put the kids to bed, dirty as they were.

We decided to take care of the cockroaches and dust in the morning. Our friends from Taiz helped out with some pots and pans, linens and towels. A friendly family of locals lived in the apartment above us. Their grandmother lived with them, and they had a child who was sick. We quickly got to know them, and somewhat later I would have an opportunity to pray for the mother and her child.

The climate in this mountainous region was mild. During the winter, the temperature rarely rose above the 80s. Now, shortly after the rainy season, everything was green and blossoming. The countryside stood in stark contrast to the desolate desert regions around Mukalla where we had lived for the past six years. For us, this fertile region was a sight for sore eyes!

And yet, all of us, including Rick, were having a hard time adjusting to this unfamiliar place. It just didn't feel like home to us. Maybe it was because everything had happened so quickly and our souls were still back in Mukalla. I hoped they would catch up with us soon.

The school year got off to a bad start. All the uncertainty had caused quite a bit of tension. And then when the school curriculum materials arrived from Germany, they were incomplete. Some of them were even for the wrong age groups!

David asked, "Mama, where are my scissors and my glue? And what about my fountain pen?"

"I'm sure we'll find everything. Let's unpack our things first."

I had actually had enough of packing and unpacking during the past few weeks. I was completely exhausted! I hadn't really had time to eat much of anything, and as a result, I had become very thin and weak.

Chris often had to travel to the capital city of Sanaa to consult with government officials. Sometimes he was gone for days. Ramadan held him up even more since some agencies were closed for the holidays. It frustrated him to have to go to so many offices and speak with numerous officials, mostly only to hear the words *"Bukra Inshallah"* time and again. He missed his family, and we missed him.

The children often asked, "Where is Papa?"

We had experienced another culture shock when we were evacuated from our home. Only a short while later, many Arabs would have to leave their home countries, too, and live in exile like us. Since we had to leave our home behind, we could identify with the refugees who had lost their homes. They were on the run and their future was uncertain. We knew what it meant to have the rug pulled out from under you.

* * *

There were advantages to living in Taiz. One of them was that we could purchase many Western products in the supermarkets and the kiosks. There was a huge variety of goods compared with Mukalla. We could even get a cappuccino, hard cheese, and various kinds of sausage here.

The language school was in Taiz. Many of our colleagues were studying Arabic there, and we had a lot of good fellowship with them. But losing our home turned into an emotional crisis for us, and I withdrew myself more and more.

Our friends couldn't understand why we were miserable. Usually we were a very happy family. But now it was as if a dark cloud hung over us. We were all homesick for Mukalla, and none of us were sure that we would ever be able to go back. I had to comfort our children regularly. They were unhappy and gloomy. And often, I had no answers to their questions.

"Mama, I want to go home. I miss my friends and our pets. I miss our house, the tire swing, and all our toys. We don't like this house here. When can we go home?"

That was a question Chris and I often asked ourselves.

"Is this just one of the obstacles we have to overcome, or is it all over now? What's next? What does God want us to do? Should we stay here and try to hold on until we can go back to Mukalla? Or should we check out job opportunities in Germany?"

The constant brooding and uncertainty robbed us of our strength. We just didn't know what to do.

Out of the blue, we received word from the owners of the house that they had changed their plans and would be returning from Canada earlier than originally planned. We would lose our shelter and needed to move on once again. Even though this place had not been ideally furnished, it had nonetheless granted us a certain sense of safety and security.

"The government hasn't given us the go-ahead to come back to Mukalla yet. What are we going to do now?"

Once again, we had to cope with uncertainty and existential questions. But soon the black clouds retreated, and the sun began to shine on our family again. Some friends of ours told us that another Western family living in Taiz would be going abroad for the birth of their baby in a few days. They would be happy to rent their house out to us during their absence. "With somebody living in our house while we're gone, it will be safe from burglars," they said.

But we had a few days between the houses. Chris had a wonderful surprise in store for us:

"Let's spend a few days down in Aden at the beach until we can move into the new place. We can stay in the Elephant Beach Hotel."

We were all very excited! We had our bags packed in no time and were happy to move out of this house. We certainly wouldn't miss it, what with its clogged pipes and all.

CHAPTER 41

Coral Reef

WE SPENT THE first few days in Aden swimming, snorkeling, and strolling through the town. Since Rick, the boys' tutor, had come along, we squeezed in a little schooling, as well.

During our stay here, Chris and I met with a Christian couple, Marscha and Dwight, who lived and served in Aden as psychologists for an oil company. They offered us professional help in dealing with the trauma of the terror attack and its effect on us and the children. We were able to talk over some painful issues and gain a little perspective for our future, which was still quite unclear.

Dwight gave us some sober advice: "No matter what you decide, an incredible risk is involved! You need to face the facts! If you decide to go back to Mukalla, it could mean that you and your children might be killed. Don't turn a blind eye to your fears and cares!"

"This is a dilemma!" I cried in despair. "If we decide to go back to Germany, we'll have to find a home and work."

"The decision is yours to make. We can't tell you what to do."

And yet their advice and support was a great help. God had often sent us "angels" like this couple to help us, pray for us, encourage us, and show us his fatherly love and care. He never abandoned us, especially in times of inner turmoil.

Shortly before noon on the third day of our vacation, Chris and I were lying in the shade reading while Tim was asleep in the hotel room.

Rick was with David and Martin on a tour to explore the cliffs. David had lost his flip-flops on the slippery boulders and was barefoot. All of a sudden he slipped. The sharp coral reef caused a deep cut and hurt his foot badly. At that moment, I glanced up from my book, and saw Rick grabbing David and carrying him back toward us as fast as he could. Even from the distance, I could see the blood dripping. I screamed, "Chris, hurry! We'll have to sterilize the wound and stop the bleeding right away! Where are the bandages? Go get the American doctor to come quickly, the one staying in the cabin next to ours!"

Gasping for breath, David and Rick arrived. We placed our son on a beach chair and took a look at the wound. It was fairly deep and ragged and went all the way across the sole of his foot.

The doctor arrived and examined David's wound. She said: "I can't stop the bleeding. He needs to be taken to the hospital right away. They will sew him up there!"

I really didn't want to take him to the hospital. I was all too familiar with the inadequate sanitary conditions there.

"Is that absolutely necessary?" I asked.

The doctor answered: "Yes, I'm afraid it is. The foot won't heal otherwise. And you can't expect a boy David's age to stay inside and rest all the time. I'm sorry, but I don't have what I need to sew him up myself."

I sighed and consented. I wished Mr. Spock could just "beam us up" to a different country.

Chris was on top of things. He usually remained calm in crises like this. His composure encouraged me and gave me strength.

I asked Rick, "Would you please stay here with Tim and Martin and keep an eye on them? There's some cold chicken in the refrigerator."

David was exceptionally brave for an 11-year-old, even though he had lost a lot of blood by the time we got to the hospital. A young female Yemeni doctor attended to his injury. She wore a black *abaya,* as well as black gloves and a black face veil with a slit for the eyes. The only things that identified her as a doctor were her white headscarf and the white apron she wore over her dark clothing.

The doctor used a surprisingly large needle to administer the anesthetics. But she refused to wait for the analgesic to take effect. When I saw the pain my son was in, I was furious. If Chris hadn't used his hypnotic stare to stop me in my tracks, I would have yanked the needle right out of her hand!

Sadly, David's swimming days were over for the rest of this vacation! He couldn't even walk on the sand. He had to wear socks and shoes to avoid infecting his wound. Whenever we went to a restaurant for dinner, either Rick or Chris would carry him. Of course, Tim and Martin really missed being able to play with their older brother.

David said he would never go to a doctor again, so after seven days had passed, he removed all of his 18 stitches himself. His brothers watched him do it, and they were full of admiration. For them and for us, David was a real hero, indeed!

"It doesn't hurt a bit!" he said proudly. "And this is good practice for when I become a doctor. Of course, I'll be more careful then. But I never want to go to a hospital as a patient again!"

* * *

Our time in Aden was quickly drawing to an end. Our talks with the professional therapists had given us new strength and direction. With mixed feelings, we headed back to Taiz. We were somewhat sad to be leaving, but we were excited to move into our new place of refuge—a little apartment on a small hill right in the middle of the city.

This apartment was nice and clean. It was also fully furnished, dishes and all. Through the large bay window in the living room, we had a beautiful view of the city. The sky in the west was breathtaking. The setting sun filled the horizon with a gorgeous shade of orange. A few dark-blue clouds stood in stark contrast to the glowing sky and the mountains behind. Next door to our house was the Taiz *qasir.*[53] During

---

53 castle, fortress

Ramadan, cannons were fired from the castle at sundown to let the Muslims know that the fasting time was over for the day.

We were so grateful to be allowed to stay here for the time being. After a few days, Chris had to leave for Sanaa for an indefinite amount of time. Together with Rick, I tried to make the school days as normal as possible. Rick lived with friends and came over for a couple of hours a day to teach the boys and to join us for meals. Our apartment was muggy and sticky since there was neither air conditioning nor a ceiling fan. We would often teach the lessons out on the terrace. Of course, there were more distractions outside.

"Look! A snake!" Martin screamed. "It just crawled into our room!"

Rick didn't believe him. "Where? I didn't see it. You just want to interrupt the class, don't you?"

Martin protested: "No, really! It's under the bed! Look! I just saw it move!"

The boys jumped up and started chasing the reptile, which seemed to have disappeared. Rick played along. He didn't actually believe there was a snake, but he didn't want to spoil the boys' fun. Even he was having a hard time concentrating due to the heat.

Somehow David finally managed to catch the slippery snake with a little shovel. The boys wanted to keep it as a pet.

But Rick had other plans. He hit the snake on the head until it was dead. The boys were angry and screamed, including little 3-year-old Tim. The poisonous snake lay lifeless on the floor, and lessons were over for the day. After such an adventure, there was no way the boys would sit still and listen to Rick any longer.

* * *

One of the highlights of our stay in Taiz was our first meeting with Joe, a cheerful young man who had seemingly come out of nowhere to organize an English faculty at the University of Mukalla and to teach English to the students.

"Only a couple of weeks ago, the university I work for in Canada told me that they were sending me to Mukalla. I had no idea where that was, so I checked the map and booked a flight to Sanaa. A couple of colleagues in the capital told me about you and said I should stop by. They said, you know all about that beautiful coastal city. So, *voilá!* Here I am!"

Since the attack on our car, foreigners had avoided Mukalla altogether. So our encounter with this young man was quite an encouragement to us.

Finally, after Ramadan was over, we received the long-awaited notification from the German embassy. The ambassador had put in a good word for us with the Interior Minister.

"This family is doing very important, sustainable development work in Mukalla. I think it's time for them to return. If your government officials don't agree, then I'll leave it up to you to tell them so!"

The ambassador had visited us only a few weeks before the attack occurred and was quite impressed with the quality of the work we were doing in the project areas. He had also quickly won over the hearts of the Bedouins by sitting around in the sand with them and playing games with them.

We decided that Chris should fly to Mukalla alone for a few days to check the situation out for himself.

The kids complained: "Papa, why can't we come with you? We want to go home, too!"

"It's too dangerous right now. I have to talk to the police. Then I want to ask the neighbors if it's okay with them for us to return. And I just want to look around and make sure everything is safe."

Martin was concerned: "But Papa! If it's too dangerous for us to go back, it's too dangerous for you, too!"

But Chris insisted: "You stay here! I have an important assignment for you—I need you to pray for me and to take care of your mother and Tim. And don't worry. God won't let anything happen to me!"

It was actually the security police who had ordered Chris to go by himself. The family could follow if everything turned out to be safe.

Unfortunately, while Chris was away, I began to experience an irregular heartbeat and chest pain. Our friend, Dr. Payo, sent me to the Baptist Hospital in Jibla to undergo various tests.

The doctors wanted to keep me longer for more extensive testing, but I refused. I didn't want to leave the boys with friends any longer than necessary, especially since they were homesick and missed their

Papa. The only thing I wanted now was to go home, back to Hadhram-aut! And somehow I knew that I would feel much better once our life in exile was over.

* * *

After a week away, Chris returned. He was excited.

"A lot of people can't wait for us to come home!"

"What about the police?" I asked.

Even though I could hardly wait to return to Mukalla, I wanted to know exactly what the police had said.

"The chief of security Abd al Hakiim was at the airport to greet me. He came up and hugged me and said he hoped we'd be returning soon!"

"What about the neighbors?"

Chris was uncommunicative, and it was like pulling teeth to get anything out of him. He searched for the right words to break it to me gently so I wouldn't worry.

"While we were gone, some of them were interrogated and had a few problems with the police. That was unpleasant for them, but they're happy that we're coming home, anyway. Why don't you call Chatija?"

The kids jumped up and down when they heard the news. Chris put his arms around me, and we all celebrated together. Nothing stood in the way of us going home now. We were all thrilled!

I called my friend Chatija right away. But when I talked to her, I noticed she didn't seem all that excited about our return.

"That's strange," I said to Chris after hanging up. "Chatija was always happy to get a call from me. Maybe it was just a bad time. Or is something wrong?"

Chris calmed me down.

"You were probably just imagining things. I'm sure everything is fine!"

And then he played his trump card:

"By the way, the International Development Aid Conference will be taking place in our beautiful Mukalla. We will be honored for our work there, and I think they want to compensate for what we went through. Anyway, it will take place three days from now, and I have been invited as the guest of honor and as the keynote speaker. The press will be there too, as well as representatives of the government."

I was impressed! Non-governmental organizations were not usually invited to attend these conferences. And now Chris was to be their main speaker!

At last our time of waiting was coming to an end. David and Martin had never quit asking:

"When are we going home?"

Now we could give them a clear answer:

"As soon as we pack our things and clean the house! Come on, boys. If we all pull together, we'll be finished in no time!"

CHAPTER 42

Back to Mukalla

WE WERE ALL in high spirits when we finally returned to Mukalla. Home again after almost two months! The children ran around the house, going from room to room, reclaiming their turf. First the children's room, of course, then the living room where the comfortable velvet *mafraj* stood in the corner by the balcony.

These square mattresses were ideal for making caves and hiding places. Our beautiful lovebirds chirped merrily from their cages to greet us. This species of parakeets was easy to take care of. The boys ran down to the playroom to make sure nothing was missing. All their toys were stored away in chests but were not very well sorted, as usual. Shariifa had kept things as tidy as she could and had taken good care of our pets. This time around, no burglar had attempted to break into our house. At first glance, everything seemed to be okay. It was only later that we discovered that the water pipes were rusty and clogged. When I looked out the window down at the courtyard, I was amazed to see that the banana plants, the bougainvillea bushes, and the oleander shrubs had grown and were blossoming. Apparently, somebody had watered them during our absence. The children weren't the only ones thrilled to be home. We all were beside ourselves with joy. We jumped up and down and sang our hearts out. And even though we were tired from the long drive, nobody thought about taking a nap!

Chris got to work unloading the car. We had packed it to the brim with bags and crates. It was amazing how many things we had accumulated while we were away! Tim had gotten a black bunny, and Chris had bought David and Martin each a colorful rabbit. By purchasing these pets, Chris had not only made the children happy but had also saved the animals' lives. The boys ran around looking for appropriate living quarters for their new housemates.

"Mama, can we build them a shelter out on the balcony? They'll be safe there from the cats and the hawks."

"That's a good idea! Take a cardboard box for tonight. Make sure you put some newspapers underneath them to keep it tidy. Tomorrow you can build a real pen for them."

* * *

The next morning we discovered that not everything was as good as we thought it was. Somebody had scribbled ugly words on the façade of our house. Apparently, not everyone was happy that we had returned! We were soon to find out why. Mohammed, our neighbor, was hesitant at first. But then he told us what had happened.

"The police interrogated many of the neighbors and even suspected some of them of being responsible for the attack on your car. They were upset. Even my wife spent several hours at the police station being questioned. That was a terrible experience for her. The whole neighborhood was talking about her behind her back. The police made some arrests, but that was just for show. Nobody will probably ever know who was responsible."

The whole situation left its mark on Chris since he was constantly concerned for the safety of our family. At first, he didn't even allow me to go outside on my own. And since he feared another attack, he told us to keep the windows closed in the classrooms on the ground floor.

But it was just too hot in there, and I protested.

"God clearly sent us here, and he'll protect us! We can't allow fear to govern our lives!"

"You're right. Come on, let's all pray together and cast our cares on our heavenly Father."

Praying together soothed our strained nerves.

Even the neighbors noticed how carefree and happy we were. It wasn't long before our boys were playing outside again with the neighbors' children. They romped around in the streets and played hide-and-seek as they used to. And soon we almost forgot the attack altogether.

We were very happy to be back. Fortunately, no new termites had taken up residence in our home. They seemed to be gone forever, which meant that my tedious work previous to our departure had not been in vain. Slowly but surely, our life began to return to normal.

The International Development Aid Conference began right after we returned. Chris was the keynote speaker there and reported to me how it had gone.

"The prime minister mentioned the attack during his opening speech. He praised our work here in Mukalla and called it very impressive and important."

That evening, Chris and I were invited as guests of honor to a gala dinner at the conference.

Chris was excited. "The conference is being held outside the capital for the first time. And it's a great honor that it is taking place in our province!"

Long, richly laden tables decorated with candles were set up around the swimming pool area of the Hadhramaut Hotel. Much to my chagrin, Chris and I were seated in the place of honor at the end of the main table. We sat between the prime minister of Yemen and the German ambassador and his wife. All the government officials and international diplomats were watching us closely. It reminded me of the promise in Psalm 23, which was being fulfilled at this very moment: *"You prepare a table for me in the presence of my enemies."* This psalm had meant a lot to us right from the outset, even before we left Germany. Many friends had warned us that we would be entering a dark valley. But God had promised that he would be with us in the "valley of the shadow of death" and that his rod and staff would comfort us!

The prime minister turned to us and said: "Please accept our apology for what happened to you. We are happy that you are back in Mukalla! We are so grateful for what you have done for our country!"

Since women usually remained in the background, this obvious honor was a bit embarrassing for me. I wished I could have become invisible at that moment. On the other hand, it amazed me to see how God was restoring our honor among the local population, as well as among the government officials.

After the delicious meal was over, the prime minister turned to me and asked me under his breath if there was something he could do to make restitution for what had happened.

I had an answer ready: "You could install a lamp on our street that would shine on our house. Our neighborhood is very dark at night."

He gave me an elusive smile and changed the subject, then turned to talk to someone else. Perhaps he hadn't understood my request or was surprised by my spontaneity.

I tried to enjoy the evening, but I had apparently forgotten how to be comfortable around strangers, especially around Arab men. This was my first time to sit with them at an elegant table!

It was late when we left for home. When we were almost there, I mentioned to Chris:

"Look how dark it is here in our neighborhood in comparison to the city with all its lights!"

The words were barely out of my mouth when a bright light came on. Everything lit up: our house, our yard, our street, and, of course, all the rubbish lying around. We could even see the recently repaired pipeline that rose through the surface of the unpaved road. The workers hadn't put it back underground yet.

Chris just laughed: "Look at that! A streetlamp and a spotlight all in one! The leprechauns must have been working overtime. This must be some kind of record. I've never seen the local workers accomplish something like this within such a short time!"

It was only now that we realized how dark it had been before. We didn't have to turn the lights on in the kitchen, the bathroom, or the bedroom anymore. Even our roof was lit up at night.

I was surprised and delighted. "I guess you just have to know the right people!"

A few days later, the multilane road along the coastline was completed, and streetlamps were installed there, too. The light from those lamps shone all the way over to our street. For years, our entire neighborhood had been pitch dark at night. Now it was well illuminated. That was beautifully symbolic of all the positive changes that had been made in our province.

Joe, the young English teacher, came and set up an English faculty at the university. That made it easier for other Western English teachers to obtain a residence permit. Two other Christian couples joined us shortly after that. Our team was growing again. We were very encouraged and convinced that each new "light" would help fight the spiritual darkness.

It was a privilege for us to see the sun rising again, even in the Valley of Death!

CHAPTER 43

Changes

WHEN WE FINALLY returned to Mukalla, the whole family celebrated. Our neighbors, friends, and the officials of the city welcomed us back with open arms. And yet we felt that something was about to change. There was tension in the air, a tension we couldn't ignore.

Would this be the beginning of the end? We loved these people, loved working with the poor, loved our home, loved our friends. We were still intrigued by this beautiful desert wasteland with its bizarre rock formations, vast ocean, and stable climate.

When we first left Germany, we thought it would be forever. We knew that God had called us, and that was all we needed to know.

But the nagging questions persisted. Would we be ready for a change? Did we even want to start something new? Changes were often strenuous, tense and unpredictable. On the other hand, a change could offer us new opportunities. Then again, it was never easy to get excited about change, and especially not now, when it was being forced on us and our plans were unraveling. We had to look at what the future had in store for us. Only then would we survive. That meant turning our backs on everything familiar. It was a challenge for each of us to embrace this involuntary change, but we would grow and learn in the process.

Even though I'm a spontaneous and sociable person, transformations have always been difficult for me. They actually scare me!

After almost nine years in an Arab environment, I felt at home here, in spite of the ups and downs, the disappointments and challenges we had faced. This familiarity gave my family and me a sense of security.

A friend of mine once said: "It's difficult to let go of something you have been holding onto, but leaving something familiar behind can be a liberating experience. It can set you free and release a new purpose and goal."

Had I been holding onto something not willing to let go? Had that kept me from seeing the new things God had in store for us? Or had God changed his mind? I was confused and had many questions.

"Things are never what they seem to be. They are always what you make of them." I was determined to make the best out of our situation—for my husband, for the children, and for myself. But it was not easy since each of us dealt with the imminent losses differently.

Although we knew that things might be changing soon, we needed to stay focused on the work at hand. We wanted to bring the "good work" we had begun here to a successful conclusion. Our desire was for the work in the project areas to continue after we were gone. The work we had lived for and sometimes fought for should not fall apart.

It was quite a challenge not to give up, to make the best of the situation, and to allow the story here to continue. But how would *our* story continue? Would we ever return to this place where we felt so at home? Or would we move to another country to begin a new project?

Meanwhile, the authorities required that a guard be posted in front of our house at all times. It would be up to us to build a guardhouse, pay the guards' salaries, and provide them with meals.

Ever since we had returned home, soldiers had been posted in front of our house. Late in the evening, they would often quietly leave their post and go home or throw a party in front of our house. Chris suspected that the soldiers were not there to guard us, but rather to keep an eye on our activities.

When other questionable restrictions were placed upon us, we realized that we were officially no longer welcome. We knew then that our time here had come to an end.

We had been back in Mukalla only a short time when an email arrived from our employer in Germany.

"Take a sabbatical! You have been traumatized and need help."

Simple and concise, yet quite radical! If only it were that easy!

Where would we go? It was always difficult to find a place to stay, even if it was only temporary. And if we planned to stay for a longer period, we needed to find a school for the kids. Two years earlier, our experience with a German school had been rather difficult. We were worried that our children now might once again have a hard time fitting in.

* * *

We were so grateful that we had been able to return to Mukalla for a couple of months. We spent the time visiting our friends and colleagues, finishing up our work, and helping our successors get adjusted. The children had to get used to the idea that we would be leaving soon. It was an emotionally difficult time for all of us.

* * *

Only later did I understand the privilege we had been offered in being able to say good-bye, as painful as it had been. I began to understand how much more difficult it must be for people who are suddenly torn away from all their relationships who never have a chance to say good-bye, and have to leave everything they ever owned and knew!

I read something during those months that really spoke to me: "Often, we can't see the many doors opening in front of us because we are so focused on the single door that is closing behind us. We are so set on the negative that we don't see the blessings." Many wonderful things happened for the first time during this time of transition. Locals came and asked us for a Bible study. Another person wanted to be baptized. It seemed that what we had planted and watered over the years was finally blossoming! Chris worked with the locals, training them to take over the teaching responsibilities. He showed them how to live the Christian life and explained to them how they could be set free from all their chains of traditional thinking.

My desire was to show families how to live out their faith in a practical way. But so far, there were mostly Christian men whose wives didn't believe in Jesus and a few women, whose men didn't believe. Chris spent most of the remaining days building trust between the local believers. That would allow them to strengthen and encourage one another when we were no longer here.

* * *

The time was ripe to place the work in the hands of the locals. We were grateful that potential leaders were available. With much foresight, my husband taught the Yemeni believers the "tools of the trade" so they could survive after we left. We had to trust that God had a hope and a future for all of our Yemeni friends and our family, as well.

It gave us great joy and satisfaction to see the first Yemeni Christian fellowship established on the Arabian Peninsula. Local believers from every tribe and province had come together to make it happen. Our friends would never be alone because God had promised to build his church and to watch over it.

During this phase of saying our farewells, many things were still uncertain. Our children asked many questions, most of which we couldn't answer. They just couldn't understand why we had to leave our beloved homeland and all our friends behind. It was painful and distressing for each of us. Chris and I were desperate as well. We were leaving everything behind and had no idea what awaited us!

On the way to the airport, I couldn't hold back the tears any longer. Our hearts were breaking, and we were filled with grief. But Chris and I had to remain strong for the sake of the children.

A verse from a Whitney Houston song encouraged me and helped me to let go: *"If I would stay, I would only be in your way... I will always love you."*

Epilogue

ALTHOUGH WE HAD to leave Yemen, the people are still close to our hearts and we continue to be involved in work impacting the country.

At the time of publishing, Yemen is in the midst of a war which has led to the worst humanitarian crisis in the world today, according to the United Nations. Civilians are suffering the brunt of the armed conflict, and even more people have died from malnutrition, cholera, and other disease outbreaks. Like when the children drowned in the ocean (chapter 34), sometimes I feel helpless. We pray continuously for our brothers and sisters in the land of Sheba, but there is more that we can do to help! If you want to be involved and help Yemen, you can do that! The most important thing you can do is pray. If you want to help save lives, donations to the "CAP Fund" will help to fuel local initiatives that serve the physical and spiritual needs of the Yemeni people.

Your donations and all royalties from this book will impact and bless Yemeni people.

Thanks

FIRST AND FOREMOST, I want to thank Jesus. He is the actual author of our story. He never left us alone!

I could include only a few episodes of our life in Yemen. Otherwise, the book would have been too lengthy. I have related the events from my personal perspective. That's the reason that they are often full of "colorful" emotions.

My father loved books and often encouraged me to write my experiences down. "People should hear about what God is doing in the Arab world!" As he was on his deathbed, I read to him from my manuscript. He smiled proudly.

My husband is the hero of this story. He is the love of my life. His devotion and dedication always inspired me. Thank you for all your practical help and your encouragement! Without you, this book would not exist.

I also want to thank our three sons who stuck with us through thick and thin. We rarely asked their opinion on matters, but rather just dragged them along with us wherever we went. Sometimes they didn't understand the decisions we made. Our lifestyle required much sacrifice from them. I appreciate you boys for sticking with us. Thank you! I am proud of you!

Thank you to all my wonderful friends and supporters.

I would also like to mention a few people who are role models for Chris and me: Tom and Edna Hamblin, Hamish E., Marge and Roger L (has already passed away), Dr. Martha Myers and "Malik", two great martyrs for their faith.

Special thanks to Tom Bragg who believed in this book, even though we did not have the chance to meet face-to-face! And thanks to YWAM Publishing and the editors Warren Walsh and Steve C. who made the work fluent.

Dear Reader, I would love to receive your feedback and comments: Amiira.Ann@web.de

For more information on specific initiatives,
please email: **info@dev-ap.com**

Tax-Deductible Gifts may be sent to:
International Christian Response USA (ICR USA)

Check or Bill Pay to:
ICR USA
P.O. Box 611
Lynden, WA 98264
Please mark CAP Fund
on the check.

E-giving:
christianresponse.org/give
Designate To: *CAP Fund*

Women in Mukalla

Neighbor kids in Mukalla

Camels on their way to Mukalla

Capital Sanaa

*Sunrise behind
our house*

*Bedouin women
learn weaving*

*Sewing
class*

Schariifa

Bedouin school

Newly built school

Habban in Schabwa

Al-Qariyah in the Project Area

Amiira with the Bedouin women at the Hajjar River

Travelling in Yemen

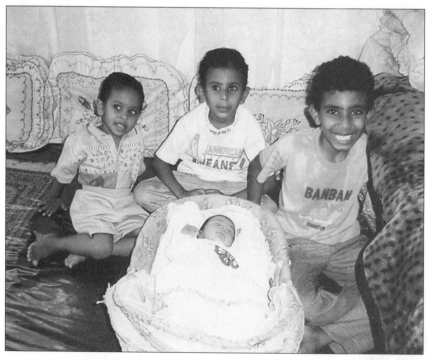

Neighbor kids

Travelling in the mountains of Taiz

Bedouin girls in Hadhramout

Sand dunes at Mukalla

View over Jibla

Hadhramout

Mukalla

283

Surviving girl of the tragedy at the beach

Daughter of the Sheik

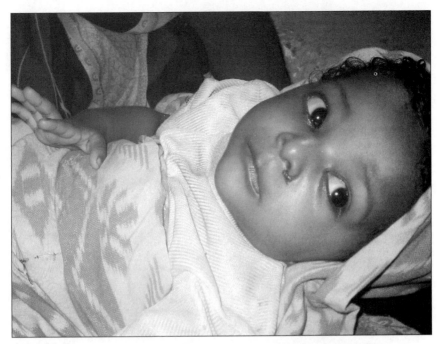

Jamila's baby

nächtlicher
Anschlag mit
Mord⭍drohung

Attack

Fishing boats

Malik

Glossary

(spelling in Arabic can be different!)

(There can be large differences in pronunciation between Arabic regional dialects.)

Aadi!	No problem!, It's normal., I'm/We're used to it! (lit. normal)
Abaya	Traditional black floor-length coat that women wear to completely cover themselves in public
Aish ilmuschkila?/aish almushkila	What's the problem?
Aish ismik? (female)/Aish ismak? (male)	What's your name?
Ajnabi	Foreigner (male)
Ajnabiya	Foreigner (female)
Alhamdulillah / Al-hamdu lillah! / Ilhamdulillah	Praise God!
Allahu akbar!	God is greater! (an expression of Islamic devotion and faith)
Baksheesh	Money given as a tip or a gift
Balto, same as Abaya	Traditional black floor-length coat that women wear to completely cover themselves in public
Chai	Tea
Daktoora	Doctor (female), but also often a respectful title given to any medical personnel
Dhuhr	Midday, but also used to refer to the prayer ritual performed at midday
Dirubalkum!	Pay attention!
Djambya / Jambiya	A traditional, highly decorative curved dagger, worn in a sheath attached to an embroidered belt
Fajir	Dawn, but also used to refer to the prayer ritual performed at dawn
Ftur / Futuur / Iftar	Breakfast, but also used for the first meal after dusk during Ramadan
Fusha	Formal classical or standard Arabic (i.e. contrasted with regional spoken dialects)
Futa	Beautifully patterned woven wrap-around skirt worn by men
Hadhrami	An inhabitant of Hadhramaut
Hadith / Hadiith	Collection of oral traditions covering the deeds and sayings of the Islamic Prophet Mohammed

Haraam	Religiously forbidden or immoral
Hurma bitsuuq!	A woman is driving!
Injiil	The Gospel (usually used to refer to the New Testament of the Bible)
Inshallah	Lit. If God wills. (Often used as an expression of uncertainty), perhaps
Inshallah bukra	Lit. Tomorrow, God willing. /Maybe tomorrow
Intabihu!	Watch out!
Isa Al-Masiih	Jesus Christ
Khat/qat	Native tree whose leaves are chewed for their mild narcotic effect
Kiif haalik? (female)/ Kiif haalak? (male)	How are you?
Lithma	Face veil that reaches to the chest, usually consisting of two layers. The outer layer can be folded back over the head to reveal an inner layer which has a thin slit for the eyes.
Madrasa/Madrasi	School
Mafraj	A traditional arrangement of narrow mattresses and cushions used for sitting on the floor in the living room
Maghrib	Dusk, but also used to refer to the prayer ritual performed at dusk
Miin maii?	Who am I speaking to? (used while speaking on the phone; lit. Who have I got?)
Mish mushkila!	Not a problem!
Nuqba	Broad headscarf that covers the hair and comes down over the shoulders
Qasr	Palace
Qauzz / Kauzz	Strong wind coming from the desert
Sabra /Sabgha	Black dye used by women to create traditional decorative patterns on the hands and feet
Salaam aleykum	Lit. Peace be upon you. (a common greeting)
Sayyaara	Car
Shaitaan	Satan, devil
Shisha	A decorative water pipe used for smoking tobacco flavored with fruits or spices
Shurba	A thick oatmeal soup that is traditionally eaten during Ramadan
Uskutu!	Be quiet! Silence!
Wadi	Canyon, valley or dry riverbed
Wakiil	Agent, e.g. land agent or property agent
Ya Allah!	Oh God!
Yella, bisuraa! Yella, bi suraa	Come on, quickly!